Managing & Measuring Employee Performance

Managing & Measuring Employee Performance

Elizabeth Houldsworth & Dilum Jirasinghe

London and Philadelphia

First published in Great Britain and the United States in 2006 by Kogan Page Limited

120 Pentonville Road	525 South 4th Street, #241
London N1 9JN	Philadelphia PA 19147
United Kingdom	USA
www.kogan-page.co.uk	

© Elizabeth Houldsworth and Dilum Jirasinghe, 2006

ISBN 0 7494 4477 0

British Library Cataloguing-in-Publication Data

A CIP record for this book is available from the British Library.

Library of Congress Cataloging-in-Publication Data

Houldsworth, Elizabeth.
    Managing and measuring employee performance/Elizabeth Houldsworth and Dilum Jirasinghe
        p. cm.
    Includes bibliographical references and index.
    ISBN 0-7494-4477-0
    1. Performance—Management.   2. Performance standards.   3. Employees—Rating of.   I. Jirasinghe, Dilum.   II. Title.
    HF5549.5.P35H68 2006
    658.3′125—dc22

2006016470

Typeset by Datamatics Technologies Ltd, Chennai, India
Printed and bound in Great Britain by Creative Print and Design (Wales), Ebbw Vale

Contents

Preface

This book is intended to serve a variety of readers. Foremost, it has been written as a book for the 'reflective HR practitioner', by which we mean the HR professional who is looking beyond the 'how to' in order to understand the origins of performance management, why it is manifested as it is and how its value might be maximized. The book's content is also likely to appeal to line managers and consultants with particular interests, responsibilities and expertise in the field. In addition, students on general business administration and human resource management specific qualifications will find something here to meet their needs.

Acknowledgements

The research for this book has received funding from the Henley Management College Research Development Fund since 2001 and support and investment from Hay Group UK since 2003. The authors wish to acknowledge the support they have received both from Hay Group, Henley and from other colleagues, particularly Professor Chris Brewster, Jill Foulds, Gavin Lawrie, Professor Arthur Money, Rachel Porter, Nick Boulter, Gina Roos, Jo Courtenay and Chris Davey. The authors would also like to thank Kate Everall for her work in the design and analysis of the line manager survey and the mini case studies, as well as Sue Burkinshaw for her input on HRM context. Additionally, we owe a debt of thanks to Helen Murlis for so generously imparting her expertise in the area of reward management and for her comments on earlier versions of the book, which have improved the content as well as enhanced our own learning and understanding. From the case study organizations we are indebted to a host of line managers and HR specialists who participated in our research; particularly noteworthy are Adrian Ward, Simon Machin, Dave Ormesher, Adrian Black, Rose Doyle, Mark Doughty, Christopher Johnson, Chris Ricketts and John Whelan.

On a personal note Tim, Phoebe and Sam are all to be credited for their forbearance, as the latter stages of the book have taken precedence over so many domestic pleasures.

Introduction

How is this book different from the many others on the subject of performance management, many of which do a highly professional job of describing practice or providing 'how to' advice for practitioners? We believe our book makes a contribution in that it seeks to adopt a strategic perspective based on the drivers behind performance management in order to meet the needs of the 'reflective HR practitioner'. We do this by looking at practice, which is contextualized through theory in order to suggest why performance management appears as it does today. Recent and discernible future trends are explained with illustrations drawn from mini case studies and longer organizational stories. Our research and personal experience as practitioners lead us to conclude that a focus on performance measures alone is unlikely to succeed in securing more than short-term compliance. Similarly, a focus on managing well and on personal development is unlikely to deliver the requisite organizational benefits. The most sophisticated and 'successful' approaches we report (in terms of making the link between performance management and improved organizational performance) appear to be those that manage to reconcile these two facets of performance: the 'hard' measurement and the 'softer' development.

Part I of the book deals with the necessary theoretical grounding required to contextualize our exploration of performance management.

It begins by describing the evolution of performance management before presenting an overview of the relevant theories and disciplines that underpin its development. This is then built on with the introduction of a 'development vs measurement' framework, which captures the different ends of the performance management implementation spectrum.

Having set the scene theoretically, Part II considers findings from field-work research. It discusses a survey of line managers and a series of mini case studies, as well as lessons from research into what the world's most admired companies are doing. This part considers how it might be possible to redraw the performance management map in order to reflect the findings from this research.

The chapters in Part III then focus on the implementation of performance management through an approach that is integrated and focused on practical aspects of the three main phases of planning, managing and reviewing/rewarding performance. Each phase is illustrated with one or more organizational story which bring to life how different organizations have striven to operationalize a range of different and topical approaches.

Part I of the book, which deals with theories and concepts, is the most academic and likely to be required reading for the student as well as the reflective HR practitioner who is continuing their professional development. Part III, on the other hand, is practitioner based, describing the elements of performance management which will be familiar to those who implement performance management systems or those tasked with re-engineering current arrangements. Parts II and III contain empirical work, including organizational stories, and are likely to be of interest to all readers of the book.

We fully recognize that readers will dip into the sections and 'grab' those that seem to serve their needs best. We have, however, sought to establish a logical flow through the book for the reader who prefers to start at the beginning and work through the whole.

Part I

Understanding performance management

This part sets the scene by describing in Chapter 1 the evolution of performance management from its humble origins in the once-a-year appraisal to become its integrated and strategic 'grown-up cousin' as seen in organizations today. It also provides an organizing framework for the reader to consider the key factors that need to be balanced for a successful performance management system. Chapter 2 then describes some of the underpinning academic theories relevant to understanding why performance management has evolved as it has. Chapter 3 suggests a framework for understanding the different 'character' of performance management implementations as having either a strongly measurement or development ethos.

1

Introduction: the evolution of performance management

Politt (2005) has described how performance management has become a universal and well-established practice in northwest Europe. This is for a number of reasons. Within the public sector the 'Modernizing Government' agenda has significantly raised the emphasis on visible outcomes and measures of success. Within the private sector, concern with increasing 'shareholder value' has put pressure on organizations to predict and deliver sustained business improvements. For whatever reasons, the increasing emphasis on efficiency, best value and performance targets has created a multitude of practitioner books and articles as well as encouraged consultants and HR professionals to seek the 'holy grail' of heightened organizational performance. It means that teachers, police officers, City 'high-flyers' and indeed the majority of the workforce have in common the fact that their performance is increasingly being managed, monitored and measured. As a result, the subject of managing performance has had something of a renaissance. It is no longer typically seen as the responsibility of the personnel department and solely as an appraisal form-filling exercise of little relevance to organizational performance improvement. Performance management has moved centre stage.

We will explain how attitudes have changed and how performance management approaches have in turn evolved both in terms of sophistication and in their degree of integration with people management practice.

Headlines from our survey of 400 line managers and more detailed research we have conducted in more than a dozen organizations cause us to suggest, like Armstrong and Baron (1998) before us, that managerial perceptions of performance management are largely at odds with the often bad press accorded to the 'dreaded appraisal'.

As social and economic pressures from most business sectors have elevated interest in managing performance, the topic has increasingly been picked up on the academic radar. In 2000 the UK's British Academy of Management formed a special interest group to consider performance management. This grouping currently numbers almost 200 in the UK, see www.bam.ac.uk for more information. On a larger and more international scale, since 1998 the Performance Management Association has taken as its aim: 'To be the world's foremost academic–practitioner association devoted to advancing knowledge and insight into the fields of performance measurement and management.' It has almost 2,000 members worldwide and hosts a large conference attracting academics and practitioners from the various subject and interest areas that deal with performance. For more information see www.performanceportal.org. What these different academic networks have shown is that performance management is both topical and multidisciplinary.

In the next chapter we shall consider some of the disciplines that are relevant to understanding the management of performance. However, it is worth restating that our emphasis in this book is on a human resources perspective on performance management as defined by Weiss and Hartle (1997): 'a process for establishing a shared understanding about what is to be achieved, and how it is to be achieved; an approach to managing people which increases the probability of achieving job-related success.'

In order to begin to contextualize this definition, the next part of this chapter will look at the evolution of performance management. We go on to suggest an organizing framework for understanding the key elements for success in performance management practice.

TRACING THE DEVELOPMENT OF PERFORMANCE MANAGEMENT

The idea of managing performance, both at an individual and organizational level, is far from new – an extensive range of literature covers the subject. A good account of the development of performance management may be found in Fletcher (2002). He traces its origins as far back as the First World War, focusing on the period since the 1950s, a decade that involved personality-based appraisal. Appraisal practice in the 1960s, he observes, shifted to a greater emphasis on goal setting and the assessment of performance-related abilities (and, more recently, competencies) rather than personality. The late 1980s, and the whole of the 1990s, saw organizations undergo a process of rapid and successive change. Almost inevitably, what Fletcher calls 'performance appraisal' became a central mechanism in a more holistic approach towards managing people and business in general. During the 1980s many organizations became more 'performance oriented'. During the 1990s performance management began to be seen as more of a core management process – capable of delivering the business vision by developing and reinforcing the key behaviours/values. Thus, performance management began to grow out of its 'appraisal' box, developing into the integrated, strategic and 'grown-up cousin'.

The evolution of performance management is shown in Figure 1.1.

The continuum diagram was developed by Hay Group in the early 1990s and has been used successfully since then in a number of different contexts. Its first application has been to encourage organizations to diagnose the state of development of their current performance management practice. Secondly, it allows the sponsors of such initiatives to map their aspirations for changing this process and also to think about the challenges they face along the way.

The vertical (*y*) axis represents the level of impact that performance management or appraisal processes are seen to have within the organization. The horizontal (*x*) axis encapsulates two elements: the degree of integration

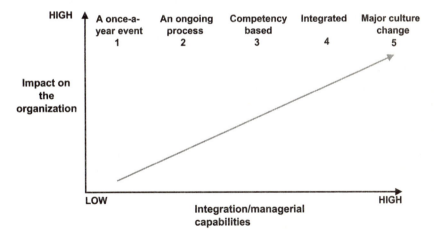

Figure 1.1 Performance management continuum or diagnostic. _Source:_ Hay Group (1995)

with other elements of the management process and, more importantly, the level of management capability required in implementation. A line has been plotted to denote a range of possible manifestations of performance management along the continuum. They may perhaps be interpreted as the evolutionary steps an organization might take in the development of its performance management process from old-style appraisal to a fully integrated process in support of culture change.

The first level on the continuum denotes an approach to managing performance that is low in terms of its organizational impact and low in terms of the degree of integration. In other words, we have a standalone appraisal process with little relevance to the needs of the business or other HR and management processes and which requires little managerial skill to deliver. This is, in our experience, where many organizations started along the road to improving the performance of their people.

The second level along the continuum is more impactful and more integrated in terms of other processes. It might best be interpreted as a phase of development associated with the 'management by objectives' approaches that first appeared in the UK in the 1970s, promulgated by John Humble of Urwick Orr consultants and the then British Institute of Management (now the Chartered Management Institute). It involves real attempts to link the business objectives to individual targets and to review these in a systematic way, perhaps linking to some other key HR processes, for example reward or promotion. Although we would not suggest this became universal, such approaches became most common in the private sector in the late 1980s and spread into the public sector in the early 1990s, owing to an increased focus on defining the outputs of jobs and on linking job performance to the objectives of the organization. Performance management began to grow out of its 'appraisal box' with the inclusion of a forward planning element via objectives set and agreed at the beginning of the appraisal period. This was also reinforced by a fundamental change in the way many people were paid over the 1980s and 1990s, to include an element of performance-related pay. In terms of managerial capability, the planning and subsequent review of performance needed for this stage of the performance management evolution is likely to require some investment in management and feedback skills in order to equip managers to fulfil these tasks confidently and in a manner perceived by their employees as fair.

Level 3 is a key stepping-stone on the performance management development continuum. At this level there is an emphasis not just on the 'what' of performance, but also the 'how', invariably expressed through defined behavioural competencies. Attempts to include competencies or required behaviours in the performance management process became increasingly commonplace in the mid- to late 1990s, as the number of organizations that had developed the necessary competency frameworks became much larger.

The background to the popularity of competencies in the UK lies in government-led initiatives to raise skill levels in the working population and those entering work in the mid-1980s. In 1986, the Review of Vocational Qualifications, which became known as the RVQ (see MSC/DES, 1986 and Hargreaves, 2000), set out to uncover the reasons for the UK's lack of competitiveness. The Review suggested that the skill base within UK organizations could no longer keep pace with the developing business climate owing to:

▌ the failure of large-scale change programmes to deliver the necessary changes in individual behaviour;

▌ a growing understanding of the link between business performance and employee skills, such that sustained business performance could be achieved only through improved management capability;

▌ the need for individuals to upgrade their skills to keep pace with continual change.

In response to these needs, a structured approach to managerial training and development geared around an emerging set of industry standards was advocated. The RVQ, in 1986, suggested that a vocational qualification should be 'a statement of competence, clearly relevant to work'. Standards of occupational competence were therefore defined across all sectors of industry. Hence the Management Charter Initiative, with its use of occupational competencies, was born in the UK. This approach to management development focused upon 'outcomes' – namely, the ability to perform a given task satisfactorily.

At about the same time, but with its origins in the United States, an approach to competencies that had grown out of the research of David McClelland was gaining momentum. This was articulated in his article 'Testing for competence rather than for intelligence' (1973). This school of thought, first deployed and popularized by the Hay Group (with its links to McClelland), adopts a 'process' approach. Competencies are defined as behavioural characteristics and attributes a person exhibits in order to be successful at work, for example influence, teamwork, analytical thinking.

Although NVQs continue as a qualification route in many fields within the UK, their popularity within management circles has dwindled. Within most organizations in private and public sectors, the 'default' approach since the late 1990s has been to seek to define 'behavioural' models

Personal effectiveness cluster	Cognitive cluster	Achievement cluster	Influence cluster	Management cluster
Self-control	Technical/ professional expertise	Achievement orientation	Influence and impact	Directiveness
Self-confidence	Information seeking	Innovation	Organizational awareness	Developing others
Organizational commitment	Analytical thinking	Concern for order and quality	Relationship building	Teamwork and cooperation
Flexibility	Conceptual thinking	Initiative		Team leadership
Interpersonal understanding		Customer service orientation		

Figure 1.2   Illustrative competency model

with competencies arranged in a number of clusters as illustrated in Figure 1.2.

Moving to level 3 of the performance management evolution represents quite a step change for many organizations in terms of the degree of management capability required. Competencies place an emphasis not just on outlining key targets or objectives, but also on **how** these are to be achieved through behaviours. We shall say more about this in later chapters. However, for many managers, making this jump requires a switch of mindset and a whole new vocabulary. For more practical illustrations of this and associated tools, see Chapters 8 and 13.

AN EXAMPLE OF COMPETENCY-BASED PERFORMANCE MANAGEMENT – BT

An example already written up in the public domain is the case of BT (IDS, 1997). This presents a description of a fairly typical performance management intervention rolled out in the mid-1990s. It describes how the performance review at BT aims to place individual achievement and competencies in the context of its business values and direction. The company structured an appraisal mechanism as a continuous process, with employees receiving regular feedback on performance. Formal meetings would take place at least quarterly, supplemented with an annual performance review. Individual objectives are linked to the company's scorecard, with a competency review being incorporated. In the case of BT, seven core management competencies were defined and in 2002/2003 a revised approach to performance management was implemented to strengthen the 'competency-based' element of the review. This was supported via a computer-based system.

At level 4 of the performance management continuum shown in Figure 1.1, we find performance management initiatives that are seen to have considerable organizational impact and which are fully integrated with key organizational processes such as human resource management, talent management, balanced scorecard and HR information technology systems. This is perhaps the highest level to which organizations would usually aspire for the long term. Level 5 of the continuum suggests performance management processes that are in transition. Here performance management is being used as a vehicle either to introduce or to reinforce a major change programme. Senior managers are sometimes surprised at the suggestion that they should think of performance management in this way. However, if one considers that the implementation of a new or revised performance management process can typically include all the elements shown in Figure 1.3, it is easy to see how this may be so.

In discussing the performance management continuum, we have been able to see a range of different manifestations. As we progress

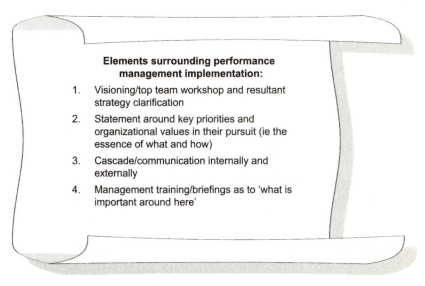

Elements surrounding performance management implementation:

1. Visioning/top team workshop and resultant strategy clarification
2. Statement around key priorities and organizational values in their pursuit (ie the essence of what and how)
3. Cascade/communication internally and externally
4. Management training/briefings as to 'what is important around here'

Figure 1.3 Elements included in performance management implementation

1991	1998
From	**To**
System	Process
Appraisal	Joint review
Outputs	Inputs
PRP driven	Development driven
Ratings common	Ratings less common
Top-down	360-degree feedback
Directive	Supportive
Monolithic	Flexible
Owned by HR	Owned by users

Figure 1.4   Trends in performance management as described by Armstrong and Baron. *Source:* Armstrong and Baron (1998)

along the spectrum of evolution we see that although current practice in performance management is related to the appraisals of old, it has evolved significantly. Some of the differences between 'older-style' appraisal and more recent performance management approaches have been described by Armstrong and Baron (1998). These are summarized in Figure 1.4.

Armstrong and Baron's conclusions suggest that during the 1990s there was a movement away from concentrating solely on the hard 'what' of performance, as evidenced by a focus on objectives and outputs, towards a greater emphasis on the 'inputs' or behaviours. At the same time they reported less enthusiasm for ratings, performance-related pay (PRP) and outputs. The 'new-style' performance management they identify also requires a switch of ownership, from a system owned and 'policed' by HR to a process designed for, and operated by, line managers. Their book in 1998 (updated with new research in 2005) provides a useful review of the literature and an empirically supported study which we build upon here. In Part II, where we present our own data, we compare our findings to theirs and suggest how the performance management map we present differs from that which they report.

AN ORGANIZING FRAMEWORK FOR PERFORMANCE MANAGEMENT

In order to support the reader consider the key elements likely to be necessary for the success of performance management implementation, we suggest below an organizing framework (see Figure 1.5).

The organizing framework contains four elements:

▌ Process

▌ Reward architecture

▌ Metrics

▌ Managerial capability

On the right-hand side of the diagram are what we later refer to as the more 'process-based' aspects of performance management. We consider success in process and reward architecture as being primarily HR professional and technical issues and we focus on them in more depth in Chapter 8.

On the left-hand side of the model are the attributes which, we maintain, must be balanced in order to secure success: metrics and managerial capability. We interpret both as being leadership issues. Accurately

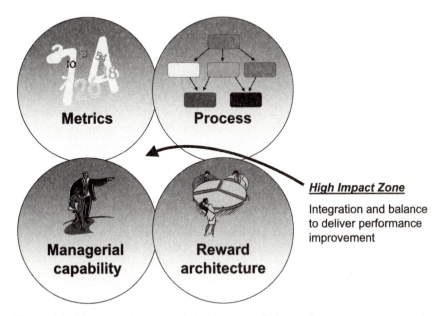

Figure 1.5 The four circle organizing framework for performance management. *Source:* Hay Group (2005)

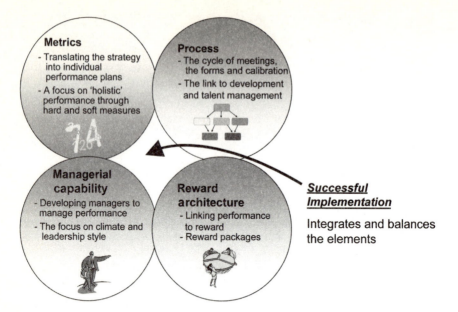

Figure 1.6   Unpicking the organizing framework. *Source:* Hay Group (2005)

defining organizational priorities and the measures around them is a key leadership task. Implementing them appropriately typically requires some real investment in managerial capability. What might be included in these is captured in Figure 1.6.

Figure 1.6 captures in more detail what might be included in both the left- and right-hand sides of the four-circle diagram. On the right-hand side we see elements that relate to the performance management process and how it is designed to integrate and support other elements of integrated HR. Aligned to this we see that the design and implementation of appropriate reward architectures are effectively linked to differential levels of performance.

The integration of these four elements is a theme that runs through the course of this book. In particular, achieving a balance between metrics and managerial capability – between measurement and development, or between 'hard' and 'soft' approaches to performance management – is a thread that runs through the book and one that we now start to explore in the remaining two chapters of this part.

2

Theoretical perspectives on managing performance

This chapter considers some of the key theoretical perspectives relevant to understanding how performance management is practised in the workplace. Its content is more theoretical than other chapters, but likely to be of value to the reflective HR manager, as well as to the performance management specialist and student.

An article in the *British Journal of Management* by Fletcher and Williams (1996) suggests that there are potentially many beneficial elements to a performance management system. These include:

▌ the development of a mission statement and business plan and the enhancement of communication so that employees are aware not only of the objectives and business plan, but can also contribute to their formulation;

▌ the clarification of individual responsibilities and accountabilities, through job descriptions, clear role definitions and so on, leading to the definition and measurement of individual performance;

▌ the implementation of appropriate reward strategies, which may include an element of performance-related pay (PRP).

However, as the authors know from experience, ask any group of managers 'what does performance management mean to you?' and their responses will typically include the following words:

▌ assessment;

▌ judgement;

▌ getting more out of people;

▌ control;

▌ raising expectations;

▌ filling in long forms;

▌ lack of consistency;

▌ time pressures;

▌ managing salary costs;

▌ chance to have one-on-one time with my people;

▌ opportunity to discuss development in role and for next role;

▌ difficult decisions (or experiences) around rating performance.

Performance management engenders a range of responses from both practitioners and researchers and the literature that surrounds it contains as much criticism as it does praise. We look at some of these criticisms later, but before we do so we begin with a look at performance itself before considering the HR context of its management.

WHAT IS ORGANIZATIONAL PERFORMANCE?

Although we have already defined what we mean by performance management in Chapter 1, arguably in so doing we have put the cart before the horse. We seek to remedy this below, by discussing work that has both challenged and helped to define our views about the nature of performance.

Corvellec (1997, 2001) has provided an interesting critique of performance. He describes how, in the English language, the term 'performance' can depict both an act and the result of an act. In recent years, the term has also evolved in the direction of referring to an accomplishment of something that is desired or intended, such as when one speaks of a performance test, the performance of a car or an aeroplane or some performance in sport. In a nutshell, performance is therefore an account of how agents – individuals, groups, departments, organizations, nations, continents or whatever – under certain circumstances, manage to get from state A to state B, the latter being in some way better than the former (Corvellec, 2001). He reminds us of how successfully 'performance' has invaded the whole of our contemporary imagination and become one of the most recurrent signs of recognition:

> We have all, regardless of whether as employees, sports practitioners, car drivers or holiday makers become susceptible to falling under the influence of performance in our ways of looking at things and people, as well as our ways of behaving. The notion of performance has become of central importance for our perception of our activities and our understanding of the world.

It is therefore not surprising that organizational performance touches on every aspect of business. Any review of the management literature would confirm this. Despite such an intense interest in the idea, and although performance has been raised to becoming the ultimate life-or-death criterion of business success, what businesses mean by organizational performance remains unclear and confusing. A search through management journals produces articles that relate an organization's performance (ie its productivity, profitability or, in the public service, levels of service delivery) to the firm's ownership or location, culture, organizational learning, top management compensation, labour force quality, team building, management control systems or balanced scorecard (Corvellec, 2001). Corvellec reconciles this by suggesting that the definition of performance is in the eye of the beholder. He points to Meyer and Zucker (1989), who conclude that 'the underlying definition of performance is rarely explicit in research studies'. Where authors originate from seems to drive the stance adopted. For example, Gomez-Mejia, Tosi and Hinkin (1987) declare that performance is 'a composite of [the firm's] financial success and the extent to which it maximizes the welfare of its stockholders'. Others do not share this commitment to a financial approach, among them Meyer and Zucker who claim that organizational performance is a function of the attainment of objectives or goals. It would seem that the standpoint of the individual and his or her functional specialism play a key role in this. For example, accountants are likely to see performance as being about return on investment, or other financial returns such as capital employed. City analysts are likely to interpret share price or earnings per share as key performance indicators, whereas operations managers might look at the efficiency of key processes and HR for evidence of improved behaviours in line with the organization's culture and values.

Corvellec concludes that for the large majority of management authors, an organization's performance is considered to be the result of its activity, as witnessed by the **measurement** of some form of output. It is perhaps useful to think of these measurable outputs as being the hard targets or the 'what' of performance. However, to focus on hard targets alone would be shorted-sighted (Corvellec, 2001). A *Fortune* survey (2004) of what the world's most admired companies do illustrates an approach that is 'more rounded' to include measures around teamwork and customer loyalty. Ethnologist Robert Jackall (1988) observed that for corporate managers, performance is not simply 'hitting your numbers'. It is about performing right on the organization's scene – that is, fitting the social rules that govern clothing or vocabulary, being perceived as a reliable team member, or endorsing the official organizational reality as the only one. So performance is not only a matter of results or outputs, but also of behaviour and process. Therefore it takes into account all aspects of what people involved in organizations do. We believe it is useful to think of these behaviours and processes as the 'how' of performance. Corvellec, along with other authors dating back to Brumbrach in 1988, have identified this distinction which we illustrate in Figure 2.1.

Subsequent chapters in this book describe in more detail how the 'what' and 'how' or targets and behavioural elements of performance have been built into performance management systems. Chapters 10 and 13 and the organizational stories in Chapters 11, 12, 14 and 15 give more examples of how this distinction works in practice.

We continue here, however, with our look at the background influences on performance management. In so doing we are keen to stress its multi-disciplinary heritage. Indeed, a forthcoming book by Thorpe and Holloway (2007) will deal with this issue. In their book these authors

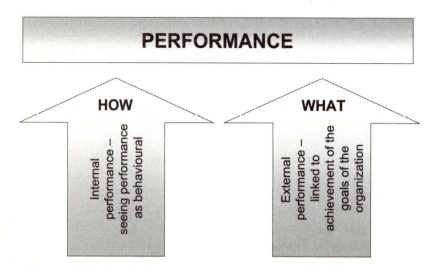

Figure 2.1   Two categorizations of performance

include chapters on performance management from the perspective of:

▌ accounting and finance;

▌ corporate strategy;

▌ operations management;

▌ information management;

▌ marketing;

▌ human resource management (HRM);

▌ organizational behaviour and organizational psychology;

▌ intellectual capital and knowledge management;

▌ operational research;

▌ project management.

Although we recognize the importance of these in defining and under-standing who owns performance, for this book we confine ourselves to the subset of these which appear most relevant in helping HR practition-ers understand current practice in performance management. We shall start with the impact of HRM before considering influences from account-ing and finance, operations management and motivational theories from economics and organizational psychology.

THE HRM CONTEXT OF PERFORMANCE MANAGEMENT

Unlike some of the other relevant underpinning disciplines, HRM does not have a long tradition to explain; indeed, as currently defined it is a rel-atively new phenomenon – although it emerged from what for 50 years has been called personnel management. As Storey (2001) has pointed out, 10 years ago the term was not widely used outside the United States, whereas he reports that by 2000 a database search revealed 448 HR publi-cations and 394 HRM publications.

In an earlier account, Storey (1992) describes how HR has developed out of its origins as a welfare-based personnel function that emerged in the mid-19th century under the philanthropic gaze of benevolent indus-trialists such as Cadbury (see 'handmaidens' in Figure 2.2) into an industrial-relations-based, often regulatory function premised around labour and collective bargaining in the mid-20th century. Both of these manifestations have been described as tactical. Storey sees HRM as having begun to fulfil a greater strategic role only in more recent years.

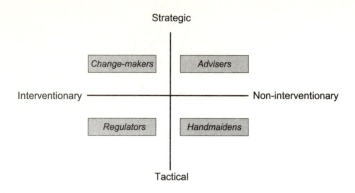

Figure 2.2 The changing nature of human resource management. *Source:* Storey (1992)

This has been achieved by individual heads of Personnel/HR positioning themselves either as a key adviser/partner to line managers – to whom all people management responsibilities are devolved, or as a strategic change-maker, realigning and reshaping the business with broad backing and high-level sanctioning.

We might expect to see different organizations operating at any one of the locations illustrated in Figure 2.2. If HR professionals are seen to be functioning as handmaidens in terms of performance management, we might expect to see them reminding or checking that line managers complete the performance management process. On the other hand, if they are positioning themselves as change-makers we would not be surprised to find them working with executives to help shape a balanced scorecard to reflect the strategic priorities of the business.

Indeed, Ulrich's work (1998) and more recently a revised version with Brockbank (2005) has described how HR might adopt a business partner role, as illustrated in Figure 2.3, which combines some of what we might have expected in the 'older-style' personnel approach as well as the more strategic 'human capital stewardship' roles required of HRM. The diagram suggests that HR leaders and professionals need to be able to lead in their own right if they are to expect these leadership skills from others in the business. In addition, they say that HR professionals must maintain the role of functional expert and employee advocate, coupling these with the roles of human capital developer and strategic partner.

Figure 2.3   Roles of HR. *Source:* Ulrich and Brockband (2005)

Ulrich and Brockbank (2005) have also suggested five steps in order for HR to add more value:

I Know your external business realities.

I Serve internal and external stakeholders.

I Craft practices.

I Build resources.

I Assure professionalism.

Numerous authors have attempted to summarize this range of activities for HRM. Keenoy (1990) has said that 'a remarkable feature of the HRM phenomenon is the brilliant ambiguity of the term itself'. He (Keenoy, 1999) said that HRM might be described as being like a 'hologram' in that it is able to appear as different things, depending largely on the viewpoint of the onlooker.

Beardwell, Holden and Clayton (2004) have sought to provide more clarity and structure by suggesting that HRM may be viewed from four perspectives, ie that HRM:

I is no more than a re-titling of the personnel management function;

I is a new managerial discipline – a 'fusion' of the traditional pluralist perspective of personnel management/industrial relations into one approach which is managerially led and unilaterally driven;

▌ represents a resource-based model of the employment relationship which incorporates a developmental focus for the individual employee, but one in which human resources are seen as a key to competitive advantage;

▌ can be viewed from a strategic perspective and is key player in driving the business forward in a highly competitive market.

We deal with each of these in turn. The first perspective reflects a long-running debate across the academic and practitioner communities as to whether HRM is just a re-labelling of personnel management ('old wine in new bottles,' Legge, 1989) or whether HRM is 'a new theory governing the employment relationship' (Beer, Mills and Walton, 1985).

As HRM has developed strategically and become a business and change partner, its name has tended to evolve from the personnel title to reflect this switch. There are long-running debates in the literature arguing that the change is often in name only and suggesting that the view that there is a commonly accepted HR prescription would be misleading as there exist obvious contradictions and inconsistencies (see, for example, Keenoy, 1996). However, it is worth while considering the main key differences we might expect to see in an HRM approach instead of a personnel one. Fortunately, Guest (1987) has done this work for us, illustrating the 'stereotypes' of personnel vs HRM. These differences are captured in Figure 2.4.

The figure shows some of the key stereotype distinctions that have been evident in many organizations as they move away from 'traditional'

Characteristic	Personnel	Human Resource Management
Time and planning	Short-term, reactive, ad hoc, marginal	Long-term, proactive. Strategic and integrated
Psychological contract	Compliance	Commitment
Control systems	External controls	Self-control
Employee relations	Pluralist, collective, low trust	Unitarist, individual, high trust
Preferred structures/systems	Bureaucratic/mechanistic, centralized, formal defined roles	Organic, devolved, flexible roles
Roles	Specialist/professional	Largely integrated into line management
Evaluation criteria	Cost minimization	Maximum utilization (human asset accounting)

Figure 2.4   Differences in emphasis: HRM vs. personnel. *Source:* Guest (1987)

personnel to HR approaches. Typically this has involved the reconfiguration of work definitions away from rigid job descriptions to more flexible role-profile approaches. As well as these 'technical' aspects there are also more profound changes evident in the positioning of the people management function. Under an HR approach we might expect to see HR specialist representation on the main board and, as a result, greater strategic influence and involvement, with associated longer lead times in terms of planning and implementation.

The second perspective suggested by Beardwell *et al* (2004) sees HRM as a new managerial discipline. This reflects the view of Torrington, Hall and Taylor (2001) that personnel may be viewed as essentially workforce centred, while HRM is resource centred. Although personnel is therefore a management function, it is not seen as being directed at meeting the needs of management in the same way as HRM. So under this perspective of HRM we might expect to view performance management as a managerialist intervention, done by managers to employees.

Beardwell *et al*'s resource-based view (2004) typically sees employee development as key in terms of defending competitive advantage. Development is an element of most performance management approaches, although in reality, as our and other research shows, the emphasis on employee development can vary considerably. We discuss in the next chapter our view that 'performance development' might be viewed as one of two broad 'schools' or styles of approach, the other one being more concerned with measurement and representing more of a strategic control approach to HRM. Much depends on who owns or has the lead power base for performance management as well as the relative influence of the HR function.

The fourth or 'strategic' perspective has been discussed since the early 'matching model' of HRM (Fombrun, Tichy and Devanna, 1984) and argues that HRM is characterized by its close alignment with business strategy (Hendry and Pettigrew, 1986). As Storey (1992) and other writers have indicated, HRM has more recently been seen to fulfil a greater strategic role. This has normally been achieved by HRM specialists holding senior board-level positions and through the devolution of many of the functions of HRM to line managers. In this way, HRM has shifted into a 'strategic/interventionary' position (as illustrated in Figure 2.2), where HRM is seen to be a strategic change-maker, helping to realign and reshape the business (Storey, 1992).

We can therefore see that the evolution of HRM has obviously impacted on performance management in terms of its positioning and how it is manifested within organizations. As HRM has 'moved up the food chain' to be aligned with business imperatives, performance management has increasingly been seen as one of the key processes around managing human resources, serving as a critical driver to help the organization achieve its business goals.

OTHER INFLUENCES ON THE EVOLUTION OF PERFORMANCE MANAGEMENT

As performance management is a major component within a framework of integrated HR, it has obviously been impacted by the development of that discipline and the increasing professionalization of those practising it. However, HRM does not exist within a vacuum, and a range of other disciplines and influences have had a key role to play. We consider the main ones in the next section.

Accountancy and operational management perspectives on performance management

Although performance management is often considered an essential element of a 'managing people' kitbag, this is not a view that is universally shared. As discussed in Chapter 1, performance management is seen as being the domain of a wide variety of subject specialists from both business and academia. Accountancy and operational management are two particularly relevant areas with their emphasis on efficiency and cost reductions.

Given the rise of management accountancy, it is perhaps not surprising that our fieldwork (described in Chapter 4) suggests an increase in the adoption of performance-measurement based approaches. It is interesting to reflect on why this is so – is the move towards performance measurement reflecting recent concerns? Has there been a sea change creating the need for performance management to lead to measurable outcomes? The appointments pages of the press reinforce this view, with a number of advertisements for 'performance managers' to fill a role that is not directly linked to the HR function but focused on service delivery improvement.

If we return once again to the HR literature we may find some clues, for example in Legge's (1978) concept of 'conformist innovators', and in Keenoy (1996). He quotes Armstrong (1987) as reporting that by 1980, over 90 per cent of companies were using some form of budgetary control and financial performance indicators. Armstrong (1987) suggests that: 'In embracing the strategic pretensions of HRM, personnel professionals will increasingly marginalize their independent contribution by subjecting their activities to the value criteria of budgetary planning and control' (Keenoy, 1996: 160).

He warns that the consequence of 'seeking to justify personnel work in accounting terms may cede too much to the dominant accounting culture' (p 160) and result in permitting line managers to turn 'the treatment of human resources into an instrument for the achievement of short-run accounting targets'.

For whatever reasons, it would appear that towards the very end of the 20th century a new template for performance management approaches was emerging that took its lead from accountancy and business process and quality movements. This move towards measurement has been noted by Pollitt (2005), who concluded that in northwest Europe, performance measurement has become almost universal and well established in practice. Performance management, on the other hand, he reports as growing steadily, but varying in form and force between different countries. The main manifestations of a measurement-based approach may be seen in the European Foundation for Quality Management (EFQM) model and the balanced scorecard (BSC).

Conceived by Eccles (1991) and popularized by Kaplan and Norton (1996) as a means of overcoming the short-termist and narrow tendencies of management accountancy, the balanced scorecard presents an approach that promises to allow organizations to measure both hard tangible and soft intangible drivers of performance. It is based on the notion that measurement motivates, drawing on theories such as goal setting (Locke, 1968) and expectancy theory (Vroom, 1964), and aims to move away from the problems created by a short-term reliance on financial measures alone. The scorecard outlines four different perspectives under which to identify performance measures and track organizational performance. These are summarized in Figure 2.5.

To produce its own scorecard involves an organization first of all identifying its key strategic drivers before articulating key measures that will predict likely business success. It is an approach built on a rational causal model. As an illustration, it is believed that measures associated with learning and growth (at the bottom of the scorecard) – for example, the fit between employees and role requirements – has an impact on the efficiency of internal processes and hence on what is delivered to the customer. These in turn impact on financial measures via a causal flow. Kaplan and Norton (2000) provide a short account as to how they see this approach to have been deployed in an HR context in the late 1990s. For a more detailed description of how balanced scorecard measures might be defined and linked to HR processes see Chapter 10. For organizational stories around the implementation of a balanced scorecard see Chapters 11 and 12.

An article by Dinesh and Palmer (1998) looked at management by objectives (MBO) and balanced scorecard approaches and suggests that

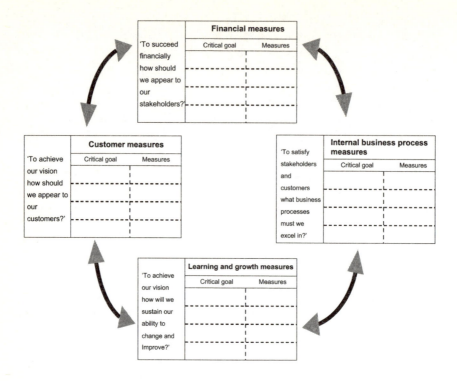

Figure 2.5 Balanced scorecard perspectives. *Source:* Kaplan and Norton (1996)

they are very similar. The authors maintain that MBO often fails because despite the hyperbole around collaborative goal setting, in reality a rational top-down model usually persists. Such a top-down approach is similar to balanced scorecard implementation unless there is a particularly skilful and time-consuming (and therefore expensive) employee involvement process linked to its design. Dinesh and Palmer observe that 'partial implementation' of a balanced scorecard is likely to preclude genuine buy-in to and acceptance of measures, and our coverage of goal theory later in this chapter supports this.

Instead of focusing on the definition of measures, the EFQM model, illustrated in Figure 2.6, operates in a different way. Rather than providing a framework for an organization to define its own measures, aligned with its strategy, it provides an opportunity to audit current practice against a European standard. The thinking behind the EFQM model is that by adhering to the standards (and there are questions to guide an organization to diagnose their current practice) higher quality and hence business performance will result.

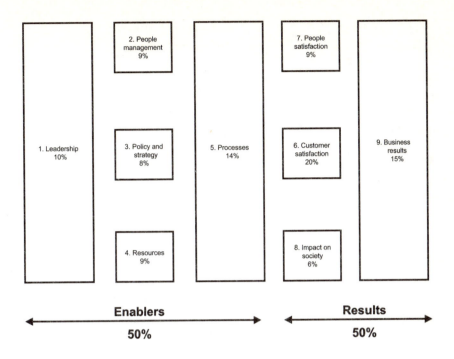

Figure 2.6 EFQM model. *Source:* EFQM (1991)

Both the balanced scorecard and the EFQM model are examples of measurement-based approaches influenced by accounting and operational management perspectives to performance management. While these approaches focus on measurable outcomes, authors such as Neely (1998), along with others, have identified how performance management systems based solely on such approaches can become overly concerned with targets and lose sight of performance. To describe this, Neely has coined the term 'measurement dysfunction', observing that 'as soon as performance measures are used as a means of control, the people being measured begin to manage the measures rather than performance'. For example, despite the 'rationality' of the approach, other authors point out that the balanced scorecard has not always lived up to its promise. The 'flood' of measures that can result from the implementation process may in fact serve to distract from what really matters to the business, and the resultant measures may well be divorced from the corporate agenda. Indeed, Neely has recently acknowledged that there is a lack of evidence to suggest how measurement-based balanced scorecard approaches actually improve business performance (Neely and Griffith, 2006).

Motivational perspectives on performance

Because of the complexity of human motivation, there is no single answer to the question of what motivates people to perform well. However, a number of theories have been used to analyse the process of managing performance within organizations. These theories come from both economic and psychological traditions.

Psychological perspectives on performance management

Although the psychological tradition is not at the root of our interests here, there is no doubt that it has contributed to our understanding of the main motivational theories applied to performance management. The preface to a recent book by Sonnentag (2002) on the psychological management of individual performance illustrates the range and nature of this significant field of research. It describes individual performance as 'one of the key variables that work and organizational psychologists want to explain and predict in their research'. The theories that emerge from these principles can be divided into two types: content theories and process theories.

Content theories – these place emphasis on what motivates an individual: the non-conscious aspects of people's needs; their strengths; and the goals they pursue in order to satisfy these desires. Content theories suggest that individuals behave as they do in order to meet their needs. Key theories include:

I *Three motives theory* (McClelland, 1973), which has a strong international research base and describes the need for achievement, affiliation and power as the three key social motives at work. People differ in terms of their profile on these three social motives and this affects what energizes, motivates and intrinsically satisfies them. Someone, for example, with a strong achievement motivation will be motivated very differently (by success) from someone for whom affiliation (good relationships and social harmony) is the dominant motive. Where power is dominant, the ability to have an impact and influence over events will be more important.

I *Hierarchy of needs* (Maslow, 1943), which identifies a five-level hierarchy of needs, starting with basic needs such as shelter and food, followed by safety and security, and then needs around belonging and feeling a member of a group. If these three 'lower' needs are met, the higher needs of esteem and desiring approval and recognition from others come into play, working up to 'self-actualization', at the highest level, when other needs are satisfied.

Process theories – these place emphasis on the actual process of motivation, ie how an individual is motivated. They are concerned with the conscious aspects of motivation: how behaviour is initiated, directed and sustained. Major theories under this heading include:

▌ *Goal-setting theory* (Locke, 1968) describes how people strive to achieve goals in order to satisfy their emotions and desires, which guides individual behaviour and therefore performance. More challenging goals result in higher levels of performance according to the theory, as long as they are accepted as valid by the recipient.

▌ *Expectancy theory* (Vroom, 1964) suggests that individuals have different sets of goals and can be motivated if they believe that there is a positive correlation between efforts and performance and that if they perform favourably they will receive a desirable reward, which will satisfy an important need.

▌ *Equity theory* (Adams, 1965) is based on the belief that people want to be treated fairly. People compare themselves with other people to see if their treatment is equitable.

▌ *Reinforcement theory* has developed from many sources. With its origins in behaviourism it suggests that people will exert higher levels of motivation in performance tasks that are reinforced. This means that behaviours that win them recognition at work will be repeated, whereas those that bring negative reinforcements or punishment will be avoided (see Luthans and Kreitner, 1985).

▌ *Procedural and distributive justice* (Chan Kim and Mauborgne, 2003), which essentially says that people are more concerned with the quality of the decision-making process and the outcome of decisions. If the process is seen to be fair then the outcomes will be more acceptable.

Economic perspectives on performance management

Economic perspectives are particularly relevant for understanding the reward and incentive elements of performance management. These include:

▌ *The effort bargain* – as articulated by Baldamus (1961). This theory suggests that pay levels and employment conditions can be subject to both individual and collective negotiation. In stressing that a reward system will not be workable unless it is recognized as fair and equitable by both parties, the theory supports the case for fairness, equity and consistency in both design and execution. Armstrong (2002) has said of this approach that 'one of the tasks of management is to assess what level of inducements it has to offer in return for the contribution it requires from its workforce. The workers' aim is to strike a bargain over the relationship between what they regard as a reasonable contribution and what the employer is prepared to offer to elicit that contribution. It is in effect, an agreement which lays down the amount of work to be done for a rate of pay or wage rate, not just the hours to be worked.'

I *Principal–agent theory* – assumes that two parties may not share the same goals or values and that the principals (employers) need to find a rational way of exerting control over the agents (workers) to secure the outcomes they desire. Sappington (1991) has suggested that it can be a simplistic theory, as it 'tends to depict the actors in agency models as self-interested individuals, often with the goal of maximizing net income. This approach may capture incentive problems but it avoids such issues as worker loyalty and pride. . . .'

I *Game theory*, now over 50 years old, assumes that each person maximizes her or his rewards – profits, incomes, or subjective benefits – in the circumstances that she or he faces in a rational manner. The insight that Neumann, Morgenstern and Kuhn (2004) and others had was that rational behaviour at the individual level might not lead to a rational outcome for the group. This has been used to explain how human behaviour has led to such problems as pollution, over-exploitation of fisheries and inadequate resources committed to research.

I *Human capital theory* – as described by Mayo (2001), which focuses on the investment costs required for a skilled and effective workforce rather than considering these to be an operating cost to be controlled and minimized.

For a fuller account of these theories see the chapter by Murlis in Childs (2005). Although knowledge of these theories is interesting for its own sake, it is important that we also consider what they mean in practice. Managing the performance of others involves both intrinsic and extrinsic motivation. The actual process of performance management relates to intrinsically motivating people through objective setting, performance reviews with constructive feedback, training and development; whereas the actual outcomes of performance management, the 'tangible' rewards of pay and recognition awards, relate to extrinsic motivation.

To maximize motivation at the planning stage, it makes sense for the goals set to be clear, specific, challenging and accepted by the individual (hence the popularity of the SMART approach to goal setting). Similarly, McClelland's work on achievement drive informs us that individuals will be motivated to work towards objectives that represent a benchmark of excellence. In addition, an individual's expectations must be managed in terms of rewards, and how his or her behaviour links to rewards must be effectively communicated.

Feedback and coaching should reinforce previous behaviour and, according to writers such as Deci (1985), may have a more positive impact than financial rewards at the end of the performance cycle. Reinforcement and equity are extremely important to motivation during the review stage. Consequently, recognizing appropriate behaviours and rewarding them is paramount. Inequities in pay awards or promotion can result in either improved or reduced performance, owing to changed motivation levels. For example, an individual might detect an inequity in bonus payments and feel that his or her efforts have been overlooked. As a result he or she may opt to do less next time. Conversely, commitment theories suggest (see, for example, Meyer and Allen, 1992) that promotion acts as a powerful reinforcer and has a significant positive impact on motivation.

The difficulties of managing the motivation of employees is just one area where performance management has attracted criticism over the years and by way of concluding this chapter we should consider some of the most vocal criticisms.

Armstrong and Baron (1998) provide a useful overview of the range of responses. They begin by pointing out the gap in knowledge around the value of performance management, reporting that the link between effective performance management systems and improved organizational performance has been difficult to establish and prove. Similarly, a CIPD research report from 2002 spells out that although the link between people management and organizational performance may be clear, there is less clarity as to what it is in HR that seems to trigger better performance and how such a connection can be sustained (Hutchinson *et al*, 2002). Related research by Purcell *et al* (2002) has found that it is line management and its capability that makes the difference, as opposed to the design and implementation of specific HR practices.

In terms of critiques, Armstrong and Baron (1998) provided a very useful review of those available and conclude that they can, broadly speaking, be divided into two camps: performance management is a good idea that doesn't work (practitioners and some academics), and performance management is a bad idea and doesn't work (academics). The heaviest criticism they found came from academics. For example, total quality 'guru' Deming (1986) described performance, metric rating or annual review as the third deadly disease of management. He believed that most performance issues in the production environments he studied related to poor systems design or poor management and his concept of performance appraisal was understandably coloured by the poorly implemented, bureaucratic paper- and ratings-driven systems which were prevalent in the US manufacturing environment where he did most of his work. Townley (1994) wrote about the issues of power relations and control, describing performance management as being at the nexus of a range of disciplinary procedures. She emphasized in 1993 its controlling nature, particularly where individuals are ranked through paired comparisons or forced distributions. The insurgence and popularity of performance management systems over the last decade have been attributed, by some, as part of a management reassertion to the 'right to manage' and that performance management processes are further attempts to secure control over the behaviour of employees (Townley, 1993; Newton and Findlay, 1996).

Barlow (1989) has similarly written about its controlling nature, in particular seeing that it relies on compliance, and Winstanley and Stuart-Smith (1996) have described the 'policing' or enforcement nature of performance management, whereas Stiles *et al* (1997) found considerable gaps between the organizational rhetoric of performance appraisal and managerial practice, particularly in the developmental aspects of performance.

In summary, although it has not been our intention here to cover all the debates in their fullness, we have sought to raise awareness of some of the academic perspectives on performance management by considering the 'root disciplines' involved and some of the criticisms which have been levelled. It would appear that, as with HRM, there is no one commonly held theory or set of theories to support an understanding of performance management. Its explanation draws on a range of theories from a range of disciplines.

In the next chapter we build on this by advancing a framework for understanding two different polarities or manifestations of performance management, with a primary emphasis upon either measurement or development.

3

Performance development versus performance measurement

In the previous chapter we talked about different underpinning theories relevant to understanding performance management. This chapter builds on some of these perspectives. It suggests a framework for understanding performance management implementation by describing the extremes of development and measurement and relating these to the concepts of 'hard' and 'soft' HRM. Although, in reality, most organizations will not consciously seek to deploy the extreme of pure measurement or pure development, we believe the concepts are worth describing as they help the managers and designers of performance management initiatives to recognize the main philosophy behind their approach. Before we discuss the framework we begin with a review of the main background influences upon it, namely the growth of an increasingly strong business results focus for HR practice.

THE BUSINESS BENEFIT PERSPECTIVE ON HR PRACTICE

Pfeffer (1998) cites evidence from the United States that HR practices can raise shareholder value by between $20,000 and $40,000 per employee. A study by Huselid, Jackson and Schuler (1997) suggested that the 'market value per employee' was strongly correlated with the sophistication of the HR practices adopted. Much of the fieldwork for this has been pioneered in the United States. However, a CIPD study in the UK by Richardson and Thompson (1999) reports that there are in the region of 30 empirical studies that have sought to address the relationship between HR practices and business performance. In reporting this return on investment, most research has focused on measures such as productivity or financial results.

In the UK, Patterson *et al* (1997) found that changes in profitability among a panel of over 60 small to medium-size manufacturing businesses in the UK correlated with adoption of certain HR practices. In the same report Patterson *et al* set out (among other things) to establish whether there was any relationship between employee attitudes (job satisfaction and commitment) and the performance of their companies and whether organizational culture predicts the subsequent performance of organizations. They found the answer to be yes, that job satisfaction does explain 5 per cent of the variation between companies in change in profitability after controlling for prior profit. Organizational commitment also explains 5 per cent of the variation. In relation to productivity, the research found that job satisfaction explains 16 per cent of the variation between companies in their subsequent change in performance. Organizational commitment explains some 7 per cent of the variation. Based on this study, it would appear that organizations would benefit more by focusing on their human resources than they would by focusing on competitor strategy, quality focus or R&D investment.

Hendry and Pettigrew (1990) explain that such an emphasis on human resources is in no way a new occurrence. In fact, they suggest that interpreting human resources as an organizational asset goes back at least to the 1950s. Perhaps part of the renewed interest in recent years has been driven by a belief that more effective people management will lead to increased business benefits. Arguably it has ever been thus – 'good leaders' have historically been able to inspire their followers to achieve great things. However, perhaps linking these achievements to quantifiable targets is a newer way of construing these outcomes. It is perhaps this change in mindset around what might be expected from 'well-run' human resources that can be best explained by the established distinction between hard and soft approaches to HR, which we explain in more detail below.

Hard and soft approaches to HRM

In the 1970s the language of 'human resources' began to creep into the vocabulary of British academics. With this came the two notions of utilitarian-instrumentalism and developmental-humanism, often now referred to as 'hard' or 'soft' HR. A simple way of viewing the distinction is to consider whether the emphasis is placed on the '**human**' or on the '**resource**'.

Soft HRM has been associated with the human relations movement, the utilization of individual talents and McGregor's 'Theory Y' perspective on individuals (McGregor, 1971). Here we see, therefore, developmental-humanism, which aims at eliciting a commitment so that behaviour is primarily self-regulated rather than controlled by sanctions and pressures external to the individual. Relations within the organization are therefore based on high levels of trust. Soft HRM is also associated with the goals of flexibility and adaptability and implies that communication plays a central role in management. Beer, Mills and Walton (1985) are commonly cited in relation to this view on HRM and have become known as the Harvard school. They place most emphasis on a 'people' focus, seeing the impact of managers on organizational climate as being at the heart, along with the relationship between management and other employees. They recognize the existence of a range of HR levers and the context of stakeholder interests as well as situational factors. The policy areas that they identified within HRM are employee influence, human resource flow, reward systems and work systems.

Other authors, including Legge (1995), have noted that employees working under such an HRM system will positively commit and give added value through labour, with employees feeling trusted, trained and developed, with control over their own work. Although for many organizations who are keen to improve performance this makes intuitive good sense, it can feel like a 'leap of faith' to invest time and resources into building commitment and motivation – without necessarily being sure of a return.

Hard HRM, on the other hand, stresses the quantitative and business-strategic aspects of managing the 'headcount resource' in as rational a way as for any other factor of production. Within HRM literature this has been referred to as utilitarian/instrumentalism and focuses on the importance of 'strategic fit' where human resource policies and practices have been closely linked to the strategic objectives of the organization with the aim of heightening competitive advantage. In terms of its view of human nature it has been seen to have an emphasis on McGregor's 'Theory X' (ie people dislike work), leading to tight managerial control through close direction. This approach as been described by Fombrun, Tichy and Devanna (known as the Michigan school). They describe the critical managerial tasks as being 'to align the formal structure and the HR systems so that they drive the strategic objectives of the organization' (Fombrun *et al*, 1984). The key

HR systems and processes they had in mind were: selection, appraisal, training and development, and rewards, and they suggest the alignment of these in specific ways to channel behaviour and create an appropriate organizational culture.

THE PERFORMANCE DEVELOPMENT/ MEASUREMENT FRAMEWORK

In this section we strive to outline a framework for understanding how the 'polar' opposites of performance management might appear in theory, suggesting how we might see linkages to the two philosophies of hard and soft approaches to HRM.

We describe the first of these manifestations as 'performance development'. This may best be summarized as being around fostering employee commitment. Its concerns are with organizational climate, managerial style, personal development and employee involvement in the objective-setting and review processes. Performance initiatives of this type take as their starting point the premise that an essential element of the role of a manager is to 'manage' the performance of others in order to ensure they have clarity around what is expected of them. The performance development approach advocates that this is good management practice, of value for the enhanced motivation of employees and ensuing higher levels of commitment, as described in Hutchinson *et al*'s CIPD Research Summary (2002). Although its end goal is still around improved business performance, it is an approach that associates more with 'soft' HR than with 'hard' or strategic HR. It is seen to deliver business benefits by virtue of the fact that it equates with good management practice and its philosophy is predominantly 'people' based. Good management practice, it is espoused, results in greater motivation and commitment from employees who are hence more inclined to deliver 'discretionary effort'. This approach is typified by management development, leadership and coaching interventions. The Belron case study given in Chapter 14 illustrates what such an approach might look like in practical terms.

Our research has shown that it is possible to discern some performance management initiatives which have a largely performance 'development' character. However, these do not seem to predominate at the current time. The recent increased emphasis on the business benefits of HRM appear to have led to a greater demand within organizations to see a tangible return from people management and a greater emphasis on performance through the delivery of specified outcomes. In the majority of instances it is no longer enough to accept in good faith the assertion that good management leads to greater employee commitment and effort and hence to improved performance.

As a result of a heightened emphasis on performance, a different 'school' of performance initiative has emerged, which takes as its starting point the goal of business benefits. We refer to this approach as 'performance measurement'. Such approaches rest on the premise that organizations struggle to clearly define, articulate and cascade their strategy. By clearly articulating what needs to be done through a set of metrics, it is believed that quantifiable business benefits will result, ie 'what gets measured gets done'. This approach has been influenced by business process approaches, as typified by balanced scorecard and EFQM methodologies. Predictive models of success are typically produced and the expected business benefits may be couched directly in financial terms (for example, economic value-add approaches) or a collection of measures, such as a balanced scorecard to combine both 'hard' and 'soft' measures. Employee motivation, commitment and development are still considered, but within the context of driving up overall business performance. There may well be attempts to quantify these 'softer' aspects of performance, for example through competency coverage, which we describe in Chapter 13, whereby an organization seeks to report these quantitatively, perhaps as a percentage of the average degree of fit of job holders against role profiles. A practical illustration of a performance measurement approach as implemented at Lloyds/TSB is presented in Chapter 12.

Performance measurement and development approaches and the main criteria on which they reside are illustrated in Figure 3.1.

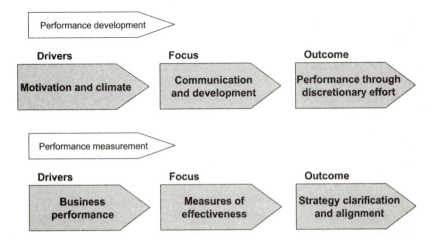

Figure 3.1 Performance measurement and performance development approaches

Table 3.1   Performance measurement and development drawbacks

Performance development	Performance measurement
Requires behavioural change and this is harder both to do and to measure	Places very high skill requirements on managers, both to interpret a scorecard or other metrics framework and to set targets and monitor progress against them
Required behaviours must be modelled from the top and often leaders see performance management as the domain of others	Requires high investment in terms of time and central (HR or OD) input to support line managers and the calibration of the process
Clarity is not always enhanced, as lacks tight focus on real business imperatives	Runs the risk of perceived favouritism if processes are not transparent and perceived as fair
Long-term approach, requires a 'leap of faith' and difficult to establish a clear link between its processes and outcomes	Requires ruthless feedback – not many managers are skilled or comfortable doing this
May be perceived to lack 'edge' and places less emphasis on ratings and reward	People feel that what gets rewarded is 'hitting the numbers'

It is possible to see that what really differentiates between the two approaches is the value-base on which they reside. Is the driver for the approach to increase motivation of employees so that they self-regulate their behaviour in order to produce extra outputs? (based on notions of developmental-humanism, McGregor's Theory Y and what is now referred to as 'soft' HRM). Or, on the other hand, is the driver about controlling and monitoring achievements against key targets, as linked to the strategy? (more in line with utilitarian-instrumentalism, McGregor's Theory X and what has become known as 'hard' HRM).

Before describing how we set about testing the framework, we set out in Table 3.1 the possible drawbacks on both extremes of either a performance development or a performance measurement approach.

CODIFICATION OF EXPERIENCE – TESTING THE FRAMEWORK

The two 'categories' or manifestations of performance in Figure 3.1 were put to the test initially by means of a codification of experience across

12 different organizations. To assist, and to provide more rigour to the exercise, a taxonomy was adapted from the one used by Truss *et al* in 1997, when they looked for examples of hard and soft HR. These authors looked at HRM practices in eight in-depth case study examples and, using a mixture of interviews, questionnaires and focus groups, they sought to establish if any of the eight were practising hard or soft HR. What they found was that there were no 'pure' examples of either. They used a framework, which differentiated between the soft and hard models in terms of:

▌ underlying perceptions of human nature: in the soft perspective they interpret individuals as being seen as a resource worthy of training and development, whereas a hard perspective implies that individuals are a cost to be minimized;

▌ managerial control strategies: in a soft model they interpret organizations as seeking to use a commitment approach, whereas in a hard model, control is through tight strategic direction. This includes communication and flexibility and adaptability.

We have deliberately followed their example when looking for examples of performance development or performance measurement approaches, as we felt that the different performance management manifestations are similar in nature to either hard or soft HRM approaches. However, we modified the approach adopted by Truss *et ul* (1997) by narrowing our focus to look at training and development (in place of a broader reflection on 'views of human nature') and communication (in place of a wider reflection on managerial control strategies). In addition, we have added three other categories:

▌ a short description of the organization and date of the intervention;

▌ an overview of the 'drivers' behind the intervention;

▌ a summative view as to whether the performance management intervention may best be viewed as 'performance development' or 'performance measurement'.

Truss *et al* (1997) conclude from their own research that pure versions of either hard or soft HRM are difficult to discern and it has been suggested that this distinction is one that works in theory but is not easily recognizable in organizational practice. Having reflected on prior experience of performance management design, implementation and support programmes, it would appear that many of the 12 interventions described in Table 3.2 include elements of both 'soft' and 'hard' HR in their intentions, focus and delivery. This is in part due to the fact that they have a number of common elements in their composition: all typically involve the three phases of performance management – planning, managing and reviewing. All therefore involve objective or target setting for both business performance and training and development. All typically include an annual appraisal. At one level, therefore, we agree with Truss *et al*, as we would not claim that we have found examples that are purely about measurement or development. However, where we differ from the account of Truss *et al* (1997) is that labels of performance development or performance measurement, as depicted in Figure 3.2, do seem to apply in most cases to capture the overall 'essence' of the intervention. In our codification exercise it was possible to discern performance management applications with a primary focus on either development or measurement, and what appears to underlie the distinction is really the philosophy, the 'intent' or 'driver' (often determined by whether the sponsor is HR or the CEO), which in turn determines the focus and probable outcomes from the approach.

In our view, the findings from this exercise are very illuminating. Although the number of companies represented is small, it was possible to see more emphasis on harder performance improvement or performance measurement approaches than on softer performance development approaches. This reflected what we felt was happening at a macro level, with an increasing emphasis on 'raising standards' across all sectors – typically through target setting and monitoring. It was also noticeable that the performance measurement or improvement approaches were most marked in the more recent projects, further suggestion of a trend from the late 1990s towards harder, more quantifiable approaches. Only one-third of the 12 projects under scrutiny in this codification may be interpreted as comprising performance development. The remainder can all better be described as performance measurement, owing to their emphasis on 'the bottom line' and measurable quantifiable benefits (Table 3.2).

In summary, the theoretical work and its application to practice caused us to believe that the increasing drive to quantify outputs from the HR professional's work has seen an accompanying move towards measurement-based performance management approaches. Just as Legge has reported on the utilitarian instrumentalism vs developmental humanist approaches which underlie hard and soft HRM, it is the value base that is really the fundamental differentiator (Legge, 1978).

What has become apparent to us is that organizations make choices around these values, not always explicitly or even knowingly, but these choices do determine the character of the ensuing performance management

Table 3.2 Reflecting on practice – codification of 12 performance management implementations

Organization description, location and date	Driver behind performance initiative	Training/development rated as 1 (low) to 3 (high)	Communication	Nature of performance drive: development or measurement
UK govt agency 1995	Following pay and grading exercise	Competency-based development as part of the process (1)	Seeking to instigate top-down strategy cascade	Performance measurement
UK govt agency 1996	Following pay and grading, but also seeking to prepare for privatization	Considerable emphasis on leadership and competency-based development (2)	Change team in place seeking feedback, including from IR representatives	Performance measurement/development
UK, engineering 1996	Common appraisal process	Competency-based (1)	Top-down	Performance measurement
UK TEC 1996-7	Management development	Leadership, some 360-degree, managerial style Competency-based development (3)	Two-way encouraged within top levels of the organization	Performance development
UK utility 1997	Merger: large change programme around business performance	Heavy emphasis on the 'enablers': feedback, coaching, active listening (3)	Working groups from across business involved in integration	Performance development with clear aim of measurement
UK retail 1995	Leadership development for business performance	Upward feedback for top managers, referencing leadership style, culture and likely impact on the motivation of others (2)	Top-down	Performance development in essence
UK element of large pharmaceutical 1998	Around living the values. Became part of massive HR change programme	Values/Competency-based (3)	Cross-business-level implementation teams.	Performance development (to drive business performance)

(Continued)

Table 3.2 (*Continued*)

Organization description, location and date	Driver behind performance initiative	Training/development rated as 1 (low) to 3 (high)	Communication	Nature of performance drive: development or measurement
European element of Japanese hi-tech 1997–2000	Integrated HR project (including renaming of personnel). Aiming for business performance and incl job definition, grading	Big emphasis on competencies in job definitions and in performance assessment. Integrated with intranet-based training (2)	Distant and with cultural differences	Performance measurement
UK govt dependency 1997	Following pay and grading exercise and part of organizational restructure	Some emphasis and movement towards competency-based (1)	Consultation process and ongoing education, but perceived as top-down	Performance measurement
UK tobacco 1996/97	Improving business performance, through alignment with strategy and effective target-setting	Competency-based (1)	Top-down	Performance measurement
Swiss/Worldwide insurance 1998/99	Massive change project around strategy implementation for business performance	Knowledge management and competency-based Coaching and upward feedback to top team on leadership style	Roadshows and workshops to input to the BSC Change project communication	Performance measurement
German/Worldwide computer solutions 1999/2000/2001	Part of large change project driven from HR, aiming for common people management processes	Movement towards competency-based development and emphasis on coaching and feedback skills	Largely top-down, but including workers' council	Performance measurement

systems and processes. In the recent past we see that many organizations have made choices that have resulted in the performance management process assuming a heavily measurement-based culture. Given the cyclical nature of fashion, many practitioners may recall that such approaches were popular during the 1980s when they were entitled 'management by objectives' or MBO.

At the outset it seemed to us that the two philosophies were so different in their grounding or value set that they could not be combined successfully. That is to say, if an organization were to pursue measurement wholeheartedly it would be very difficult to mitigate against the drawbacks of the approach, so dissatisfaction and measurement dysfunction would ensue. On the other hand, we were unsure whether a truly development-based approach could ever be perceived as having 'teeth'. This is a theme that we will return to later, as our thinking has evolved. Before we do so, it is worth while spending a few moments considering some case examples that illustrate in more detail performance management implementations at either end of the development/measurement spectrum.

CASE STUDY

Our first example is of a performance development approach linked to soft HRM and our first organization (which we will refer to as 'Company A') is a former government agency, now working more closely with the private sector and increasingly being charged with profitability targets. The organization was established six years ago under an enthusiastic and entrepreneurial chief executive. From its small-scale origins (with 10 staff initially) it has now grown in size to 200 employees. This has meant that a range of more professional 'support services' have been implemented. The management services director has recently appointed a full-time HR manager who has been assigned the priority of working on motivation and morale and performance management. Many of the staff within the organization are young and for many this is their first job. They report informally that the culture is one of 'blame' and 'name and shame'. Staff turnover is surprisingly high for the local area and exit interviews suggest lack of development and support from managers as key reasons for leaving.

Against this backdrop the organization decided to review its approach to performance management, moving away from the older-style 'Civil Service' approach that had been used before. This allowed for a redesign of the whole process and Company A (via a steering group of the most senior managers apart from the CEO) determined that it would focus on both objectives and development plans. There would be no overall 'rating of performance', although managers were all to be asked every six months for their current assessment of potential among all their direct reports. The organization did not have a highly geared performance-related pay (PRP) system, but a link did exist at a subtle level between the performance discussions and resultant salary increases.

In order to emphasize development, the organization decided to include a 'compulsory objective' for all people managers around conducting timely performance reviews, quarterly reviews and the production of development plans. At the same time, the HR manager persuaded the board to look at culture within the organization – to determine what needed to change in order to meet the increasingly commercial operating environment. This work led to the creation of a competency model, linked to the new values of 'Succeeding Together'; 'Serving the Locality'; 'Honesty and Integrity'; and 'Delivery Focus'. Not only were these competencies incorporated into the development and performance review sessions, but at the same time a 360-degree feedback tool was piloted with the executive. It produced interesting results. Most of the executive received feedback which did not surprise them – with the exception of the CEO. His feedback pointed to a strongly autocratic and 'controlling style', one likely to engender a climate of fear. The new HR manager feared for his life, but upon reflection the CEO began to recognize elements of this behaviour and to discuss ways of better managing and masking these. He took the surprising decision of finding a personal 'coach' and worked with her to complete a further range of diagnostics and (for the first time ever) a development plan.

Eighteen months later, the HR manager was happy still to be in post and was able to report on progress. Staff turnover had reduced considerably, and staff feedback suggested this was a motivating place to work. Objectives in an increasingly commercial and competitive marketplace were tough, but development went hand in hand with this trend.

CASE STUDY

This is an example of a performance measurement approach linked to hard HRM, from a European-wide logistics organization operating in nine countries across 200 sites in the UK, Belgium, France, Germany, Ireland, the Netherlands, Italy, Portugal and Spain.

In 1999, business results were poor and despite an excellent year in 2000 the downward trend re-emerged in 2001 and looked set to continue in 2002. At the end of January 2002, 30 members of the senior management team met to discuss and work on developing ideas for urgently improving the organizational performance of the company. They decided on three core principles to improve organizational performance:

▌ a shared company scorecard;

▌ an integrated group-wide performance management system;

▌ a revised approach to reward linked to the above two points.

The group was influenced by Jack Welch's ideas of the 'vitality curve' and, as a result, sought to differentiate between staff. The intention was to 'raise the performance bar' by eliminating the bottom 10 per cent of performers each year. Essentially a 'hard' approach to performance management emerged, with a primary focus on the 'what' of performance. The 'how' was also included via a new leadership competency model which was to form a 10 per cent element of the final review.

As a starting point, a set of core business imperatives were identified and from them flowed eight key performance indicators (KPIs) across the four balanced-scorecard categories. These key measures became the improvement numbers and targets for every part of the business, from group to division and regions through to site levels. As a result, everyone within the business knew the targets and what was being expected from them for this year. The approach was supported by a new performance management process, underpinned by a revised reward architecture aiming to:

▌ link individual performance contribution to overall company performance contribution;

▌ assess individual manager performance contribution across all four scorecard categories;

▌ differentiate between performance in terms of three types across the peer groups (the top 20 per cent, middle 70 per cent and bottom 10 per cent).

The new reward system was designed for introduction one year into the new balanced-scorecard performance approach. This was in order to give the business one year to become familiar with the process before any hard monetary rewards were associated with it. The new bonus system was underpinned by weightings, which stressed the importance of the achievement of financial measures in the first instance. It was also designed so that it would only pay out if overall company performance reached a pre-defined percentage of the target levels. This percentage could be set at the beginning of each year.

For readers interested in considering their own organization's practice in terms of the development/measurement framework, we have devised a simple diagnostic. This self-score instrument may be found in Appendix 1.

This chapter and the one before it have provided a more academic framework for understanding performance management as it is currently manifested within organizations. In Chapter 2 we presented a review of some of the main disciplines which have contributed to its development and in this chapter we have described a framework for understanding based on two very different 'faces' of performance management: one grounded in measurement and improvement philosophies and one that is more grounded in developmental and motivational approaches. As we have described these different manifestations we have introduced the debate as to whether they are discernible in practice (we have decided that they are) but also whether they might be reconcilable. We have sought to make the two different approaches 'tangible' via a framework against which the reader may consider our findings from the empirical work, which we report in the next part.

Part II
Evidence from fieldwork and redrawing the performance management map

This part describes the fieldwork we have conducted to date in order to describe the nature of current performance management practice. In Chapter 4 we detail a survey of line manager perceptions of performance management, which was conducted towards the end of 2003. This was followed up by five 'mini' case studies described in Chapter 5, where we explore emerging trends. Chapter 6 provides a summary of our fieldwork and attempts to redraw the performance management 'map' in order to illustrate what we know about current practice. The emergent picture is very different from what we knew and experienced around performance management five years ago, and appears to typify where many organizations are finding themselves at the current time. For those readers who want to move beyond this, however, and benchmark themselves against the 'best in class' companies, this part concludes with what we can learn from research into what the most admired companies are doing around performance management.

4

Line manager survey

This chapter is concerned with performance management as it applies to, and is experienced by, line managers. When this research began in 2000 it was our intuitive view that an increased emphasis on the business benefits of HRM and the growth of HR accounting had led to a greater demand within organizations to see a tangible return from performance management. We were keen to explore this in more detail by means of a survey, for which we wanted to make line manager perceptions our focus, rather than the HR manager who is so often held accountable for implementing performance management.

DESIGN AND SAMPLE FOR LINE MANAGER SURVEY

We started the fieldwork with certain preconceptions and questions that we were interested in exploring. These are presented in Table 4.1 as a set of themes. The table also indicates the outcome we expected the survey might reveal.

Our survey questionnaire was designed with 50 items, mainly containing Likert-style responses in terms of agree or disagree. We opted for a telephone survey conducted via a third party and utilizing its pre-existing

Table 4.1   Survey themes and anticipated outcomes prior to data collection

Theme to be investigated	What we anticipated survey would reveal
1. Line manager perceptions as to effectiveness of performance management (PM)	Low managerial perceptions as to its effectiveness
2. Prevalence of measures and evidence of measurement dysfunction	Increase use of measures since 2000 and associated measurement dysfunction
3. Accountability of performance and ownership of PM process	Senior management ownership and PM no longer seen as domain of HR
4. Driver of performance management	Emphasis on measuring and 'hard' character of initiative
5. How goal and objective setting is linked to the organizational strategy	Evidence of 'harder', more measurement-based tools such as scorecards
6. Line manager capability in terms of motivational and development aspects	Room for improvement
7. The use of ratings to differentiate between levels of performance	Ratings to be in use in support of measures
8. The use of reward practices based on differentiating between levels of performance	A moderate reward link

databases of managers. This approach proved to have both strengths and limitations. We sought to ensure consistency by agreeing a fixed interview schedule and certain qualifying criteria for participants (working for an organization with a performance management process and having six or more direct reports). From 2,200 telephone approaches, there were 398 individuals who both agreed to participate and met the qualifying criteria. This may be interpreted as representing a response rate of 18 per cent. Using the model of standard error proportion, the 398 respondents allow us to be 95 per cent confident that results are within + or −5 per cent of the population value.

Breakdown of responding organizations

The 398 respondents were drawn from 216 UK organizations in total representing a mixture of private-sector organizations and government

Table 4.2 Distribution of organizations by type represented within survey

	Private sector	Government bodies	Total
Frequency	155	61	216

Table 4.3 Breakdown by sector within private sector organizations

Industry	Frequency	%
1. Pharmaceutical	5	3
2. Financial services	35	23
3. Utilities	2	1
4. Professional services	13	8
5. Manufacturing	2	1
6. Retailing	20	13
7. Telecommunication	3	2
8. Transportation	12	8
9. Construction	7	5
10. Food producers + processors	9	6
11. Chemicals, oil, gas, mining	8	5
12. Engineering	2	1
13. IT/Software, Computer Services	7	5
14. Media and Entertainment	11	7
15. Leisure and Hotel	15	10
16. Unspecified	4	3
Total	**155**	**100**

bodies. The breakdown in terms of sector and organizational size is shown in Table 4.2. Tables 4.3 and 4.4 provide additional information on the composition of the sample.

LINE MANAGER RESPONSES TO THE SURVEY

Although there were a number of instances where more than one individual responded from the same organization, we shall focus here on

Table 4.4   Participating organizations by company size

Employees	Private sector		Government bodies		Total	
	Frequency	%	Frequency	%	Frequency	%
Under 500	17	11%	16	26%	33	15%
500 to 999	17	11%	11	18%	28	13%
1,000 to 2,999	22	14%	6	10%	28	13%
3,000 to 9,999	30	19%	5	8%	35	16%
10,000 or more	56	36%	3	5%	59	27%
Unspecified	13	8%	20	33%	33	15%
Total	**155**	**100%**	**61**	**100%**	**216**	**100%**

managers' perceptions in the seven thematic areas presented in Table 4.1, rather than on cross-company comparisons. Where we present overall percentages we are giving the numbers who indicate a strong or very strong view or preference (ie a preference indicated by level 7 or more on a 9-point scale).

Managerial perceptions as to the effectiveness of performance management

As performance management has anecdotally received a mixed press, we expected a range of low–medium ratings as to the perceived effectiveness of performance management from managers in our survey. We discovered that, like Armstrong and Baron (1998, 2005) before us, our findings are largely at odds with the anecdotal bad press often accorded to the 'dreaded appraisal'.

Sixty-eight per cent of the 398 respondents indicated that performance management within their organization was very effective to excellent. This struck us as a very positive response, which resonates with that of Armstrong and Baron who found similar high levels of support for performance management processes, with almost two-thirds perceiving that performance management was either very or mostly effective.

Prevalence of measures

We expected measures to be prevalent and to have increased in recent years. Here our intuition proved accurate. In terms of trends, 72 per cent

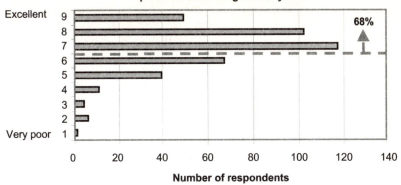

Figure 4.1 Effectiveness of performance management

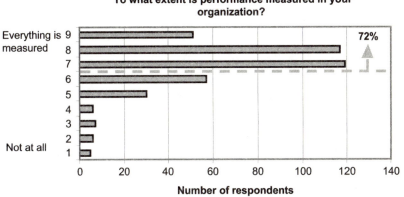

Figure 4.2 Prevalence of measures

strongly agreed that everything was measured within their organization and 64 per cent reported that the use of measures has increased over the past two years. Sixty-seven per cent reported that the measures they use are centrally dictated and three-quarters (75 per cent) strongly perceived that measures keep people focused on what is important. However, unlike certain academic critiques, we could find little evidence that measures were equated with disempowerment or micro management. As many as three-quarters reported that measures keep people focused on what is important.

In the last two years have the number of measures you have ....

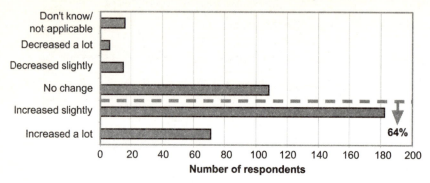

Figure 4.3   The increase in measures over past two years

'Using the measures and discussions about them keeps people focused on what's important'

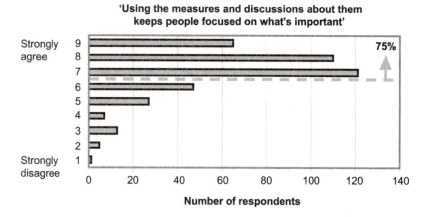

Figure 4.4   Measures help focus on what is important

Academic critiques have suggested that measurement is a controlling mechanism that might be perceived to dis-empower. The concept of measurement dysfunction has emerged in consequence, where the concern is with managing the measure instead of managing performance. Although there was some evidence of this in existence, the level that reported it was lower than expected. As illustrated in Figure 4.5, only 22 per cent believe that people are more concerned with manipulating the figures so they look good, rather than doing a good job.

Accountability for performance and ownership of PM process

In Chapter 2 we considered Corvellec's (1997) writings around the number of ways organizations define success. Our research data indicated that

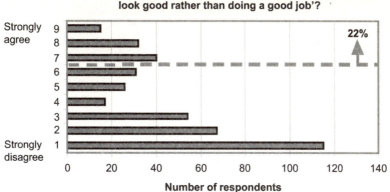

Figure 4.5 Evidence of measurement dysfunction

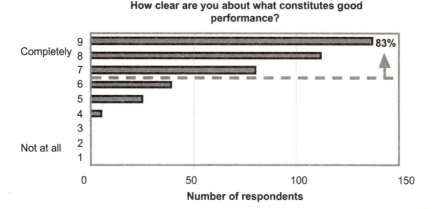

Figure 4.6 Clarity over performance requirements

despite the lack of a common framework, 83 per cent of managers who responded were clear about what constituted good performance within their own organization.

Although the earlier (1998 and 2005) surveys by Armstrong and Baron reported a shift in perceived ownership from HR to line managers, we did not discover such a strong sense of this. We did find evidence that 78 per cent strongly believed that the senior management team within their organization was involved in the performance management process. However, when we asked a question as to who 'owns' performance management in your organization, 13 per cent of respondents indicated that they did not know and over half (58 per cent) suggested it to be the role of HR. The impression that line managers might be responsible was limited to 9 per cent, with 7 per cent believing it to be the responsibility of the individual. This is similar to findings from the CIPD Reward Management Survey (2005), which confirmed that despite board and senior manager support, the involvement of line managers was disappointingly low.

Driver for performance management and character of initiative

Despite its sometimes bad press, we also did not find a sense that performance management was perceived to be about driving down costs. In fact, we found that in almost half of cases (46 per cent) the main driver was perceived to be around motivation.

We were expecting to see an increase in the use of measures (and indeed we did) and thought this would emerge as a dominant characteristic of the performance management experience. We therefore asked managers whether they perceived their performance management system to be more about motivating or more about measuring. When forced to choose, however, between motivation and measurement, 71 per cent opted for motivation as the more dominant driver behind the performance management process in their organization. This seems to disprove some of the more academic critiques that link measurement with perceptions of employees being overly controlled.

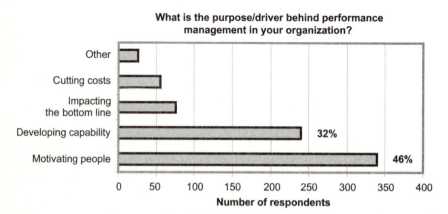

Figure 4.7 Main driver for performance management

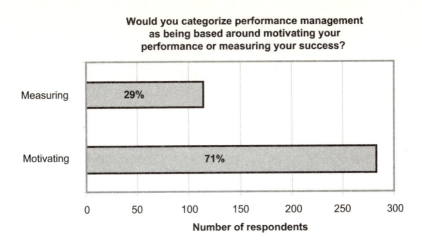

Figure 4.8 Motivation or measurement focus?

How goal and objective setting is linked to the organizational strategy

When asked what processes were used to help the planning cycle, 48 per cent reported that they used a business plan methodology, 25 per cent a team-planning approach and 21 per cent reported that they were using a scorecard. Overall, 65 per cent of respondents reported a strong belief that their goals were aligned with organizational strategy. Over half (56 per cent) reported that they were using a mix of goals combining financial and behavioural. Seventy-six per cent reported that they set SMART goals.

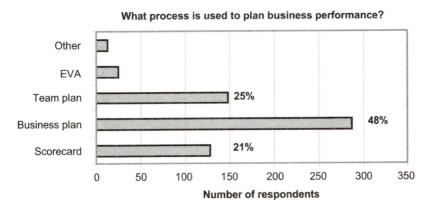

Figure 4.9 Linking goal setting to organizational strategy

Line manager capability in terms of motivational and development aspects

Despite the fairly 'hard' and business-focused character of performance management processes, 67 per cent of line managers surveyed here believed that their performance management process focuses on career development.

Three-quarters of respondents (79 per cent) reported that they had regular discussions with their manager about their performance.

Sixty-four per cent stated that they were motivated by the performance management process and over 93 per cent reported being motivated to

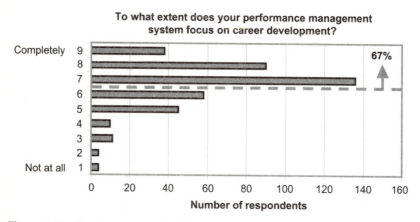

Figure 4.10 Focus on career development

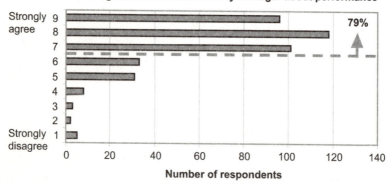

Figure 4.11 Focus on performance

some degree by their last review discussion. These findings are broadly in line with Armstrong and Baron's earlier surveys (1998 and 2005), which report around three-quarters of their respondents as finding performance management to be motivational.

The use of ratings to differentiate between levels of performance

We found no evidence of ratings going out of fashion and over half (55 per cent) reported that the rating of performance was important within their organization. This is very similar to the figure reported in 2005 by Armstrong and Baron (59 per cent). However, we found considerably more evidence than they did for a 'forced' distribution of ratings; 49 per cent of managers who responded here indicated that they were encouraged to allocate their direct reports into 'quotas' of above average, average, below average, etc. Of the line managers we surveyed, 42 per cent reported that their organization considers 'letting go' the lowest-rated individuals, as in the forced distribution approach popularized by Jack Welch at General Electric (GE).

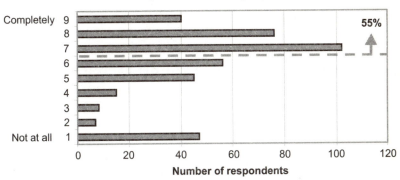

How important is the rating of your performance?

Figure 4.12   Importance of performance rating

The use of reward practices based on differentiating between levels of performance

Across all sectors, 69 per cent reported a link between performance and bonus or base salary. The 2005 reward survey by the CIPD suggests that a similar number (64 per cent) see one of the main drivers of reward to be identifying and rewarding high performance. Our survey suggests that there is a gap between ambition and effective practice, with only 46 per cent reporting that pay was really differentiated on the basis of performance. Sixty-one per cent strongly believed that performance management meant people are rewarded fairly, with 36 per cent saying it had no bearing. The issue of fairness is a perennial one for performance management processes and 72 per cent of the respondents report that their organization held calibration meetings to support the fairness of the process and its reward links.

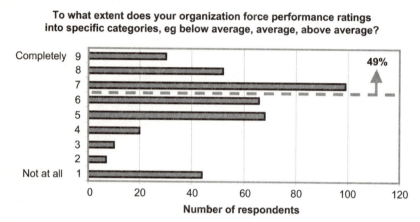

To what extent does your organization force performance ratings into specific categories, eg below average, average, above average?

Figure 4.13   Use of forced distribution

Criticisms of performance management

The survey also provided us with an opportunity to ask line managers what were the main issues they had with performance management. Despite the encouraging tone of much of the findings, there were nonetheless issues with performance management. The following emerged as the most common themes: time consuming; inconsistent; inflexible; poorly communicated; insufficient reward link; and a lack of management capability to do it well.

CONCLUSIONS FROM THE LINE MANAGER SURVEY

Although our survey preceded the *Fortune*/Hay Group research into what the most admired companies do and we embarked on our survey of

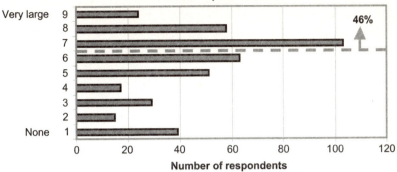

Figure 4.14 Differential reward based on contribution

line managers to investigate somewhat different themes, we do discover a significant degree of congruity across our findings, as discussed later in Chapter 7. We find fairly high levels of awareness and understanding of organizational imperatives, despite the range of techniques that organizations deploy to decode and operationalize their strategy. We see that measures play a key role in helping both to achieve this clarity and to make both manager and employee accountable for delivering what is required of them in performance terms. In terms of measures we find that organizations are increasingly measuring more than financials, with almost three-quarters reporting that 'everything is measured' within their organization. Despite the heavy measurement focus, we do not necessarily see this to be having an adverse impact on culture, motivation or development initiatives. Measures appear to be providing the much-needed clarity that line managers require to keep performance management motivational in nature.

In summary, the survey findings confirm a trend towards 'harder' and measurement-based approaches, in place perhaps of the emphasis on incorporating competencies which was so popular in the late 1990s. Competencies and development are still included, but not at the expense of being highly focused on the organization's main deliverables. The climate is therefore one where human resource departments are increasingly required to predict and deliver business improvements. Our findings are encouraging, as they suggest that in many organizations this is being achieved without sacrificing employee motivation and career development approaches. For practitioners we consider that the challenge for the future is to continue in this vein, seeking to combine the best of performance measurement with good management and development practices.

5

Deepening our understanding through mini case studies of practice

While the survey of line managers described in Chapter 4 identified some patterns and trends in the data presented, we were left with many questions in order to understand more fully some of the facts and figures we had uncovered. In order to pursue this, we followed up the survey in 2003 with a round of mini case studies.

Five European organizations participated in this second phase of data collection, with three operating on a global basis. They were:

1. Metro AG – the third-largest retail group in Europe, headquartered in Germany;

2. Philips – the third-largest consumer electronics company, headquartered in Holland;

3. A recently formed UK regulator;

4. Abbey – the UK's sixth-largest retail bank;

5. Department for Trade and Industry – the government department focusing on the business environment in the UK.

In order to allow us to probe in depth some of the areas highlighted through the earlier literature and empirical studies, the mini case studies focused on:

▌ the sense of clarity and direction built into the performance management process and the use of measures to clarify this message to staff and managers;

▌ the impact of any process on defining or supporting the existing or proposed culture;

▌ the reinforcement of organizational values through what the performance management process asked managers to do;

▌ how the performance management process sought to build motivation, as well as ensure that outputs were measured and tracked; was the performance culture essentially measurement or development focused?

▌ how the performance management process linked to reward, if at all, and how these organizations ensured that reward and recognition were differentiated on the basis of contribution;

▌ the perennial problem of dealing with underperformance;

▌ what senior leaders within the organization did that helped/hindered the success of any performance management process.

The case studies focused on interviewing the 'architects' of the performance management process (the HR department in each case) as well as talking to a small sample of line managers – the 'end users' of the process. This enabled us to understand whether the strategic intent of the process – the purpose and philosophy behind its design as well as the mechanics of intended implementation – matched the reality of how people were viewing and conducting the process 'on the ground'.

THREE CONTEXTUAL THEMES

Across all five organizations, three contextual commonalities emerged. The most striking was the degree of change, with all describing performance management in transition. All the organizations we talked to were improving, re-engineering or refreshing their performance management process. This echoes a point we alluded to earlier in Chapter 2, the fact that most organizations are focusing at the present time on getting human resources – and therefore the performance management process – to deliver more, and to be aligned to what the organization identifies as its key priorities. The dissatisfaction with a process that was seen primarily as an annual ritual or an ongoing system of planning, managing and reviewing performance, but not focusing sufficiently on the business agenda, had led these organizations to focus on specific aspects of their systems, which differed for each organization. This points to a more general requirement to do an accurate audit as a first step of what needs changing and how, to ensure that the biggest benefit is derived from the most cost-effective change.

The second theme follows on from the first, in identifying a clear role for 'professional HR' to orchestrate this transition. In all five case study organizations the role of HR had changed, from the traditional role where they were at best the custodians of design principles and best practice providing advice to line managers, to at worst hassling people for the return of forms and administering the process. The change was often a subtle one that retained the guidance and counselling role but demonstrated in a noticeably different way – as a business partner rather than as a best practice adviser – and a noticeably harsher stance that was about 'policing' the process and ensuring consistency. The latter often meant that conversations with line managers were about offering guidance around distribution norms or how to differentiate and tackle poor performers. (The shifting nature of the HR role was examined in more detail in Chapter 2.)

Finally, and perhaps not before time, performance was seen as being owned by senior managers within the organization and the board had a key role in endorsing aspects of the process. For many of the case study organizations, key performance measures, decisions about performance ratings, the proportions that would be expected within each rating group and the key messages that would be propagated within the performance management process were now being actively debated at board level. There seemed to be a greater awareness than ever before that driving organizational performance was about driving performance among people, and the vehicle that any organization had to do this was its performance management process.

FIVE DOMINANT THEMES AROUND PERFORMANCE MANAGEMENT

As well as the contextual commonalities, a number of themes occurred across the organizations examined. For descriptive purposes we have grouped these into five dominant themes, although overlaps entail a number working in combination to successfully re-engineer a performance management process:

▌ Theme 1 – Measurement and hardening of 'intangibles';

▌ Theme 2 – Dealing with underperformance;

▌ Theme 3 – One company, one approach;

▌ Theme 4 – Strengthening clarity and HR 'line of sight';

▌ Theme 5 – Differentiation of reward linked to level of performance.

Each of these themes is explored in detail below, using one of the case studies to exemplify how a particular organization has made this a reality. It should be noted, however, that the themes were not exclusive to the organization described but were common to a number of the mini case studies.

Measurement and hardening of 'intangibles'

In support of our earlier hypothesis about a shift towards a measurement culture, nearly all of the five case studies had clearly defined objectives and key result areas as the bedrock of their performance management processes. This did not end simply with the 'harder' measures around objectives but now also extended to an attempt to quantify those factors traditionally considered to be 'intangibles', ie values, competencies and 'softer' factors that holistically constituted performance. This aim of quantification removed the perception of these being 'softer' and sanctioned their use in the performance assessment. This seemed to be underpinned by an inherent belief that by measuring these elements in the same way as objectives, any vestiges of subjectivity would be further removed.
Key elements of this theme included:

▌ a concern to align personal and business objectives;

▌ a strong systems approach focusing on prescription, structure and process;

▌ treating all measures as equal and open to the same 'laws' of assessment;

▌ a quantification of 'softer' elements to legitimize their use;

▌ an attempt to integrate different elements within the organization that referred to how people should perform or behave under one common umbrella.

This theme was exemplified by **Philips**:

Philips has a people performance management process that focuses on KARs (key areas of responsibility), drilled down into personal objectives and further defined into measurable performance targets for the year. An example for an IT manager role is shown in Figure 5.1.

The key area of responsibility and personal objectives – traditionally considered a hard measure – is here combined with an assessment rating (and supporting comments) against the four Philips values – usually considered too 'soft' to measure in a direct way. The results of KARs and personal objectives together with the values rating combine to create a performance–value rating on a 5-point rating scale ranging from 'excels' to 'requires action' (illustrated through the performance management grid in Figure 5.2). This measure of personal contribution applies to all staff and is linked to reward.

In addition, a separate score is assigned to indicate the promotability of an individual, indicating the expected future career progression in terms of grades or pay scales as illustrated above. This rating is applicable to all staff and 15,000 employees participated in the process

PHILIPS

Example – for IT manager role:

- **KAR:**
  - *Ensure availability of applications and access to hardware, network and local PCs to support the business*
- **Personal objective:**
  - *Increase up-time of the network of business unit X in 2006*
- **Measurable performance target:**
  - *Increase up-time of the network of business unit X by 3% in 2006*

Figure 5.1 Example for an IT manager. *Source:* Philips, reproduced with permission

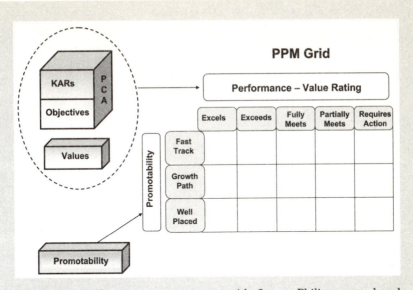

Figure 5.2 Performance management grid. *Source:* Philips, reproduced with permission

and used this performance management tool in 2004/05. The promotability rating – Fast Track, Growth Path, or Well Placed – projects an individual's ability to operate at a higher grade within guidelines of specific periods of time. Both ratings are inputs for reward decisions. The promotability rating is also based around an assessment of the individual's performance against proven competencies. Philips utilizes a mix of the Philips leadership competencies and functional competency models, with reference role profiles used to help people identify required performance levels against the competencies for their particular role.

Development plans therefore include a comprehensive mix of objectives, strengths and development needs, development objectives, career aspirations and mobility. Leadership competencies and functional competencies are also used as input for the development plan.

This is a highly structured and systematic process. The focus on intangibles – values and competencies – has extended to measuring these, which is likely to make them feel like any other target. The highly structured process has strong elements of control but offers clarity around performance expectations and organizational benchmarks of performance.

Dealing with underperformance

The issue of dealing with poor performers is one that we come across in whichever sector – public or private – we work in. It has always been the thorn in the side of managers and HR alike. In our case study organizations we found active attempts to confront poor performance, with a focus by the architects of the performance management process both to support line managers through this difficult issue and also to police and enforce measures aimed at getting line managers to meet the issue head-on.

Key elements of this theme included:

▌ a tougher line and commitment that this issue had to be tackled – for reasons of emphasizing excellence and equity to others who were doing their best;

▌ the introduction of forced distributions of performance;

▌ board-level involvement in decisions about performance distributions or what constituted good performance;

▌ 'policing' of, and support to, line managers;

▌ calibration across departments and areas to ensure consistency in the way performance standards were being enforced.

This theme was exemplified by The Department for Trade and Industry:

The UK Department for Trade and Industry (DTI) had a reputation, like much of the nation's Civil Service more generally, for a performance management process that was rigidly conducted with discussions around performance but which did not yield differentiations in terms of performance among individuals. There was a tendency for line managers to be restricted in the range they used to give performance ratings, resulting in the majority of people being viewed towards the high end or middle of the scale and very few, sometimes none at all, at the poor performance end of the scale. These results did not seem to match the reality of the situation, where some members of staff were clearly not performing as the organization expected. Allied to this, line managers were finding it hard to give difficult messages to staff or to confront them about their performance.

To tackle this, the DTI initially focused on establishing greater clarity and consistency around individuals' objectives. It moved towards a smaller number of departmental strategic objectives that were linked to objectives for individual work areas, which in turn drilled down into individual performance plans. There was a clearer link between these elements and also greater 'policing' of these; senior managers now review samples of individual objectives to ensure that staff set objectives around a mandatory set of key areas.

A guideline distribution of performance has been introduced, with 'Highly Successful' (expected to be around 20–25 per cent of people), 'Successful' (65–75 per cent of people), and 'Improvement Needed' (5–10 per cent of people). There is also an 'Unacceptable' category – likely to apply to only a very small number of people – that invokes the inefficiency (disciplinary) procedure. These performance distributions have been discussed and signed off at board level, displaying a commitment from the very senior levels of the organization to accurately identify and recognize the performance of staff. Although this approach has been criticized by some staff as a quota, the DTI has taken pains to emphasize that it is a guidance distribution only, derived from what you might typically see in the organization. Historical data around performance distributions has enabled the organization to say roughly what proportions of staff have been categorized at different performance levels. This has also enabled the department to say what proportions it would realistically expect to see moving forward, resulting in an incremental approach to tackling poor performance and based on the starting point of previous years. Annual reviews of this guideline performance distribution allow the organization to make changes to the proportions expected within each category, enabling it to build on successes from previous years.

In the first year of the new scheme, the DTI found that the Improvement Needed category was underused and reported this back to line managers the following year; it has subsequently found that this category has helped line managers address poor performance more openly and honestly. The category is less penalty driven (not linked, as before, to disciplinary measures) and leads to a Performance Improvement Plan that is seen as fixing an issue, with the expectation of a return to satisfactory levels of performance.

The setting up of the 'Performance Management Unit' has also helped. This is clearly branded and is used to support line managers only (or challenge them); other staff that have issues with the performance management process receive help elsewhere. The unit has three caseworkers that support line managers with performance issues, offering them the advice and guidance needed to ensure they take responsibility for confronting the performance issues within their own teams.

Much of this work had led to perceptions within the DTI changing – there is a harder line, underscored by distribution guidelines and a seriousness signalled from the very top of the organization. It is a good example of a performance management process that is not radical but has introduced a number of features that have made a difference in setting standards and tackling underperformance.

One company, one approach

Among the case study companies that were international, all were concerned with moving away from a state of high autonomy (in relation to performance management) among regions and/or different businesses, to a state that relied on a common and more standardized approach. This was often characterized by a need to ensure consistency in the way performance was assessed, to deploy common templates and establish benchmarks of performance across the organization. It was often fuelled by the need to ensure people delivered the global brand in the same way across constituencies and was underpinned by a belief that although there were benefits in 'acting local', the strength of the business lay in the group and 'thinking globally'.

Key elements of this theme included:

❙ a move towards one common process, with shared language and consistency for assessing performance;

❙ clear commitment and timescales by which to adopt the new process company-wide;

❙ a staged approach, piloting a new process in a few regions before rolling out globally and allowing regions time to migrate;

❙ all materials and tools available on intranet or central HR system.

This theme was exemplified by Metro AG:

Metro AG is a German supermarket chain, now the third-largest supermarket in the world, with more than 2,300 outlets and a distribution network across 26 countries including China, eastern and western Europe, as well as Vietnam, India and Japan. Although 40 per cent of its turnover is generated outside Germany, the business is still based in Düsseldorf.

Metro AG has experienced several years of growth and consolidation within its main markets and now includes 29 companies, employing 240,000 people. Recently there has been a move to implement EVA (economic value added) approaches across the business, resulting in staff information being reported to the board as a cost. From the central HR function there is a growing desire to represent personnel as more than a cost. The latest approaches to performance measurement have therefore attempted to establish the key value drivers in terms of how HR issues directly influence the business.

In order to address this need, five business drivers with appropriate measures have been identified. One of these drivers is the measure of commitment/engagement within the organization, and this driver has been recognized by Metro as being key to its future business success. In order to measure this, the company has deployed an approach developed by the Gallup Group that asks just 12 questions around engagement to the organization. The approach has been validated via earlier Gallup research and has established links to EVA as well as to profit and customer satisfaction.

The concern of central HR was to ensure it influenced the use of this approach company-wide. As a starting point, pilots were completed across a number of different companies, each with 15,000–20,000 people. Take-up by different businesses has relied on providing success stories and case studies from the pilot sites as well as providing a toolkit for managers and staff. Through this approach, central HR has begun to provide a template for measuring commitment and engagement across a large and disparate organization.

This is an example of an innovative way of tackling performance management which not only accepts that measurement should be used for hard financial outputs but also attempts to incorporate some key lead measures around commitment and motivation. It also charts an organization striving to propagate 'one company, one approach' along a still-evolving performance management transformation journey.

Strengthening clarity and HR 'line of sight'

A theme that underpinned much of the transition work around performance management in our case study organizations was the need to align the performance management process, conducted at a one-to-one level by line managers, more clearly to the needs of the organization at a higher level. This was being achieved in different ways, for example through tackling underperformance at the DTI, or through measurement at Philips. All were about strengthening clarity around what the performance management process was required to deliver for the organization, and ensuring the actions of line managers and staff were aligned to this. This was achieved through the actions of HR, as architects and enforcers of the system, supporting people to see this 'clear line of sight' between their individual actions and the needs of the organization.

Key elements of this theme included:

▌ establishing clarity between business objectives and individual actions;

▌ a focus on getting the planning part of the performance management cycle right, so that objectives were set around the areas required by the business as well as the individual;

▌ time spent on clearly articulating what was expected and why.

This theme was exemplified by Abbey:

A need to reinvigorate business performance has led to Abbey investing in the design and implementation of a new approach to performance management. The new approach aims to be aligned much more closely to the corporate brand of 'keep it simple' and to link business objectives more clearly to individual performance plans. Clarity has been enhanced through a three-part plan – termed 'do, be and develop' – designed to ensure that objectives are set around behavioural, development and business goals. This has been reinforced through planning workshops for all managers to support them in setting business-focused objectives with individuals.

The thread established through the planning stage is followed through with mandatory quarterly performance reviews, in addition to the standard formal mid- and end-of-year reviews, to ensure that managers hold people accountable for delivering against objectives agreed at the outset of the year. Linking performance development to regulatory requirements has also enabled compliance to be seen not just as a necessary financial regulatory process but as something that also contributes towards high performance in role.

Buy-in and endorsement by senior management have been a critical part of the new approach to performance management. All of the above activities, while being essentially simple in their design, have in combination helped Abbey revise the performance management process to adopt a clear results focus, predicated on the need to improve business performance.

Differentiation of reward linked to level of performance

One of the issues that emerged from the survey of line managers described in Chapter 4 was the lack of effective differentiation in terms of rewarding level of contribution. While most organizations had a link between performance and pay, there was less evidence of them ensuring that those who received greater rewards were the people who had actually contributed more in performance terms throughout the year. Consequently, this was an issue with which many of our case study organizations were grappling. Most of the organizations we talked to recognized that the answer to the question rested less with the design and engineering of the performance management process and more with the capability of line managers to assess performance accurately and have honest conversations about the level at which that performance would be judged.

Key elements of this theme included:

I guidance about expected performance distributions, ratings and reward implications;

I investing in training and development for managers to help them differentiate performance within their teams;

I reconfiguring the way that bonuses and/or performance-related pay are distributed;

I widening the scope of reward to encapsulate others forms of recognition such as access to training and development, secondments, work–life balance, etc.

This theme was exemplified by a UK regulator:

> The UK regulator was created through the amalgamation of a number of different agencies and consequently had a performance management system that had evolved through the different practices of the merged organizations. The regulator's main aim was to move away from the previous system, where managers adopted the guidance around the process as a set of 'rules' to be applied rigidly. Instead, efforts were focused around developing an approach that encouraged flexibility, recognized the contribution the individual was making to the organization and supported an honest conversation between manager and employee. One of the biggest issues for HR had been the misuse of performance ratings, with lower ratings rarely being used and high ratings being used as an easy means of motivating people.
>
> The revised approach facilitated managers' ability to 'get on with it' by removing bureaucracy and building manager confidence. The latter was achieved by ensuring that all managers received coaching and training designed to give clarity around reward and bonus. This included input for managers around the expected ratings distribution and how to use bonus ranges for each performance rating as a means to encourage a more even and balanced differentiation of the performance contributions of different team members.

SUMMARY

The five mini case studies suggest that we are observing a move towards formality and structure around process. It seems that it is no longer acceptable to allow leeway and freedom in the interpretation of guidelines or to put up with idiosyncrasies of style according to cultural differences or historical starting points. The concern for standardization and consistency, while producing laudable benefits, is also about control and setting clear standards of 'corporate' performance. The critics who decry the creation of 'identikit' managers have been silenced by the lobby of 'one global enterprise with global methodologies'.

The emphasis appears to be on setting standards, describing in detail the performance areas and levels required and measuring individual achievement against these. But far from finding this precision regarding performance expectations demotivating, our findings suggest the opposite; its use is providing clarity, focus and a clear line of sight around what needs to be done and how, raising levels of motivation to perform effectively.

For organizations, this emphasis on defining performance dimensions and clearly measuring these has provided an opportunity to address one of the thorniest issues in performance management – managing at the extremes. Clarity around performance standards and greater central control have provided an opportunity long missed to tackle underperformers and to identify and manage talent.

6

Redrawing the performance management map

The evidence emerging from our survey of line managers and the follow-on mini case studies has enabled us to start piecing together a picture of what performance management looks like in practice now. The picture we see is markedly different from what we experienced as practitioners and consultants in the late 1990s. It has led us to 'put a stake in the ground' and attempt to redraw the map of performance management as represented by current practice. The discipline of psychology tells us that this 'map is not the territory'; it is a chart of our view of the world, rather than a 'truth'. While this is inevitably the case, we believe we are able to present with some confidence new trends and patterns in the way performance management is currently being delivered in organizations and to identify some of the root causes of these developments.

REDEFINING PERFORMANCE MANAGEMENT REALITIES

Previous research-based attempts to chart a shift in performance management realities in the UK have been limited. The most recent systematic research comes from Armstrong and Baron, in their 1998 book

Performance Management: The new realities, updated in 2005 (*Managing Performance: Performance management in action*). Their late 1990s research for the Institute of Personnel Development (IPD) charted the considerable changes in the approach to performance management that have taken place since 1991. It probably represents the best published 'snapshot' of performance management at the end of the last century.

Our findings differ from theirs in a number of key areas. For example, Armstrong and Baron in 1998 reported a shift during the 1990s away from older-style top-down appraisal towards more inclusive and development-based approaches. In their updated research for the CIPD in 2005, they saw little change to their original picture:

> Overall, there has not been a great deal of movement in the kind of practices employed by organizations to manage performance since the 1997 survey was carried out. Practices such as team appraisal and 360 degree appraisals had become more popular, and it appears that more organizations had become more sophisticated in their approach and in the integration of performance management with other HR practices. However, the vast majority still relied heavily on the tried and tested practices of objective-setting and review, accompanied by development plans and performance. (Armstrong and Baron, 2005: 78)

However, the findings from our survey and the subsequent case studies suggest that the pendulum has swung from development-based approaches to those more centred around measurement.

Our findings suggest the following shifts, as shown in Figure 6.1. When we expand on the 1998 findings of Armstrong and Baron to suggest what the picture looks like in 2006.

1991	1998 *	2006
System	Process	Structure
Appraisal	Joint review	Integrated HR process
Outputs	Inputs	Measurement of results
PRP driven	Development driven	Measurement driven
Ratings common	Ratings less common	Forced distribution
Top-down	360-degree feedback	Holding people accountable
Directive	Supportive	Capability building
Monolithic	Flexible	One company, one approach
Owned by HR	Owned by users	Owned by organization

Figure 6.1 Redefining performance management realities
Source: Armstrong and Baron (1998)

From process to structure

The late 1990s showed a shift from a mechanistic 'system' of rules and techniques that could be applied rigidly to an organization towards a more integrated set of 'processes' focusing on how the performance management process is carried out. Our work suggests that the ongoing process Armstrong and Baron identified is still in place, but if anything it has become more formalized and structured in response to moves towards a common cross-company methodology – often underpinned by intranet-based systems which themselves demand more conformity. Although the move is not towards a set of rigid rules to be applied, and line managers are encouraged to take ownership of the PM process, there is a focus on everyone following the same structure to provide greater assurance of consistent standards in the delivery of the performance management process.

From joint review to integrated HR process

The concept of 'joint review' now seems fairly standard across organizations, the annual appraisal event involving unilateral judgements on the part of line managers having been relegated to the past. Our work suggests that most organizations have now moved further beyond this to integrate the joint review process much more clearly with other HR processes, such as training and development, talent or succession planning, and reward.

For example, at BAT, the joint review process is more fully integrated with the 'Leadership Pipeline' – the process that defines the work requirements of BAT's leaders at particular levels and identifies what is needed to make the transition from one level to the next (see Chapter 11).

From recording levels of inputs to measurement of results

The 1990s were characterized by many organizations investing in developing behavioural competency frameworks and consequently by the end of the decade there was a strong belief that a fully rounded view of performance must embrace 'how' people do things (inputs) as well as what individuals need to get done (outputs). The focus on inputs – competencies, skills and behaviours – is sometimes overshadowed in emphasis by the measurable outputs – the results people were expected to achieve. We have observed a swing-back of the pendulum to a greater focus on achieving job objectives and the quantification of these in the form of actual results that impact on bottom-line performance or delivery targets (in the public sector).

This has been achieved by a strong emphasis on giving clarity around performance expectations – for example, through the balanced scorecard at Lloyds/TSB (see Chapter 12), or the measurement of 'intangibles' such as values at Philips (see Chapter 5). Even in our most development-based performance management story at Belron, the organization has developed a 'leadership KPI' on the climate created by a leader and the leadership styles exhibited, resulting in this behavioural target being viewed as a measure of results just like any other (see Chapter 14).

The exception to this trend is perhaps among the most admired companies who appear to be succeeding in deriving a more 'rounded' and holistic set of measures, as we shall discuss in the next chapter (see Chapter 7).

From development-driven to measurement-driven

Allied to the above, we have already set out the contention of a movement towards more measurement-driven performance management (see Chapters 3 and 4). In our survey of line managers, nearly three-quarters of those surveyed strongly agreed that everything within their organization was measured and two-thirds reported that the use of measures had increased. This is a significant difference in emphasis away from the development-driven approach described by Armstrong and Baron in 1998, a theme to which they report little change in their updated research for the CIPD in 2005. Our findings suggest that while personal development plans and access to training and development still form a significant part of successful performance management, development alone no longer seems to be a key driver for the process. Development still features as a key component of many performance management processes but the emphasis is placed on measuring and recording of development objectives.

From ratings being less common to forced distribution

While there is still hostility among some staff and line managers to performance ratings, our research suggests that ratings remain commonplace and it is unusual to find an organization that does not have some form of rating process in place. One of the most interesting trends that has begun to define current practice in performance management is the rise in the use of forced distributions or at least flexible guidelines on the expected distribution of performance ratings. These are used to guide line managers as to the proportions of people that would normally be expected under each performance rating. While often presented to managers as guidance, rather than a prescriptive 'quota', many of our case study organizations were using forced distributions as a means of managing performance at the extremes, to tackle underperformers or to bring on and identify talent as well as reward very high achievers. For an example of a forced distribution system in the public sector, the reader should refer to the performance management story featured in Chapter 18 on the UK Senior Civil Service scheme.

From 360-degree feedback to holding people accountable

Many of the organizations in our research were using 360-degree feedback to support performance evaluations and development planning primarily against competencies. This was often linked to another trend we observed – a much greater push to hold people accountable for their performance. As we shall see in the next chapter, the issue of holding people accountable is a key differentiator between those companies that are successfully implementing performance management processes that make a difference and less successful companies. In our research, holding people accountable was linked specifically to a willingness to manage and tackle underperformance. With the majority of organizations having many of the basic aspects of performance management in place – such as the use of competencies, annual and interim joint review discussions – organizations are turning to the more complex and challenging issue of getting line managers to hold others to account. Some of the most sophisticated leadership competency models contain 'holding people to account' as a specific differentiating behaviour – for example, the Leadership Qualities Framework (LQF) developed by Hay Group for the senior management of the UK National Health Service.

The use of performance distributions, a top-down organizational intolerance with the status quo and greater policing and support from HR are all being used to mobilize managers into action on this issue. For an example of an organization attempting to manage underperformance, see the mini case study at the DTI in Chapter 5.

From a supportive approach to one of capability building

As the next chapter in this book presents in more detail, research into the most admired companies shows that the ability of line managers to develop and manage talent is a key differentiator between average and excellent companies. However, we seem to have some way to go in conducting performance management that is truly supportive, focusing on giving feedback and coaching people to optimize their performance and realize their potential. That said, great strides have been made over the past decade in moving from a directive to a much more supportive approach to managing performance. In our survey of line managers, 79 per cent of respondents reported they had regular discussions about performance with their line managers and 64 per cent said they were motivated by the performance management process.

Recent trends suggest that for the best organizations the focus is on capability building, moving beyond simply being supportive to staff in the conduct of performance reviews to being much more proactive around supporting them in their career development, to actively tuning into spotting talent, nurturing it and being planful in the way it is managed within the organization. However, our observation is that this is an area where there may be a gap between what the best companies are doing and what we have observed in the field among many more mainstream organizations. Building long-term capability requires line managers to move beyond simply offering support and seems to represent a significant challenge for many organizations surveyed in this research. We will pick up on this when we talk about some of the implications for practice around managing staff (see Chapter 13).

From being locally flexible to 'one company, one approach'

In the late 1990s Armstrong and Baron observed the relaxing of bureaucracy and the offer of guidance through fairly simple forms and procedures rather than a set of prescriptions that everyone must follow to the letter. They also commented on a growing recognition of performance management as a tool for managers to apply in their own particular way in accordance with their own particular systems. It is our observation that for some organizations this approach has backfired, leading to at worst unacceptable variations in the way managers have interpreted guidelines and – for some – a lowering of the level of commitment they have applied to conducting rigorous reviews. It has also meant local variations in practice in different geographical locations, business divisions and functions, resulting in the adoption of either harsh or lenient standards of performance rating and accusations of unfairness.

Perhaps unsurprisingly, this seems to account for many of the global organizations that we examined, such as Metro Group and Philips, introducing more standardization and less flexibility into their system. This has meant them moving towards one common process across the organization, with shared language and consistency for assessing performance.

From being owned by users to owned by the organization

Finally, although performance management is still seen in our survey by over 50 per cent of respondents to be owned by HR, we can perhaps see that this perception is changing. Our survey suggests that senior managers are now involved in the performance management process, although line managers could increase their perception of accountability (less than 10 per cent reported that line managers were responsible for performance). The mini case studies are encouraging as they suggest that a key role is now being played by the board, which is increasingly involved in debating and endorsing aspects of the process. The performance management stories we describe later in the book at Lloyds/TSB and Belron all have as a common thread the re-engineering of the PM process at the behest of the CEO and their commitment and involvement in it. Thus the performance management process is moving from being seen as a tool for line managers to have individual conversations with staff in order to manage them effectively to an organizational tool used to align people's performance with its direction, goals and priorities. There is a greater recognition than ever before that performance management plays a critical role in delivering the strategy of the organization, a theme we will expand upon in the next chapter on what the most admired companies are doing in this area.

THE ANTECEDENTS FOR CURRENT PERFORMANCE MANAGEMENT REALITIES

It seems that many organizations are still reluctant to commit fully to the assertion that good management leads to greater employee commitment, effort and therefore improved performance. There is an increased expectation from stakeholders to see an economic return from improved people processes. The short lead times for CEOs to start adding value and pressure emanating from the City have meant an impatience to rely on traditional performance management methods. Similarly, in the public sector, increasing governmental demands for accountability among public servants and for performance standards in service delivery have led to the need to measure and monitor more than ever before.

All of this has led to a climate where measurement of results is valued and structured processes are in place to ensure that individuals' performance targets are agreed, monitored and tracked on a consistent basis. This is often about publicly reporting rises in standards or quantifying improvements for the political value this produces. It has also, at best, ensured that there is greater integration between performance management and the other business processes to ensure that duplications of effort are reduced and efficiencies maximized.

It is a climate that has not been resisted by HR professionals but often promulgated by them in response to internal and external pressures to quantify the value of their own work. The present climate around measurement owes much to the movement to show the business 'value-add' of the HR function.

Some of the antecedents to the current realities in performance management are due to the influence of some key and highly publicized global players on the way they manage performance, with General Electric (GE) leading the way. The enormously influential book by Jack Welch (Welch and Byrne, 2003) signalled a 'hard-line' shift in managing the extremes of the performance curve, with a focus on investing in star performers and ruthlessly eradicating the bottom 10 per cent – an approach GE called the 'Vitality Curve'. The 'trickle-down' effect of this thinking is probably being realized only now, for example in our observations about many organizations opting for forced performance distributions. Ironically, there is evidence to suggest that the originators of the approach may themselves be moving on from the methodology while others attempt to implement their own performance management system in GE's image.

Much has also been made of the trend for globalization in HR practices in recent years, and we can see its influence on multinational organizations as they standardize methodologies and reduce the freedom of line managers to 'do their own thing' unless there are culturally important reasons for 'keeping local'. Where there are links between performance and pay, local inconsistencies have increasingly led to concerns around equal-pay legal requirements being met. All of this, allied with an even more fundamental need to simplify and strip out complexity from the system, appears to have led the way towards 'one company, one approach'.

However, we should not denigrate the advances that have been made in performance management in the past five years; they have been significant. The focus on integration, managing at the extremes of poor or 'star' performance and forced distributions can only take place with a solid bedrock of sound performance management practice. It is because many organizations have made major inroads into many of the issues mentioned by Armstrong and Baron in 1998, such as the need for joint reviews, a focus on inputs as well as outputs and a system that is supportive/owned by users, that we now observe a greater sophistication in the issues that preoccupy organizations at the current time.

7
The secrets of the world's most admired companies – how they implement performance management

In the last chapter we presented a picture of what we feel performance management looks like currently from the evidence gathered from our fieldwork. We described the trends and patterns we observed as good current practice. For many readers this picture in itself represents an ideal towards which they are steadily making progress. However, for those who aspire one day to move beyond good practice to align themselves with the 'best in class' organizations, we focus in this chapter on what secrets we can uncover from some of the most highly admired companies in the area of performance management. We present the key success factors that characterize the performance management processes within these admired companies and consider implications for practice for those who may wish to emulate these processes.

So what do we know about effective performance management practice from those companies we most admire? Rankings of 'highly admired companies' have long captured the attention of practitioners and academics alike, appealing to natural instincts around competitiveness and the desire to benchmark own practice with the 'best in class'.

For some years *Fortune Magazine*, in conjunction with Hay Group, has conducted a global survey of corporate reputations to identify the most admired companies and to determine what they do that separates them from the rest. This annual survey was conducted in both 2005 and 2004. We present here the listing of the most admired companies for 2005. In 2004 the survey included follow-up work to consider the key factors around performance management and strategy 'execution' and we therefore report, in addition, the findings from this 2004 survey (*Fortune* in association with Hay Group, 2004, 2005).

For the 2005 survey, Hay Group surveyed more than 10,000 directors, executives and managers at 357 companies around the world. The companies all came from *Fortune* 1,000 and Global 500 listings, with separate rankings for the United States' and the world's most admired companies. All organizations had revenues of at least $8 billion in 2003 or were former industry leaders.

Respondents were asked to rank the other companies in their particular industry on nine attributes (shown in Figure 7.1). Companies were thus judged by those who knew them best and those who might be the harshest judges – peers and competitors. Respondents were also asked to rank their 'top 10' companies across all industry groups – termed the 'All Star list'. The All Star list, showing the US 'global most admired' and the non-US 'global most admired', is presented in Figure 7.2.

It is well documented that the most admired companies outperform industry peers and the market as a whole. For example, in 2004 shareholder

Attributes:

1. **Innovativeness**

2. **Quality of management**

3. **Long-term investment value**

4. **Social responsibility to the community and the environment**

5. **Ability to attract and retain talented people**

6. **Quality of products or services**

7. **Financial soundness**

8. **Wise use of corporate assets**

Global only:

9. **Effectiveness in doing business globally**

Figure 7.1 *Fortune* survey of most admired companies: attributes on which companies are ranked. *Source: Fortune Magazine* (2005)

Global most admired	Global most admired (non-US)
1. General Electric*	1. Toyota Motor*
2. Wal-Mart*	2. BMW*
3. Dell*	3. Sony*
4. Microsoft*	4. Honda Motor*
5. Toyota Motor*	5. BP*
6. Procter & Gamble*	6. Nestlé*
7. Johnson & Johnson*	7. Nokia*
8. FedEx*	8. Singapore Airlines *
9. IBM*	9. Canon*
10. Berkshire Hathaway*	10. L'Oréal*

* Company also included in Top 10 list in 2004

Figure 7.2 Global 'All Stars' for 2005. *Source: Fortune Magazine* (2005)

returns for the top 10 US 'global most admired' were 5.8 per cent versus the Standard & Poor's 500 at −5.6 per cent over the previous three years. So what is it that distinguishes these companies from the rest?

KEY SUCCESS FACTORS

Research by *Fortune Magazine*/Hay Group on the most admired companies suggests that these companies are characterized by a number of key success factors around performance management.

Key Success Factor 1: Strategy – clarity and implementation

Both the most admired companies and others in the sample felt that clarity around the strategy was important. Most of these organizations also had a plan to realize the strategy but the two groups differed in the success with which they were implementing this plan. The most admired companies were fairly confident that all of the functions within the organization that would be required to implement the strategy effectively were in place. Most critical, however, was their ability to translate strategic goals into

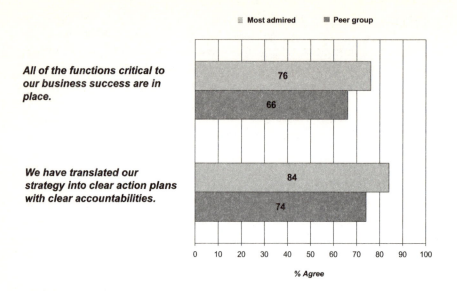

Figure 7.3 Organizational structure is driven by strategy. *Source:* Friedman *et al* (2004)

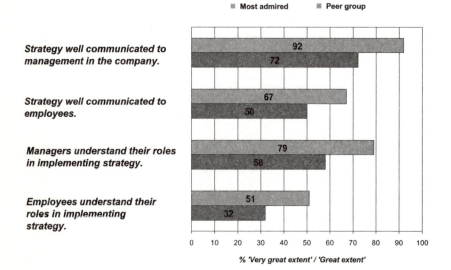

Figure 7.4 Clarity is driven deep into the business. *Source:* Friedman *et al* (2004)

clear action plans with specific accountabilities. Executives, mid-level managers and employees all understood the corporate objectives, and equally important, how they were expected to contribute to the achievement of these objectives (see Figures 7.3 and 7.4).

Implications for practice

The most admired organizations are confident that the functions required to execute the strategy are in place, raising the question of 'fit for purpose' organizational design. It is widely recognized that organizational design can have a profound impact on strategy implementation and competitive success, yet most chief executives have embarrassingly few good answers when pressed to justify their organizational designs, and most managers tend to put organization design into the 'too difficult' box (Goold and Campbell, 2002). As a starting point, organizations will therefore have to examine the organizational structure that prevails and consider whether this is supporting or detracting from the ability of managers and staff to deliver the strategy. Are the structure and organization around regions, functions, business segments or matrix relationships truly supporting the implementation of business imperatives? If jobs are in place that are not aligned to the key priorities of the organization, why are they there? In creating new jobs or examining old ones, the most admired companies are critical in evaluating their relationship to the implementation of the strategy. Typically, however, jobs appear to be 'nice to have' rather than 'mission critical', and are often created around the people in place or for the purposes of 'empire building'. This, of course, hampers performance planning since roles are not then based on logic and their purpose is likely to be unclear.

If the organizational structure supports the implementation of the strategy, is the strategy then translated into clear accountabilities for people? In the most admired companies, employees at all levels understand the three or four priorities that the organization has to get right. It is often said that an acid test of whether an organization has cascaded its strategy effectively is asking individuals at different levels what the three key priorities are for the organization and how they contribute to the achievement of these. This raises the importance of getting right the _planning_ aspect of the performance management cycle (described in more detail later). Aligning the planning of individual objectives with clarity around the strategy as well as the business planning process is likely to be critical for this first key success factor. We shall say more about how an organization might achieve this 'drill down' of strategy when we describe balanced scorecards in Chapter 10.

Key Success Factor 2: Holding people accountable

The world's most admired companies excelled at driving accountability right down through their organizations, while the rest of the sample were

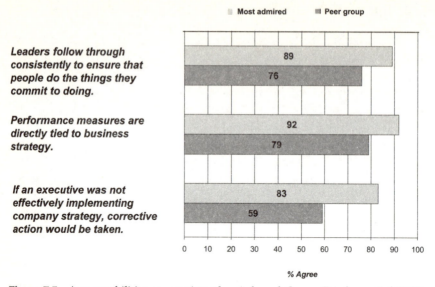

■ Most admired   ■ Peer group

Leaders follow through consistently to ensure that people do the things they commit to doing.
89
76

Performance measures are directly tied to business strategy.
92
79

If an executive was not effectively implementing company strategy, corrective action would be taken.
83
59

0 10 20 30 40 50 60 70 80 90 100

% Agree

Figure 7.5 Accountabilities are consistently reinforced. *Source:* Friedman *et al* (2004)

significantly less good at holding people accountable. The other companies tended to hold people accountable for metrics, instead of delivery of the strategy, and did not follow through, letting executives 'off the hook' (see Figure 7.5). The most admired companies reinforced accountabilities by monitoring and managing performance. As we saw in Chapters 4 and 5, where we presented our own findings from surveys and case studies, the best organizations reinforce accountabilities through a very strong focus on managing poor performance, through the use of forced distributions, and through standardized global processes (see Chapter 5).

Holding people accountable is also likely to be more challenging in the complex, team-based and matrix structures that characterize many organizations. The most admired companies were managing these interfaces more effectively than others, ensuring there were no gaps in accountabilities across roles or processes and managing interdependencies through team-working and collaboration (see Figure 7.6).

Implications for practice

This key success factor leads to implications for practice in two areas: first, being clear about individual accountabilities for a particular role (and managing interfaces where there are overlaps between jobs), and second, managing performance to hold people to account for delivery of these accountabilities.

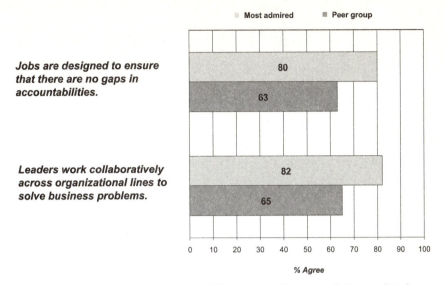

Figure 7.6 Interdependent accountabilities are well managed. *Source:* Friedman *et al* (2004)

The first requires a systematic approach to understanding jobs and roles – 'what is done to what/whom and with what end result?', or put another way, 'what are the main areas in which this job must get results in order to achieve its purpose?' This concept of accountability, the starting point for 'job evaluation', establishes how the role adds value and is a necessary prerequisite for holding people accountable. We look at the mechanics of this in Chapters 8 and 10. The best organizations know what they want to hold different people accountable for. This will link to Key Success Factor 1 – the best organizations hold people accountable for those things they do which contribute to strategy execution and delivery. It is unlikely, however, that individuals, particularly managers, will have primary responsibility for delivery of all objectives; for some objectives this will require shared responsibility with others. The most admired organizations – such as Proctor & Gamble, Asda/Walmart – effectively define inter-accountability, with matrices delineating accountabilities as 'prime', 'shared' and 'contributory'. Some organizations – such as Tesco – have for many years adopted the 'RACI principle' to define work, ascribing who is Responsible (who will do the work), who is Accountable ('where the buck stops'), who needs to be Consulted, and who needs to be Informed.

Defining accountabilities is only part, however, of holding people accountable; it also relies on the capability of managers to manage performance over time. People need to be monitored against set accountabilities, given feedback and coaching to help them realize these responsibilities and be evaluated on the extent of their achievement. Thus processes need to be put in place to ensure that people are not 'let off the hook', that performance against key accountabilities is measured, and that if it falls short there is a consequence to underperformance.

Key Success Factor 3: Cross-organizational working culture

All the companies surveyed expressed a desire to achieve a similar 'ideal culture' that fostered:

▌ teamworking;

▌ customer focus;

▌ taking initiative;

▌ treating all employees fairly.

However, the *Fortune* research found that the most admired companies were three times closer to achieving this target than the other companies (see Figure 7.7). The best companies, it appears, have a closer match between the espoused (desired) culture and the culture in practice (current). While all companies aspired to the qualities listed above, the Peer companies tended to have cultures that reinforced and rewarded achieving budget objectives and supporting management structures and decisions.

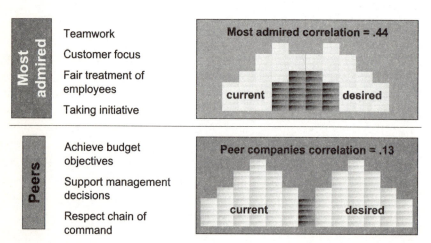

Figure 7.7 Current vs ideal culture

Implications for practice

What is important here is less what the most admired companies and the other companies said were the important attributes they wanted to foster within their organizational cultures, but more the extent to which the admired companies were actually doing some of these things. It is not surprising, in any survey of aspirations around culture, to have team-working or customer focus, but what is significant is the extent to which the respondents recognized these attributes as being part of the company they worked for.

Indeed, in terms of culture it is better to strive for consistency and agreement between members of the organization (for example, the members of the board) as to what sort of culture they want to foster 'around here' and the kind of culture they currently have. It is better to have small gaps around these perceptions rather than to have confusion as to what the ideal culture should be and in some cases a lot of disagreement surrounding the prevailing culture. The latter is indicative of a board, or others within the organization, not pulling in the same direction, and this may be the presenting issue of deeper disagreements about the organization's strategy, its positioning and what it needs to do to realize its ambitions. Thus it is not a question of what people actually say in relation to their desired culture but the clarity and consistency with which they say it that is likely to be the critical factor in enabling an organization to move towards the culture it desires.

Key Success Factor 4: Developing and managing talent

In the most admired companies, people development is a core accountability for line managers. Leaders devote a significant proportion of their time to talent management and provide ongoing coaching to their people (see Figure 7.8). These organizations expressed satisfaction with their leadership development processes and had greater confidence in the quality and depth of their leadership talent. Leaders were informed about the capability of their managers and there was confidence in the way individuals were matched to roles based on their skills as well as their career aspirations. While both the most admired and the other companies had equal proportions of in-house training, the most admired companies had significantly greater use of planned career assignments, one-to-one coaching and competency models.

We explore the themes of developing and managing talent further in two stories from organizations that have built these into the heart

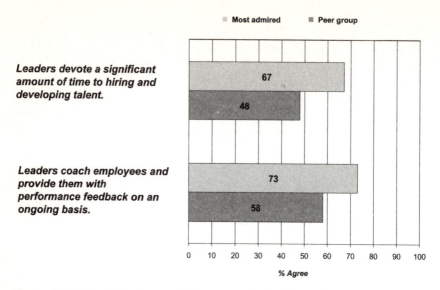

Figure 7.8 Talent development is a core leadership task. *Source:* Friedman *et al* (2004)

of their performance management process – *A focus on development at Belron* (Chapter 14) and *The performance management cycle a BAE Systems* (Chapter 9).

Implications for practice

For talent management to be seen as a core accountability for line managers, organizations need to move this activity from being seen as an add-on to a managerial role to one that is central to effective role delivery. There is inevitably a certain kudos associated with moving the talent within your team on to bigger and better things, and managers need to feel there is an incentive to move away from the traditional habit of trying to keep their most talented people. Line managers will also need a clear lead from the organization as to the kind of person it regards as talented. Who are the people that the organization wants to keep and promote? What attributes do they have and how can line managers spot these people?

Average organizations anchor their talent management in their current strategy or set of circumstances, whereas the best organizations are able to translate their strategy into what this means for the kinds of roles and accountabilities they require and the behaviours that will take them forward (Hay Group White Paper, 2005). They make greater efforts to ensure their people processes – organizational design, performance management and reward – are all aligned to reinforce the talent management process.

The identification of talent is, however, not the same as its management; once spotted, it is all too easy for organizations to rely on traditional forms of development (such as training courses or line managerial support) to help individuals realize their potential. The best organizations work hard at growing their talent; for example, mapping workable career paths for individuals, providing lateral moves to enhance skills, and offering coaching to people making difficult transitions.

Finally, identifying and managing talent requires follow-through. The best organizations regularly review the talent within the organization and act on the implications for role realignments, development and exits. This involves having not just internal standards but incorporating external benchmarks to keep the bar raised; it also implies rigour to the assessment of talent and acting on the results of talent reviews.

Key Success Factor 5: Balancing measurement and development

In Chapter 1 we charted the evolution of performance management, citing the move from purely financial or metrics-based objectives to a more balanced assessment of performance through the consideration of development objectives and behavioural (or values) requirements.

Despite this evolution, average companies appear to have performance management systems that encourage their senior executives to focus on easily quantifiable measures that reflect direct impact on the bottom line: profits, growth and operational excellence. However, the most admired companies have created performance management systems that take a more rounded approach, and include measures on teamwork, long-term thinking, building human capital and customer loyalty. For example, Figure 7.9 shows that the most admired companies are almost three times as likely to include a customer measure in their performance management systems as others in the sample. Senior executives within these companies were also more likely to be remunerated according to a variety of measures, including employee satisfaction, than other companies.

Our observation described in the previous chapter of a swing of the pendulum towards measurement-based approaches to performance management, characterized by financial targets and metrics, is therefore typical of the majority of average organizations. The best in class, however, are those that are able to reconcile the measurement and development interfaces. The most admired companies set expectations that move beyond purely financial metrics to include the extent to which leaders build human capital (develop and manage talent) and motivate employees and customers alike.

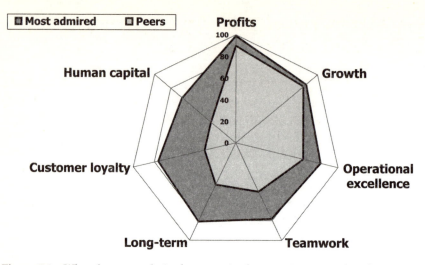

Figure 7.9   What the most admired companies focus on in terms of performance management

Implications for practice

Arriving at a balanced set of performance measures that reconcile the measurement and development aspects of an individual's role is therefore a critical factor contributing towards success in the most admired companies. The key appears to lie in working backwards from the desired outputs, for example revenue, to understand the key factors that actually drive this. This is not dissimilar to the balanced scorecard approach (as postulated by Kaplan and Norton and discussed in much greater depth in Chapters 2 and 10 of this book). The balanced scorecard in its purest form is about translating the strategy of the company into the key processes that help to realize it. It moves beyond purely financial measures to build in metrics around internal processes, customer engagement, and learning and development. It also makes a distinction between lead measures (what really *drives* the achievement of business goals – such as new accounts opened, staff retention rates, climate feedback, etc) and lag measures (the things that *indicate* the achievement of business goals – such as net operating profit, loss index, etc). While average companies tend to focus only on lag measures, the most admired companies look at both lead and lag measures. A simple analogy would be driving a car relying only on the use of the wing mirror to look backwards rather than moving forwards looking through the windscreen but also using the wing mirror. For more detailed information on the practical aspects of balancing measurement and development in planning performance, see Chapters 10 and 13.

Key Success Factor 6: Integrating strategy, performance and compensation

In addition to paying for performance that is more 'holistic' (rather than purely financial), the top companies also pay their people less, a finding that may seem surprising at first glance. In comparing the base salary levels between the most admired companies and their peers, the most admired paid on average 5 per cent less at each job level. These companies appear to able to do this because they offer their employees a more diverse set of rewards, including access to wider development and learning and the opportunity to work for a successful brand. They have clearly accepted and put into practice the concept of 'total reward' – identifying what it is that employees see as their reward 'deal' and optimizing the value of this as part of their focus on raising employee motivation and engagement. The exceptions to this pattern sit at the top of the most admired organizations, where senior directors are paid more than others in the sample. These individuals receive higher salaries as well as better bonuses than their peers at average companies (see Figures 7.10 and 7.11).

This appears to be in part due to the recognition of the value that 'top talent' brings to an organization, and of the role of such individuals in ensuring sustained high performance. It is also a feature of another key attribute that differentiates the most admired from average companies – their ability to align pay to performance and, in turn, performance to strategy. When companies within the survey were asked how strongly they linked executive compensation, performance and strategic priorities,

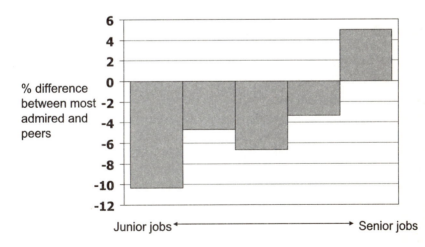

Figure 7.10   Most admired companies pay 5 per cent less

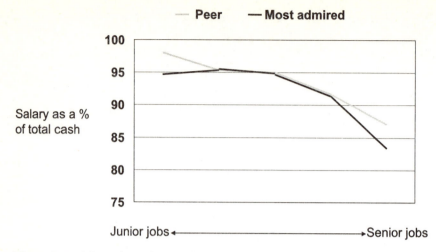

Figure 7.11 Most admired companies use bonuses more

the most admired companies had a link between these factors that was twice as strong as average companies. So successful companies are better at translating the company strategy into individual objectives (as we saw in Key Success Factor 1 above) and executives are encouraged to maximize their personal pay packet by delivering on activities that are of strategic importance to the organization. Strategy, performance and compensation are better integrated and working in the same direction, rather than on divergent paths that do not reinforce each other.

Implications for practice

One of the secrets of the most admired companies that enables them to differentiate the reward on offer – paying people less on average than other companies but offering substantial awards to senior directors – is their ability to segment the reward offering. This segmentation is achieved on the basis of a deep insight into the nature of their workforce and the factors that motivate people at different levels of the organization. When an organization truly asks the question: 'what motivates our high performers?', the answer is often that the monetary reward is usually a temporary retention tool, with career development, learning opportunities, work – life balance, and a belief in the values and aims of the company figuring highly in what motivates people to stay. So the key lies in knowing what motivates your high performers and targeting rewards accordingly, and this may not cost as much as imagined. Less effective organizations are often characterized by obsessive benchmarking with other comparable companies and attempts to stay competitive within the market. The more effective companies, however, take a more holistic view of the reward on offer, asking what is it that really motivates people around here and investing closely in the findings.

The most admired companies may also pay less base salary and more bonus but this is used as a deliberate strategy to recognize excellence, although it must be 'achieved excellence' (for example, targets exceeded, outstanding business unit performance, etc). This does not mean that base salaries will be behind the market, but it represents a strategy, for example, of aiming to be at market median for base salary but towards the upper quartile (or higher) on total cash rewards (including bonuses) to recognize high achievement. This approach recognizes the reality that a focus on base salary competitiveness alone leads to higher fixed costs and paying people who may not ultimately perform. The focus on bonus, however, enables these organizations to pay for performance that is achieved and they are able to dictate quite clearly the areas in which performance should be achieved or exceeded. This is essentially around delivering the strategy. Therefore these companies are able to reinforce the message that delivering what we believe is important will lead to the largest compensation. It is this alignment between the strategy, the commensurate performance required and the compensation for achieving this that makes the difference in these organizations.

SUMMARY

It appears that the most admired companies achieve high levels of clarity in roles and responsibilities, linking individuals' accountabilities at all levels to strategic priorities. They are able to drill down the strategic plan to individual performance plans and then to align compensation to successful delivery of those goals. Goals, however, are not focused on profits, growth or operational excellence alone; measures are more balanced to include customer loyalty and building people's capability. The latter is about people development and talent management being seen at the heart of a line manager's core accountabilities. The most admired organizations do not therefore seem daunted by the development agenda involving factors that are harder to measure objectively or to quantify and that require longer lead times to see to fruition. The best organizations reconcile the two faces of performance management – measurement and development – avoiding the trap of focusing on extremes and actively ensuring that performance is judged in a holistic sense rather than in purely financial terms.

Delivery against these specified accountabilities is monitored and managed, with individuals at all levels being held accountable. Poor performance is acted upon and line managers are not 'let off the hook'. It appears to be these factors that enable the most admired companies to achieve a culture that in reality matches more closely their aspirations around team-working, customer focus and sustainable successful performance.

The picture presented above of what the most admired companies are doing around performance management is reassuring in a number of areas in its corroboration with the trends we have observed within many organizations at the current time. For the most part, these organizations can be characterized as 'good' or 'average' as opposed to 'outstanding'. The trends we have picked up from our fieldwork (described in Chapter 6) showed moves towards:

▌ integrating what was the 'review discussion' to be much more closely linked to other HR process such as development, talent management/ succession planning and reward;

▌ holding people accountable through rating and ranking performance and the use of forced distributions, as well as tackling underperformance;

▌ aligning people's performance with the organization's direction, goals and priorities through the use of the performance management process as a tool owned by the organization emphasizing structure, consistency and control.

Many companies, it appears, are making real progress in emulating the practices of the best companies in the above areas. However, we have also observed that there are some significant risk areas where recent trends have not kept pace with what the best companies are doing or, at worst, are moving in the opposite direction. The success of the most admired companies in building capability for the longer term through actively developing and managing talent represents a challenge for the majority of organizations we surveyed. Access to training or development opportunities is not the same as putting in place processes to identify talent, to manage it and to follow through with career progression. The most significant gap, however, is in the area of balancing performance measurement with performance development. The most admired companies avoid the pitfalls of falling into the extremes of measurement or development, adopting a rounded, more 'holistic' approach. The swing of the pendulum towards measurement-based approaches is therefore clearly at odds with what the best companies do.

Having started the discussion around the implications for practice, we now look at supporting the reader in implementing the findings from our research as relevant to their current situation, as well as emulating the key factors for success as displayed among the most admired companies we have described here.

Part III
Managing and measuring performance – a guide to implementing a balanced approach

This part of the book is about practicalities – how to design, build and maintain performance management processes that are both leading edge and 'best fit' for your organization. It builds on the two previous sections by providing practical advice on how to enhance performance management practice while working with the realities of where your organization is currently. Chapter 8 gives an overview of the foundations required for performance management to be implemented in a fully integrated way and Chapter 9 showcases the integrated approach at BAE Systems. Chapters 10, 13 and 16 then describe implementation strategies in terms of the three main phases of performance management: planning, managing and reviewing. Our aim is to help the reader understand how both measurement and development approaches can be achieved in a balanced way. Throughout, we aim to link theory and practice and intersperse the chapters focused on implementing theory with organizational stories to demonstrate how this has been used in practice. We conclude in Chapter 19 by identifying the current trends and future directions of performance management as surfaced by our research and experience.

8
Understanding the foundations of integrated performance management

In this chapter we describe in detail the elements of the core performance management 'process' – those that can be designed into the architecture and where technical 'experts', both in-house and on a consultancy basis, may advise. Subsequent chapters focus on key phases within the performance management cycle of planning, managing and reviewing. Chapter 10 is more relevant to the metrics circle of our organizing framework (introduced in Chapter 1 and shown here again in Figure 8.1) as it is concerned with the planning phase and how organizational strategy is translated into objective setting. Chapter 13 is concerned with capability and examines the managing phase of the performance management cycle, and Chapter 16 deals with the reward architecture.

THE PERFORMANCE MANAGEMENT CYCLE

Within any organization professing to have a performance management system, it is usually possible to discern three key stages: planning, managing and reviewing; see Figure 8.2. These three stages may be emphasized to greater or lesser degree, depending on the current design of the process, its state of evolution and the organization's culture. In the section that follows

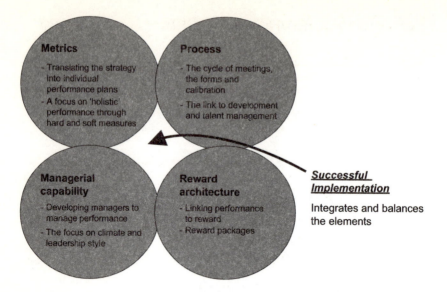

Figure 8.1 The four-circle organizing framework. *Source:* Adapted from Hay Group (2005)

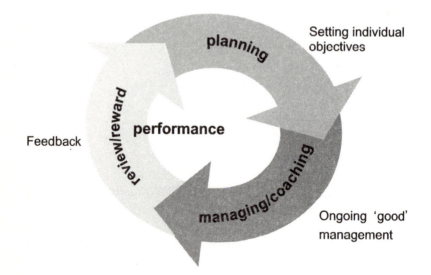

Figure 8.2 Performance management cycle. *Source:* Hay Group

we will provide a brief overview of each element of the cycle; more detail on each of the phases may be found in subsequent chapters. For a real-life illustration of what each phase might entail within an organization, see Chapter 9 which tells an organizational story about the performance management process at BAE Systems and in so doing provides an insight into each phase.

Performance Management Stage 1 – Planning

When an organization implements performance management, the first part of this process is usually performance planning. This stage typically embraces:

▌ definition of job/role responsibilities;

▌ setting performance expectations;

▌ goal or objective setting and agreement (people need to own their goals!) at the beginning of the period.

Historically, in many organizations this stage occurred on the 'anniversary date' of an individual joining the company as part of a 'rolling review' process. However, more recently and often in tandem with the growth in performance-related pay, the trend has been towards a convergence around the business planning cycle of the organization, which makes a lot more sense in terms of aligning plans and goals. Although this places a heavy burden in terms of workload on managers – particularly those with a number of direct reports – it does support the notion of using performance planning to cascade the strategy. In order for this cascade to be effective, the business plan for the year and a set of objectives need to be communicated **prior** to the objective-setting period. Wherever possible, senior managers should set and agree their own objectives before they discuss objectives with their direct reports and so on. The objective-setting and performance-planning discussion can, and often does, include reference to development planning, or this may be carried over to a formal development discussion specifically provided for in the process.

Performance Management Stage 2 – Managing

Once objectives have been set, the next phase of the performance management process is usually that of managing performance. To call this a 'phase' in its own right is sometimes seen to be misleading. At its simplest, this phase of performance management may be difficult to identify separately; it may not involve any 'formal' reviews but may be perceived to be about good management practice, regular short 'one-to-ones', informal feedback and effective coaching and mentoring. In organizations where performance management is not yet that well embedded, this cannot be assumed to be happening, or where more structured processes are thought to be required (to improve manager engagement with PM), it is common to have mid-year, quarterly and even monthly reviews of progress. One or more of these discussions may be set aside specifically to discuss development plans.

The managing stage typically embraces:

▍ monitoring performance and achievement towards objectives – at best a jointly owned process;

▍ feedback and coaching;

▍ competency review;

▍ development discussion.

As a part of the performance review process, competency-based approaches have become an increasingly common tool for considering both managerial and employee capabilities in terms of skills and behaviours. It is at this stage of the performance cycle that the emphasis will be on capability, both in terms of the manager's ability to motivate his or her staff and also the employee's ability or competency for the role in question. This is the part of the performance management process where managerial aptitude and willingness to work beyond a pure task focus are really at the fore, and we shall look further at the challenges this raises in Chapters 13 and 14.

Performance Management Stage 3 – Reviewing

Managers and staff alike often have the most vivid feelings and recollections about performance management around this third stage of performance review. Try asking any group of managers to rate their last review against a scale of 1–5 (5 being the highest) and you will find few scores higher than three, with the majority being ones and twos. It can be quite sobering for the same group of managers to be asked to speculate on the likelihood of their own performance review skills being sufficiently superior to make the experience for their direct reports a positive one.

The reviewing stage typically includes:

▍ formal performance review, resulting in a rating, if used, or a narrative summary if not;

▍ links to reward – in terms of base salary and/or incentive pay where these are in use within the organization;

▍ possible 360-degree feedback around competencies or other feedback.

What is assessed in the annual review differs depending on the design of the process; we shall discuss this more fully when we look at the links to reward in Chapter 16. Achievement against objectives will invariably be assessed. Some organizations also include a full competency review (looking at the individual's fit with the competency requirements of the role, as specified in their job description or role profile); others review the achievement of development objectives.

DESIGNING INTEGRATED PERFORMANCE MANAGEMENT

Having looked very briefly at the elements of the performance cycle, we shall now drill down to understand how the different components interact. It is our belief that performance management offers most value as a fully integrated HRM process, and in order to illustrate this we find the metaphor of a house useful to capture its components (see Figure 8.3).

The house model suggests that core aspects of HR exist as the building blocks of a people management process. Performance management exists as a key element of the integrated structure once individuals have been

Figure 8.3 Performance management as a fundamental business process

recruited and roles defined. It then serves to drive reward, training and development, promotion and career progression. The result should be motivated employees, aware of and committed to the mission and strategy of the organization.

Everyone who has responsibility for people management will require some familiarity with the building blocks shown in the model. In particular, the management of performance is key because it integrates and coordinates across the whole gamut of people management processes within an organization to deliver business performance. It is also, of course, a critical area where managers can make a real difference to team culture – and hence team performance – through leadership style and the application of motivational techniques. We will now work our way through the 'rooms' in the house that comprise the foundation and consider how they support and are integrated into performance management.

PERFORMANCE MANAGEMENT BUILDING BLOCKS

The building blocks of integrated HRM practice include job definition statements, competency frameworks, profiling devices to link an individual to a specific role, plus infrastructure support, particularly database services and HR management systems. Each of these will be explored in more detail in the paragraphs below.

Definitions of work

Job definition is really all about organizational design. This has to start at the top. Nethersell (2005) has suggested applying these five key tests to benchmark management job design practice against best in class:

Strategy alignment – Is the structure as a whole clearly aligned with key performance objectives? Is it clear who is delivering what and how individual managers contribute to overall business performance?
Added value – What is the nature of the value added by managerial positions individually and collectively? Is it clear, and are you getting appropriate value from the management input?
Linkage – Where the realization of objectives requires coordination between management units, are the linkages truly necessary and are they clearly defined?

> **Coherence** – Are the roles coherent in the sense of being focused on the management of related activities, or are the management agendas too diverse? Is short, are the roles doable?
>
> **People** – Is organization and role design adapted to reflect the strengths, weaknesses and motivations of people available within the business?

This thinking can then be taken down to all employees within the organization. We assume for the purpose of this chapter that most employees, apart from those in the smallest or most informal of organizations, will have some sort of document (a job description or role profile) that strives to clarify how they fit into what the organization is trying to achieve and what their unique contribution is intended to be. We are well aware that the nature and applicability of this document may vary from organization to organization and even from department to department. More traditional job descriptions contain a set of responsibilities, often listed as a set of activities for that unique job. More recently there has been a trend towards more generic role profiles which apply to any number of individuals performing similar roles. See, for example, the one shown in Table 8.1.

Role profiles such as this capture the main outputs required from the job – usually as a set of accountabilities with some indication as to how success will be measured. Both job descriptions and role profiles relate to the 'day-to-day job' and are unlikely to change much over time, unless the job itself has changed. Where role profiles tend to differ is that they attempt to capture the 'what' and the 'how' of performance, as illustrated below in the example for a team leader.

Table 8.1 Sample role profile – team leader

Key accountabilities	Skills	Competencies
Lead project reviews with customers	Project management (projects £200K+)	Customer focus (4)
Manage 'project X' to deliver on time and in 'X' budget	Expert reputation in Staff and financial management	Planning and organizing (3) Concern for quality and order (4)
Manage contract staff to budget	Broad understanding of strategy business	Achievement drive (5)
Maintain own network in specific area of technical expertise		Organizational awareness (3) Flexibility (3) Teamworking (5)

Competency-based performance management

Competencies are located at the base of the integrated HR house (Figure 8.3) as a key building block. We now describe some of the groundwork likely to be required in order to support the roll-out of competency-based performance management. Having produced a competency framework (as illustrated in Chapter 1), a starting point for most organizations as they strive to include competencies in performance management is likely to be the profiling of roles in terms of their competency requirements. This enables a gap analysis between job holders and their current or future roles. Once the competencies and their performance levels have been identified for a given role, it is possible to use the appraisal and development discussions to explore the competency gaps that emerge and capture any areas for improvement. The example in Figure 8.4 shows how this might be captured on a computer-based system.

The example shows how a role profile might be used as the basis for a fuller assessment. It is based on a position described as being in Job Band S2ii. It indicates the required performance level of each competency for

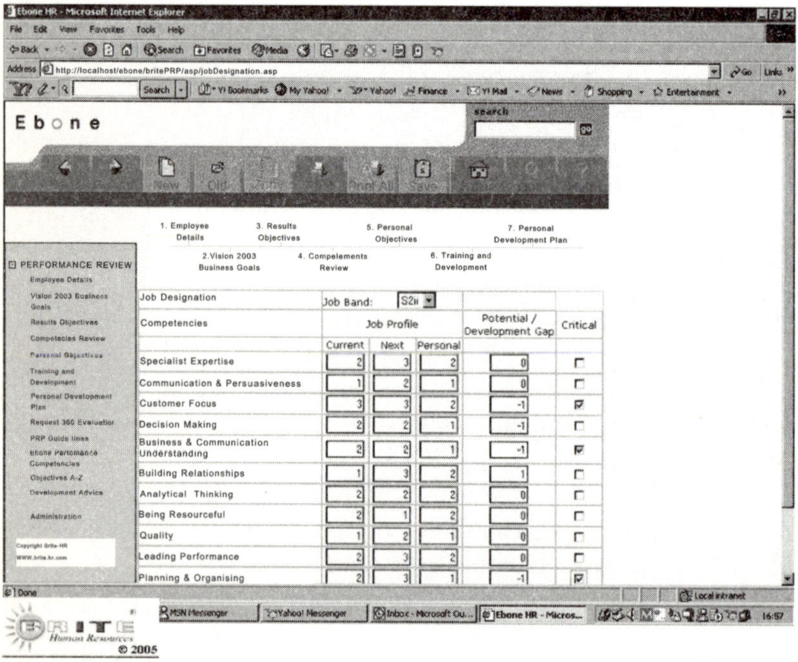

Figure 8.4 Example of a computer-based competency role profile. *Source:* BRITE HR (2005)

the current role as well as those required for promotion to the next level. It also tells us how the individual has been assessed in terms of his or her existing personal competency level against the job requirements. A gap exists between the levels required for:

▌ customer focus (level 3 is required for the role and the individual's personal level has been rated at 2 in this competency);

▌ decision making (level 2 is required and the individual's personal level has been rated at 1);

▌ business and communication understanding (level 2 is required and the individual's personal level has been rated at 1);

▌ planning and organizing (level 2 is required and the individual's personal level has been rated at 1).

Having successfully completed the building blocks of defining the actual competency framework and profiling roles against this, it becomes possible for organizations to integrate this fully into the performance management process. This requires the profiling of each individual against the competency framework as illustrated above. Support for this style of approach and the necessary record keeping is likely to require technical support, hence the increasingly important area of computer-based HR systems comprises the last of our building blocks.

HR systems to support performance management

Performance management has increasingly been seen within organizations as far more than a bureaucratic process associated with a form that must be completed according to a timescale provided by an HR department. Instead, it is being recognized as an opportunity for dialogue about organizational and individual performance enhancement.

For performance management to be meaningful, however, organizations must be able to link personal objectives to organizational strategy as well as accurately and equitably record what has been agreed.

Proprietary tools have begun to emerge to fill this need, typically combined with wider people management database services. Some of these are now very creative in making the whole process more attractive and 'user friendly'. In addition, many organizations have opted to produce their own bespoke version, which links to other employee record systems. These have the benefits, usually, of using the organization's own 'language' around performance and delivery. Although all applications are likely to have their own look and feel, common elements of functionality are likely to include:

I common job or role profiles menu on screen;

I history function to store what was agreed at the last meeting;

I on-screen 'form' to type in objectives and save;

I capability to search for objectives either by job holder or objective type (such as financial, customer, learning and growth, etc);

I on-screen version of competency dictionary showing range of different job types within the organization and profiles required;

I development planning structure and advice;

I links to development planning resources/catalogues of books/videos/ courses, etc.

More sophisticated versions may also have on-screen visual career pathways as discussed in Chapter 13.

Given the reality that only a small minority of companies do not now have access to company intranets to support such approaches, we expect this trend towards computer-based performance management to continue, in line with, and as part of, integrated HR approaches.

The next chapter builds on some of the themes introduced here by presenting an organizational story from BAE Systems. It further illustrates the three phases of performance management: planning, managing and reviewing, as well as a number of the HR building blocks we have described in this chapter. Subsequent chapters then deal in more detail with each of the three phases and are interspersed with relevant organizational stories to illustrate theory in practice. Chapter 10 considers how the planning phase of performance management can be integrated with broader business processes and outcomes. Chapter 13 then focuses on the management phase with its emphasis on capability development and coaching, and Chapter 16 focuses on reviewing and rewarding performance.

9
Organizational story: the performance management cycle at BAE Systems

In this chapter we showcase BAE Systems, an organization that has sought to maximize value from its performance management scheme, both in terms of engaging the workforce to complete the process and also in ensuring its integration with a number of other key people-management processes which include: development, potential rating, reward, and talent management.

BAE Systems is the premier transatlantic defence and aerospace company delivering a full range of product and services for air, land and naval forces as well as advanced electronics, information technology solutions and customer support services. The organization has major operations across five continents and customers in some 130 countries. Annual sales for the group amount to over £14 billion, making it the largest European defence company and placing it in the top 10 defence companies in the US. The workforce across the group is currently in the region of 90,000, spread across eight major businesses. Leveraging performance and talent across these business streams is therefore fundamental to future success.

DESCRIPTION OF PERFORMANCE MANAGEMENT AT BAE SYSTEMS

The business year within BAE Systems is January to December, with the performance management (PM) cycle following a similar timeframe. The performance management process is clearly driven from the integrated business planning process (IBPP), which is signed off each year by the end of October. Every December the Executive Committee work through this in order to determine the CEO's Top 10 Objectives – thus effectively starting the cascade of the strategic goals.

The actual performance management process commences for each new business year in January. It is supported by an online system. This system is actually 'open' all year, unlike some other organizations where there is only open online access for a small window of time. Despite this fact, managers and their direct reports are reminded by HR at the start of the process that the 'online' system is available and that they need to complete the planning process for staff by the third week in January. The HR department at BAE Systems are strict about chasing up completion of the online form and run a number of reports, which they issue to show the rate of completion across the business. Although this may be construed as 'naming and shaming' they do manage to achieve a completion rate approximating to 100 per cent for the planning element of the performance management process.

Planning performance

At the initial meeting in January the manager and employee conduct both the review of performance for the previous year and plan what is required for the year ahead. We shall deal with the review element in a later section. The planning element of the discussion is supported by the availability of the CEO's Top 10. This list of key business objectives is always a good mix of financial, capability and customer priorities. The process is based on the individuals completing their own performance plan ready to discuss with their manager for sign off. The online system prompts them to write the objectives in a format which is SMART. With each objective there is a box which must be completed before the system will allow them to continue. Participants must state what will they do, what is the deadline for completion and what is the measure of success. During the planning discussion in January, the focus is upon setting objectives in the priority areas for the year ahead. Typically, around 10 objectives are set. These relate to both the 'what' of performance, in alignment with the business priorities for the year ahead, and the 'how', via one or two development objectives that are intended to support the individual achieve his or her business goals.

To support development planning – a key element of the process within BAE Systems – an extensive development resource 'the integrated development portfolio' has been created which may also be accessed online. The portfolio contains a range of function-specific and also more generic learning opportunities. For example, each function such as HR and Engineering has its own 'suite' of development options in line with functional/technical skill requirements. These functional offerings are captured in the 'Developing You' section as illustrated in Figure 9.1 below. In addition, the integrated development portfolio also contains the range of generic leadership programmes, which are offered centrally as part of the performance-centred leadership offered by central HR.

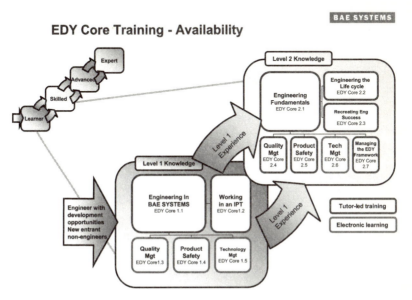

Figure 9.1 The engineering 'developing you' menu from the integrated development portfolio

Managing performance

It is recognized that the management of performance is an ongoing process and indeed in one business within the BAE Systems Group there is a trial being held of two weekly 'quick fire' performance reviews. However, the performance management process requires a minimum of one interim review and this is conducted in June/July each year, with a reminder being sent out that the online system is available to record comments on progress.

Reviewing performance

In order to ensure that the performance development review is able to focus upon both the 'hard' targets and the 'soft' behaviours, a short 360-degree feedback tool has been introduced to the business which is called behavioural performance feedback (BPF). This focuses on the five core competencies, which are linked to the overall vision and goals of BAE Systems. These five competencies are: achieving high performance, focusing on the customer, developing others, working together and, continuous improvement. Individuals are invited to nominate their 'raters' using a scroll-down list. They must nominate their boss, at least one subordinate and some peers, with an average of 10 to 15 raters. Their initial list of raters is forwarded by the system to their manager for approval before the individual completes a self-report and the respondents are asked for their feedback.

The individual then receives a report, which provides for feedback on each competency in terms of whether he or she is:

▌ Band 1 – the top 15% (approx) of employees display behaviour at this level

▌ Band 2 – the middle 70% (approx) of employees display behaviour at this level

▌ Band 3 – the bottom 15% (approx) of employees display behaviour at this level

As well as the banding, the individual also gets to see any comments made by the raters and, unusually for this sort of 360-degree feedback tool, this feedback is attributed to the respondent. BAE have found this is a useful way of ensuring that respondents 'own' the feedback they provide and also that they ensure they use specific behavioural examples.

The behavioural performance feedback process (BPF) is completed by the end of October so that the data is available for use in performance development reviews (PDRs). As well as the BPF, the review phase of the performance management process also has data from the employee survey (EOS), which is conducted every two years. In addition, in the UK the 'customer voice' tool provides feedback from the customer perspective. Similarly in the US, feedback from the Department of Defense (which is linked to contract payment) gives a clear indicator of the degree of customer satisfaction. For senior managers, this data is a statement of their own performance and leadership; for more junior managers, the employee and customer perspectives provide context and information on the 'mood' across the business.

The review phase of performance management at BAE Systems begins in December, when the online system again sends a reminder of the need to complete the performance development reviews by the last week of the following January. There is a five-point rating scale and lots of guidance is provided to help the manager arrive at their decision, which takes into account performance against objectives and development objectives. The ratings are: All exceeded; Some exceeded; All achieved; Some achieved; and, None achieved.

LINKING PERFORMANCE MANAGEMENT TO POTENTIAL RATING, REWARD, TALENT MANAGEMENT AND LEADERSHIP DEVELOPMENT

The BAE Systems example is an excellent introduction to our section on integrated performance, as it provides an illustration of both the 'typical cycle' but also how it may be linked to other key managing people processes.

Potential ratings at BAE Systems

Performance management links to the potential rating process – which in BAE Systems is known as 'spectrum'.

Linked to the performance management process, and following soon after the planning/reviewing meeting, the manager considers each direct report in terms of their potential and performance in order to rate them using the distributions agreed by the Executive Committee for that year (for the senior management population), and the Chief Operating Officer of each business (for the lower levels of managers). The spectrum categories and typical distribution are listed below

▌ Deep gold – top 5 per cent who demonstrate sustained exceptional performance and have potential to take on significantly more responsibility.

▌ Light gold – 20 per cent who exceed objectives and have potential to take on larger roles.

▌ Green – 66–72 per cent who are experienced and fully competent, but have the capacity to change their role.

▌ Orange – 3–9 per cent who are not currently performing to the required standard.

▌ Blue – used for individuals who demonstrate unacceptable performance and were previously rated as orange, but have shown no discernible improvement.

Once the spectrum ratings have been input they are abstracted from the online system and calibration meetings are held, either centrally or within the business units. Once calibration has been completed managers inform their direct reports of the spectrum rating. Interestingly this all takes place before the reward cycle is initiated and there is no formal right of appeal. After the potential ratings have been articulated to the individuals, some actions are instigated for those rated as orange or blue. It is unlikely that anyone rated as blue would remain within the business. All those rated as orange would receive a performance improvement plan in the first instance. Data from the last six years shows consistently that of those designated as orange, 50 per cent leave the business and the other 50 per cent make changes either to their role or to their performance.

Linking performance management to reward at BAE Systems

There are various elements to reward at BAE Systems. In the first instance the incentive plan is used, which is mainly driven by the previous year's results. The budget or 'pot' for this is determined by the company's financial performance, and is distributed according to the individual's performance rating as well as their behavioural performance feedback. The potential bonus is multiplied by a ratio from 0 to 1.5, depending on the behavioural performance feedback, thus underlining that hitting targets or achieving the 'what' of performance is not enough – behaviours are also a key requirement. The incentive plan applies to all managers.

The salary review looks at the spectrum rating (which in itself provides a composite view of both potential and performance) in order to determine a salary increase. Again, these increases are set in line with the budget, as determined by the company's ability to fund it and the market conditions.

Long-term incentives are another option, and these are also used to reward performance at BAE Systems. Spectrum ratings are again used here, with the intent to tie-in individuals of high potential in order to secure their longer-term contribution.

The management resource review BAE Systems

This process is an approach to talent management. Known as the management resource review (MRR), like performance-centred leadership (PCL) and the PDR it is a mandated process.

The HR Director for organizational development and learning takes responsibility for the Top 100 managers across the company, and elsewhere HR teams within the business units run it. It is conducted twice a year and its focus is on development rather than performance management. These meetings involve a visual overview of the potential ratings from Spectrum, and the colour-coding supports this process. Clearly one would expect to see the majority of gold-rated employees featuring on succession plans.

Performance-centred leadership development

Just like the performance management process and the management resource review (MRR), the performance-centred leadership framework has full endorsement from the Executive Committee.

A framework of options has been designed to support the development of senior leaders as illustrated in figure 9.2 below.

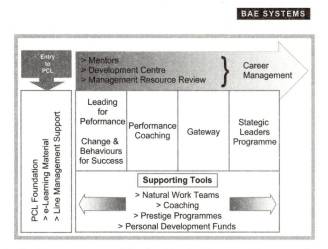

Figure 9.2   Performance-centred leadership development framework

Figure 9.2 shows the leadership development framework for those managers within the performance-centred leadership population. It encompasses programmatic solutions and supporting elements such as coaching and mentoring. The framework recognizes that both hard and soft skills are necessary for leadership and draws on a global faculty of academics and consultants to provide these. In order to show support and also to interact with the leadership population, executive committee members are present at virtually all of the programmes run under the performance-centred leadership framework.

BAE Systems provides a very interesting example of an organization linking performance management directly to talent management strategies. Despite the technological elements of the process, it is important to note that the aim of managing performance for the leadership population is clearly seen as being far more than just completing the 'online forms', although there are checks and balances in place to ensure that this does take place. Performance management is just one element of the performance-centred leadership framework – the key tool for managing the performance and career development of the top 5,000 managers within the group, in order to support BAE Systems in pursuit of its vision.

10

Planning performance and measurement-based approaches

We set the scene by describing the main phases of performance manage-ment and considering the underpinning elements of HR architecture that are likely to be required to support successful implementation. Now we look at designing and implementing the first phase of performance management – performance planning. It is perhaps with the planning phase of performance management that we most associate measurement-based approaches, in the target- and objective-setting activities necessary for assessing an employee's contribution. We begin by considering ways in which organizations strive to link their strategy to individual perform-ance plans and we then focus more particularly on measures and measurement-based approaches. Since the balanced scorecard is one of the most popular tools for attempting to achieve the 'balance of measures' affecting organization performance, we shall focus on it in this chapter.

LINKING THE STRATEGY TO WHAT PEOPLE DO

Making the link between what the organization has identified as its main priorities and the day-to-day activities of individual employees is a key challenge for managers and leaders. Performance management method-ologies are a key tool in making this link and reinforcing appropriate activities and behaviours. We know from our research into what the world's most admired companies are doing that strategy clarification and holding people accountable are key success factors in differentiating the best from the rest. Our survey into line manager perceptions of perform-ance management, as described in Chapter 4, revealed that the common-est way for organizations to seek to link an individual's objectives to business priorities is via the traditional business plan route, with almost half of the respondents reporting this as the method used. Team-based approaches were used by one-quarter and scorecards by one-fifth. Elsewhere in the book we refer to the background to balanced scorecard approaches and also to an example of implementation from Lloyds/TSB (see Chapters 2 and 12).

Setting objectives

In setting objectives the aim is to link what the business needs to achieve to the planned and agreed actions of individuals. Done well, the objective-setting process should heighten motivation (goal theory) as long as the objective is suitably stretching, within the individual's sphere of control, and achievement of it is reinforced (reinforcement theory) in ways appro-priate to the individual's motivational needs (content theories such as McClelland's). Objectives are therefore about specific things that need to be done in a performance period (usually a year) and, as a result, should not be simply a restatement of accountabilities. A common misunder-standing of objectives is that they might have to capture all of an individ-ual's accountabilities, but this is not the case. The accountabilities exist year on year to reflect the ongoing boundaries and responsibilities of the job holder. Objectives provide an opportunity to focus more directly on what the individual can realistically be expected to contribute this year in pursuit of overall company/organizational goals, as communicated by some sort of corporate cascade or balanced scorecard. Good practice will see an individual with not more than six key objectives to pursue within the course of a year. However, when performance is reviewed a manager is likely to take into account not just the achievement of objectives but also **whole** job performance, including the full scope of the job as defined in the accountability statements for it and any competencies agreed as key to the success of the role.

The choice of objectives thus depends primarily on business priorities. An awareness of these should suggest a natural focus as to which of a job holder's areas of responsibility are given most prominence this year.

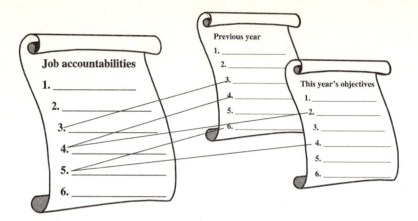

Figure 10.1 Linking accountabilities and objectives

Figure 10.1 illustrates this. It suggests that for any one year an individual may have two or more objectives linked to the achievement of one of their accountabilities. However, it is likely that not all accountabilities will have an objective set. This does not mean that the individual is free of this responsibility this year, but that this is wrapped up in the concept of whole job performance.

The figure illustrates how in successive years an individual might have objectives that link to different accountabilities in the job profile. The objectives will focus on the ways in which this individual will be making a contribution to achieving the priorities of the business in this perform-ance year. For example, an IT team member at the time of an equipment upgrade might have several objectives around managing the installation of new hardware and managing the training of colleagues in its usage.

When setting objectives it is useful to think about where best to target efforts – the most effective objectives are generally considered to be those that will have a large impact on the business and are within the job holder's sphere of control. Locke's (1968) goal theory tells us that people are motivated by specific, challenging goals which they accept as valid. A useful tool to support this thinking is captured in Figure 10.2 and has been entitled the 'leverage matrix'.

The matrix suggests considering each objective in terms of its potential impact on the business, if successfully completed, and also the relative degree of influence the job holder can exert to ensure successful achieve-ment of the objective. Q1 objectives are therefore likely to have a low orga-nizational impact and would be difficult for an individual to influence, being outside his or her normal sphere of control – they would make very inappropriate objectives. Q2 objectives are 'easy' for the individual to

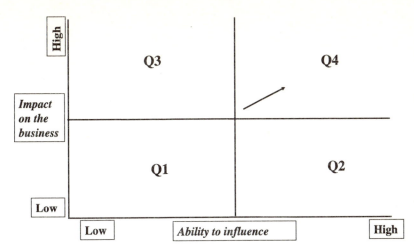

Figure 10.2 The leverage matrix: supporting effective objective setting

achieve in terms of their influence, but are the sort of objectives that make little real difference. Q3 represents objectives which are of high organizational importance and impact but which are not within the job holder's sphere of control – these equate with high stress. Q4 objectives are the most desirable as they have high organizational importance and are also within the job holder's normal scope of authority and influence. For example, an individual who works in Accounts may be able to influence the successful implementation of a new process for streamlining the month end. A reasonable objective in Q4 of Figure 10.2 might therefore be: *'By end first quarter devise new process for collating expense returns and determine roles and responsibilities by individual colleagues in order to ensure the implementation remains on track. Run a briefing session at team away day to communicate to colleagues.'*

Objectives around ensuring colleagues in other departments comply with requests for information may be more difficult to influence and would be placed within the Q3 quadrant – potentially a source of stress since impact on the business is high but ability to influence its achievement is low.

In order to provide clarity, objectives should be expressed in a format that allows for simple identification as to whether they have been achieved or not. The 'SMART' formula, which has achieved widespread acceptance, requires that objectives be set which are:

▌ Specific;

▌ Measurable;

▌ Achievable;

▌ Relevant to role;

▌ Time bound.

Given that over 75 per cent of our survey respondents reported (see Chapter 4) that they are already using the SMART approach, we expect its use to be well understood already and will not be expanding on it further here.

Setting performance standards

Directors are likely to have objectives traced directly from business plans, whereas for senior managers and their direct reports the directorate plan is likely to drive objectives. For other staff, typically those in front-line jobs, it is likely to be less appropriate to try to set individual objectives. A more appropriate focus might be to identify and monitor the achievement of key and agreed performance standards. In order to complete this effectively, it is necessary to draft common performance standards for all these employees.

All accountabilities are likely to have been drafted in such a way that their success can be assessed, for example on time, within specification. Performance standards look to formalize the monitoring of these.

So, for example, an individual working in security in a busy regional airport might have a mix of performance standards to adhere to, linked to the *accountabilities* contained in the *role profile*. One accountability might be: 'to manage equipment and queuing systems in order to maintain an even throughput of passengers'. Performance standards for this could quite reasonably include:

▌ number of passengers per minute through the screening station;

▌ customer satisfaction (as reported on feedback questionnaires);

▌ passenger queuing time;

▌ a zero target around lapses in security.

Performance planning therefore is essentially about measures. It is about agreeing the objectives, standards and measures against which individual job holders will be judged to have succeeded, exceeded or failed to live up to expectations of the role. In Chapter 2 we considered a number of the underpinning theories relating to performance management. Goal-setting theory is particularly relevant to the objective-setting process undertaken in organizations and managers should remember its principles when engaged in the planning stage of performance:

▌ goals should be clear and specific;

▌ goals should be demanding;

▌ goals should be accepted by employees;

▌ there must be feedback on performance.

In short, these principles tell us that objectives cannot be set by the manager in a vacuum. To be successful they must be jointly agreed and owned by the job holder, who feels he or she is being coached towards the achievement of the stated outcomes.

MEASURES AND MEASUREMENT-BASED APPROACHES

A considerable number of organizations have adopted an approach to measurement which is rather more sophisticated than the fairly traditional performance planning approach described above. Indeed, 21 per cent of respondents in our line manager survey reported that their organizations were deploying some sort of scorecard approach, as described in Chapter 2 and illustrated in our organizational story about Lloyds TSB in Chapter 12. Given that scorecards have become one of the main vehicles deployed by organizations seeking to rationalize both the link to strategy and the target/measurement process, it is worth while considering in more detail how measures are set within a scorecard approach.

The balanced scorecard was originally conceived by Kaplan and Norton (1992) as an approach to performance measurement that combined traditional financial measures with non-financial ones to provide managers with richer and more relevant information about organizational performance in relation to strategic goals.

It complements traditional financial accounting measures – earnings per share, return on capital employed – with operational measures on customer satisfaction, internal processes, and the organization's innovation and learning activities. It is based on the premise that measurement motivates but that traditional measurement-based approaches have tended to favour the things that are easy to measure (for example, financial results). As a result, these do not represent the 'balanced' picture of performance which the four quadrants of the scorecard promise, illustrated in Figure 2.5:

financial, customer, process, learning and growth/innovation. Balanced scorecard approaches are not without their critics and indeed in the years since the introduction of the approach many authors have suggested ways of improving its efficacy – including its original proponents (for more information, see, for example, Lawrie, Cobbold and Marshall, 2004).

Scorecards do, however, provide – in concept at least – a mechanism for moving beyond financial measures and can serve as a useful tool in the quest to balance measurement and development. For the purpose of this chapter we shall work through some of the underlying principles of the 'original' approach. We say more about new directions – the so-called second-generation scorecards or 'strategic scorecards' – in the concluding chapter of the book.

Before the organization can arrive at what might seem like a sensible set of measures under a traditional balanced scorecard approach, it will usually need to work through a series of steps similar to those described below.

Step 1: Strategy clarification

Before attempting to locate measures in a balanced scorecard format it is likely that the organization will require some form of strategy clarification exercise. In a balanced scorecard project this is typically achieved through the creation of what has been coined a business 'driver' model as shown in Figure 10.3.

The 'bubbles' on the driver model are intended to illustrate key strategic priorities for the business in a causal manner, grouped according to the four balanced-scorecard categorizations: financial, customer, internal, and learning and growth. For example, the illustration below suggests that for

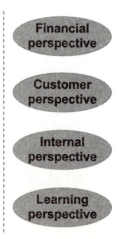

Figure 10.3 Layout of a simple driver model

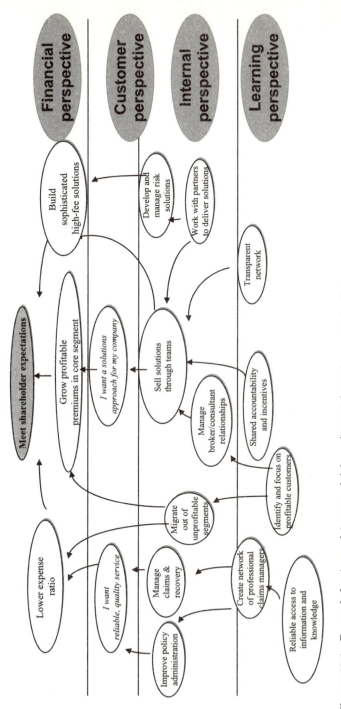

Figure 10.4 Example business driver model for a financial services organization

this organization enhanced IT capability in the learning and growth category is likely to be required to support product development and process efficiencies (in the internal category) in order to acquire and retain customers (customer perspective) and therefore to contribute to the required profit growth through a greater level of sales and cost management (financial categorization). Figure 10.4 indicates what a driver model might contain for a real organization – in this case a financial services organization.

The business driver model contains an 'at a glance' overview of what the management team building the scorecard think to be the important strategic interdependencies and drivers. After completing the strategy clarification exercise it becomes possible to establish what the strategic objectives might be for the organization during the next 12 to 18 months.

Step 2: Identification of strategic objectives and measures

The first round of strategic goal setting might involve the identification of many goals which together represent the organizational recipe for success. Sample objectives for each scorecard category are shown in Figure 10.5. For simplicity, our example shows only one objective per scorecard area and good practice suggests five objectives in each perspective are likely to be sufficient. In reality, less is more and for any one year the organization is likely to have to focus on those which are most critical this year, rather than attempt to do everything.

Moving from the driver model to the objectives and measures of a balanced scorecard might seem a difficult step, so to help structure your

	Objective			
Financial	Profitability			
Customer	Brand awareness			
Internal	Cross-sell our products			
Learning	Enhance capability culture			

Figure 10.5   Scorecard objectives in each of the four categories

Table 10.1 Checklist for development of a balanced scorecard

Financial	Who are your stakeholders? What do they expect? To meet these expectations, what must you do well in relation to: revenue, costs, asset utilization?
Customer	How would you describe the segments that define/will define your customer base? What must you do to improve market share in each segment? How should you measure progress towards each objective?
Internal	Considering the financial and customer objectives, which internal processes will be most critical to achieving these goals? For each selected process, what needs to be done? How should progress be measured?
Learning	In what areas must people learn and improve in order to meet the internal process objectives? What must be done to improve in those areas with an identified gap? How should progress be measured in this area?

thoughts, Table 10.1 contains a list of suggested questions to work through during the development phase.

	Objective	Lead Measure	Lag Measure	
Financial	Profitability	Transaction size	Gross profit growth	
Customer	Brand awareness	Customer activity	No. branded items sold	
Internal	Cross-sell our products	Sales meetings based on referrals	% revenue from new products	
People	Enhance capability culture	Culture survey feedback	Internal promotions (vs plan %)	

Figure 10.6 Illustrative scorecard lead and lag measures

Figure 10.6 then captures what might be *measured* for each scorecard objective from our previous example in Figure 10.5, which also illustrates how an organization might set both lead (contributing or driver) and lag (final outcome) measures. So, for example, to meet the internal process objective of cross-selling products there might be a lead measure around monitoring the number of sales meetings based on referrals from one product area to another. This lead measure is seen to contribute to the final outcome or lag measure of an increase in percentage revenue from new product sales.

Having identified what to measure, the challenge for organizations – if measures are to be meaningful – is to move to Step 3 of the process and establish how success for each measure will be judged in any one performance year.

Step 3: Defining targets against scorecard measures

Once a measure has been defined, it becomes necessary to establish a baseline (the current picture) and a target for the coming year. See Figure 10.7 for an illustration of this in the internal process area of the scorecard. The example suggests how, if 2006 were the year of introduction of the target, we might expect the percentage revenue from new products to equal around 15 per cent. However, we can see a target for 2008 that is 50 per cent of revenue from new product sales.

Figure 10.7 also illustrates how it may be necessary to put in place certain actions to deliver against the scorecard measures. In our example the

	Statement of what the strategy must achieve and what's critical to its success	How success in achieving the strategy will be measured and tracked	The level of performance or rate of improvement needed	Action required to achieve objectives
	Objective	**Lag measure**	**Target**	**Initiative**
Financial				
Customer				
Internal	Cross-sell our products	% revenue from new products	2006 15% 2008 50%	Data sharing to support cross-selling culture
People				

Figure 10.7   Target-setting for each measure of the scorecard

increase in revenue from cross-selling is likely to require support for a change in culture to one of cross-selling. This in turn is likely to have a knock-on effect on the people category of the scorecard, with a target being set for training on new products and data sharing in support of the cross-selling objective.

TRYING TO BALANCE MEASUREMENT AND DEVELOPMENT

By its very structure the balanced scorecard methodology encourages organizations to think beyond traditional financial targets that are easy to quantify. In theory, therefore, it should be ideal for encouraging an equal focus on both 'hard' and 'soft' deliverables.

We provide now a case study example which considers the challenge of implementing a balanced scorecard and in particular of really aiming to make quantifiable some of the intangibles of people management such as capability and development.

Case study: devising a measure of development within a balanced scorecard

Our example focuses on an international insurer we will refer to as Company Z. The organization, recognizing its difficult trading conditions, undertook an extensive strategic review, employing consultants to support this. The balanced scorecard emerged as a framework to support translating this strategic review into action. It was recognized that in order to implement the new strategy a radical change programme would be required. This involved changing the focus of work, redefining roles accordingly, building the appropriate information technology and people infrastructures and defining measures for success against which to measure and reward performance.

The initiative exemplifies the integrated performance management 'house' metaphor, described earlier in Chapter 8. In order to align a workforce with organizational strategy, the building blocks of job definitions, competency and skill profiling and HR infrastructure and process support were identified as the foundations with which to enable the performance management process. This process is then the driver for reward architecture, training and development, career planning and high-potential recognition.

Once the strategy had been clarified, it was possible to drill down to identify a number of priorities, essential for its successful delivery:

▌ key account management;

▌ the claims process;

▌ leadership across the organization;

▌ putting in place an effective monitoring and measuring function.

There was obviously a financial element to a number of these; for example, the cost-ratio was defined as an important lag measure within claims. However, there was also an awareness of the need to change behaviours in line with the demands of the new strategy. This culture change required a focus on customers, internal process and, in particular, on people development and their learning.

In order to achieve these changes a number of actions were required which resulted in a wave of implementation projects. These started at the bottom of the integrated house with job definitions and competency profiling.

If we look at the example of key account management, a priority area from the strategy clarification exercise, it is possible to see how the business driver model shapes both the scorecard and the new competency and skill definitions. In turn, these are used as the basis for revised job definitions (in this case a role profile). This is illustrated graphically in Figure 10.8.

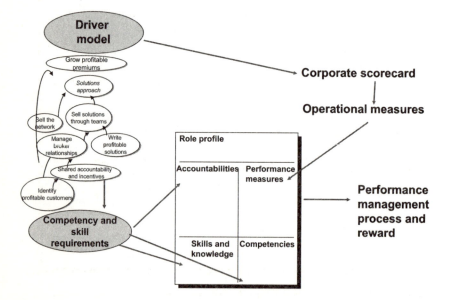

Figure 10.8   Linking the new job definition to balanced scorecard

Role profiles were therefore redrafted so that they covered the key priorities reflected in the business driver model and measures included in the scorecard. The new role profile for key account managers included seven accountability statements with associated performance measures, skills and competencies, as captured in Figure 10.9.

In addition, the role profile contains skills and knowledge required for the position and also the competencies drawn from the Company Z competency model. In our example we list only the competencies associated with the first of the accountabilities: Monitor customer awareness. The behaviours associated with this accountability were around

Role Profile
Key Account Manager

Accountabilities	Performance measures
1.Monitor customer awareness	Number of visits/contacts Participation at events
2. Prioritize targets against criteria	Updated target list
3. Create/progress target plans	Plans updated
4. Meet new business targets	Agreement ratio Net growth per business line
5. Extend customer relationships	Customer satisfaction and cross-referral
6. New ideas/project contribution	360-degree feedback
7. Knowledge sharing	Contributions to know-how database

Skills and knowledge	Competencies
Qualified probably to degree level Financial /insurance experience Insurance certificate	Impact and influence Conceptual thinking Relationship building

Figure 10.9   Illustrative role profile reflecting scorecard and driver model

actively seeking opportunities to impress potential customers in target segments and taking practical steps to enable introductions. The competencies required to deliver this behaviour were defined as being: impact and influence, conceptual thinking and relationship building. It was recognized that the mindset and associated behaviours for this crucial role of key account manager would in fact take some time to develop. Here therefore lay a challenge as to how to measure progress towards this development objective. Interestingly, Company Z decided that the easiest way to incorporate this within the scorecard framework was to quantify it, just like any other measure. What emerged was a learning measure all around capability and development, entitled 'capability coverage'.

A measure for development – capability coverage

Capability coverage was devised to serve as a set of measures illustrating the extent to which the organization had the right people to fulfil the strategy, that is, the fit between the competencies and skills of the current role holder and those required in the role. It could be expressed at an individual or at an organization-wide or team-based level. So, for example, assume that a key account manager has five core competencies required for the role. If during the performance discussions the individual is judged to be achieving three of the five competencies set out in the role profile then his or her overall score would be 60 per cent. At a team level, capability coverage is an average of individual percentage scores, with 0 per cent for each unfilled post. As measures can be provided at all levels, from teams to the whole organization, comparisons may be made across teams and departments and trends tracked over time.

Table 10.2 outlines the capability coverage measure.

Our account management case study provides an illustration of how the scorecard methodology can help to achieve the much-desired balance between 'hard' (typically financial) measures and less tangible 'softer' ones. If this can be achieved then the two categories of performance, 'what' and 'how', as introduced in Chapter 2, might be combined and effectively managed.

Chapter 2 also saw us raise some reservations about placing too much emphasis on managing measures at the cost of managing performance itself. Indeed, defining employee capability in such a quantifiable way is at best a crude measure. For example, what does a 1 per cent decrease in overall capability coverage actually mean and should the data be presented in such a composite/organization-wide manner?

Table 10.2 The capability coverage measure

Step 1: Resourcing required vs actual	Establish a resource budget for all levels in each function, tracking against actual headcount (desired vs current) Set recruitment targets/limits
Step 2: Skill and knowledge audit	Produce skills and knowledge inventory for function, drawing on role profiles Audit against inventory to produce percentage fit with profile by using amalgamated performance management data Highlight development needs by role/function and set recruitment/training plans accordingly
Step 3: Overall capability	Produce overall percentage of total capability (skill, knowledge and competencies) by combining analyses of each function to determine requirements vs actual

However, such approaches serve to indicate how it is possible to define the causal links between the strategy of an organization and its workforce. In organizations where there is a commitment to work with a scorecard approach, or indeed where there is simply an apparent dominance of measurement-based approaches, then approaches such as capability coverage have a key role to play. They provide a seemingly rational picture on which to base investment decisions around developing and managing talent, in line with any areas of apparent risk within the business. Indeed, by quantifying capability and development the approach provides an example of how it is possible to legitimize and 'set among equals' the contribution of human capital.

The next chapter remains with this theme and provides a different account of how one organization has set about measuring capability – this time specifically for a leadership population.

11

Organizational story: measuring capability at BAT

Most of the organizations we studied in researching this book recognized the importance of measuring the capability of their leaders and supporting their development within the performance management process. The previous chapter also raised the importance of an organization ensuring it had the right people (or leaders) to fulfil the strategy. However, not all of the organizations we examined had put in place a coherent strategy to address these issues. British American Tobacco (BAT) – showcased in this chapter – was an exception to this, applying a new and different approach to measuring and developing leadership capability and managing the supply of its future leaders to ensure that the right people were in place to deliver a step change in performance.

With revenues of around £34.2 billion, BAT operates in 64 countries and is the world's second-largest tobacco company, behind Phillip Morris, with a 15 per cent share of the market. Selling to around 180 countries, BAT owns more than 300 well-known brands, such as Lucky Strike, Pall Mall, Kent, Dunhill, State Express 555 and Benson & Hedges.

In 2003 the management board of BAT outlined the work they saw as necessary to take the company from a good, successful company to a truly global enterprise. They identified five work-streams: Strategy and Process, Organizational Structure, Overheads & Indirect Costs,

Leadership & Alignment and Communications. In Leadership & Alignment, a number of key deliverables were identified, including:

▌ reviewing the performance expectations of managers, providing clarity on the performance dimensions relevant to each level of the organization;

▌ reviewing senior role definitions, to ensure they reflect the requirements of the new organization;

▌ reviewing the reward architecture to focus on performance expectations at individual, unit and group level, and reinforcing the behavioural expectations of leaders.

To meet some of the above demands, BAT decided to reconfigure all of its people processes around the work conducted by Charam, Drotter and Noel (2001) on the Leadership Pipeline.

THE LEADERSHIP PIPELINE AT BAT

BAT had traditionally been very good at developing people in functional silos, and excellent performance had been measured in terms of 'delivering the numbers'. The focus had historically been on objectives, relating mainly to operational targets, and competencies had been used for development purposes only.

The Leadership Pipeline model is aimed at capitalizing on the potential of all managers within the organization by discerning the real work requirements at key leadership levels and identifying what is needed to make a successful transition from one leadership level to the next. The model concentrates on levels of leadership rather than specific jobs, moving away from a focus on the technical/professional outputs of jobs to the managerial and leadership duties associated with the role.

The pipeline describes six 'leadership passages' (illustrated in Figure 11.1), beginning with Passage One – from managing self to managing others, and culminating in Passage Six – moving from group executive to enterprise manager.

These passages define expectations and output required of every manager in BAT, differentiated by each leadership level. The passages are referred to as 'turns' an individual is required to make, each turn representing changes in skill requirements, new time applications and new work values.

For BAT, understanding the challenges and potential pitfalls associated with each turn is essential for planned career development of individuals

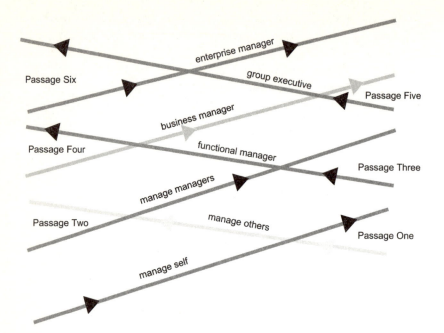

Figure 11.1 The leadership passages. *Source:* BAT, reproduced with permission

and for better coaching to ensure individuals are 'ready' for progression into new roles. It is also crucial for clear delineation of what needs to be delivered in a given role, providing a sounder basis to make decisions around the performance of leaders.

Each turn requires a new way of managing and leading, implying change in three main areas:

- **work values** – what people believe is important and so becomes the focus of their effort;

- **skill requirements** – the new capabilities required to execute new responsibilities;

- **time applications** – new time frames that govern how one works.

The challenge for BAT is to ensure that leaders are working at the level that is appropriate to their skills, time applications and values. Leaders in many organizations may be working at the wrong level either because what they value around the role – often the technical and professional component – is less important at this level; or because they lack the managerial and leadership skills that they increasingly need to rely on; or because they do not fully appreciate the need to raise their time horizon, to take action now to create growth opportunities for tomorrow.

BAT, in recognizing this challenge, has realigned all its core people processes to this new leadership framework. Performance management is the first people process to be aligned and, in time, all jobs will be positioned to one of the pipeline levels (manage self, manage others . . . etc), providing a great deal of clarity around what is expected of people.

For BAT, the new model fundamentally raises the bar on what constitutes effective 'performance', and delivering great numbers alone is no longer considered to be good enough. In addition, the new model:

I identifies clear performance standards and reviews against these;

I identifies gaps and produces focused development planning;

I ensures that the work required to deliver the BAT strategy is aligned and executed at the appropriate leadership level;

I helps build skills cumulatively throughout careers;

I builds a 'leadership' pipeline;

I enables more precise, proactive planning as leaders get ready for transition.

MEASURING PERFORMANCE

For all six passages shown in Figure 11.1, performance dimensions define the five core areas against which tangible results have to be delivered, and these form the basis of performance objective setting. Thus objective setting encompasses the five areas of:

I business/operational/technical results;

I leadership results;

I management results;

I relationship results;

I innovation results.

This represents a departure for BAT, an organization that has been less prescriptive in the past around the areas for objective setting, often resulting in objectives that neglected the relationship, management and leadership aspects in favour of operational priorities. By mandating that managers set objectives in five key areas embracing a more holistic view of the leadership role, BAT has set itself on a road towards changing the

Performance Dimensions	Required Work Values	Full Performance
Operational/Professional & Tech/Financial Results Improved Effectiveness/Efficiency/Productivity/Quality Strategy. Contribution to development and execution Information for Strategic and Business Plans & decisions	Results through other managers	Meets both individual and aggregate department KRAs/goals and makes appropriate adjustments Customer/client requests met as promised Assures all work meets professional/technical/operational standards for quality Contributes to functional strategy development, and drives its execution
Leadership Results Clear Direction Department Leadership Pipeline Right People in Right Job Building/Developing First-Line Management	Leadership capability within department pipeline Direct reports accountable for leadership work/results	Ensures all department members understand and support the vision and the strategy Drives cross-functional team-working to drive business integration and performance delivery Identifies, retains, coaches and develops future leaders and future managers of managers Ensures whole team understands how their roles fit into overall corporate vision and strategies Role models and builds enthusiasm for change with passion Builds and values a diverse team Shows high level of self-awareness of their leadership role Seeks opportunities for growth and development and produces written development plans for self and direct reports
Management Results Operational Plans and Priorities Performance Management/Standards and Expectations for First-Line Managers Progress Review/Results Measurement/Follow-up Appropriate Delegation/Resource Allocation Project Management	Management competence of direct reports Lateral integration	Holds first-line managers accountable for management work Keeps team focused on key priorities/projects by setting measures and milestones to ensure things happen as planned Causes work to flow smoothly throughout the unit/ department Holds direct reports accountable for their own results and obstacles Makes the hard decisions promptly, even when they may be unpopular Produces a positive, cumulative result from all unit projects and KRAs
Relationships Results Internal Net working – within and across functions Understanding Others' Agendas/Perspectives Knowledge Sharing/Learning Across BAT Communication Upward and Downward	Cross functional relationships Peer relationships with all peers	Readily shares information with peers & throughout the function Proactively supports peers in own and other functions Builds effective network (internally and externally) to get things done Models relationship building for direct reports Effectively uses existing opportunities/vehicles to communicate information upward, sideways, downward and outward
Innovation Results Technology Leveraged to Drive Business New/Improved ways of adding value through work done	Continuous improvement of processes Challenge from direct reports	Measures direct reports on changes and improvements Tries out new ideas and technologies – challenges the status quo Takes calculated risks and learns from mistakes Optimises and improves systems and work processes to drive productivity and reduce cost

Figure 11.2 Performance dimensions and associated performance criteria for a 'manager of managers' at BAT. *Source:* BAT, reproduced with permission

culture of the organization. Performance dimensions have been further drilled down to specify the required work values and indicate what 'full performance' would look like against each indicator. The performance dimensions, work values and full performance measures for a 'manager of managers' are presented as an example in Figure 11.2.

BAT has also focused on providing role clarity, an important factor if individuals are going to understand the scope of their role and the level at which they are required to operate. Thus the organization has developed some generic role profiles with key accountabilities defined in terms of the five performance dimensions above, providing further clarity around what is required from leaders in their roles. For example, for functional managers, the differences between regional roles, global roles at headquarters and market-based roles are specified; similarly, for directors, a functional and regional set have been identified, highlighting the areas of shared focus as well as the differences.

Finally, BAT has re-engineered the reward architecture for leaders, recognizing its powerful role in reinforcing the changes the organization is attempting to embed. This redefinition has been useful in that it has enabled BAT to select the most appropriate areas to focus performance objectives, the optimal unit of measurement (the individual, the market, or corporate performance) and the preferred reward outcome (cash or shares).

BAT appears to be at the 'cutting edge' in aligning all of its people processes against the Leadership Pipeline model, which attempts to raise capability and performance through clarity. The work done by the organization has greatly increased the clarity around roles, expectations, performance measures and progression to the next level. It has also helped to underpin a cultural shift away from quantifying and developing capability around operational performance/results delivery to a more 'balanced' approach that also sets clear expectations around managerial and leadership skills.

12

Organizational story: measurement using a balanced scorecard at Lloyds TSB

In this chapter we showcase Lloyds TSB, an organization that has adopted a primarily measurement-based approach to managing performance through the development of a balanced scorecard. This organizational story effectively brings to life some of the implementation issues around balanced scorecards that we raised in Chapter 10.

Lloyds TSB is a leading UK-based financial services group, created in 1995 following the merger of the TSB Group and the Lloyds Bank Group. Lloyds TSB Group's total group assets are over £252 billion; it employs over 71,500 people and has over 15 million customers. Its activities are organized into three businesses: UK Retail Banking and Mortgages, Insurance and Investments, and Wholesale and International Banking.

As with the Belron story reported later, the performance management process here was transformed at the behest of the CEO, in this case with the advent of a new CEO, Eric Daniels, in 2003. Daniels introduced the concept of the balanced scorecard into Lloyds TSB as part of a strategy of organizational renewal aimed at restoring confidence in a business that was seen as performing under par. He recognized that pursuing a strategy of growth by acquisition was no longer an option and that organic growth would be dependent upon how well the organization moved away from narrow objectives around sales volume and operating costs to being driven by the customer agenda and the processes to fulfil these expectations. He recognized that the company had become too narrow in its focus and instigated a strategic shift that forced a fundamental rethink of business performance measurement.

THE INTRODUCTION OF THE BALANCED SCORECARD AT LLOYDS TSB

The balanced scorecard (BSC), introduced by Kaplan and Norton in the 1990s (see Chapters 2 and 10 for background and more information on implementation), provides a way for an organization to balance its strategic priorities around finances, customers, processes and people. In theory it ensures that performance metrics at both an organizational and individual level are 'balanced' rather than skewed towards financial targets alone. The scorecard at Lloyds followed these broad principles, tailored to meet the particular business environment, and focused on five new areas: Contribution, Franchise Growth, Customer Satisfaction, Risk, and People.

Having identified the corporate priorities for the business via the balanced scorecard, individuals were then expected to cascade these into an individual 'personal' scorecard. At his first conference for senior executives across the Group in May 2003, Daniels asked all executives to ensure that every member of staff had just such a performance contract by the end of the following month. However, the timescales for implementation meant that while people initially embraced the concepts and complied with this request, individual scorecards were often no more than cosmetic repackaging of existing objectives. There was little understanding across the business of how balanced scorecards worked, why they were good for Lloyds TSB and how individuals should change their current practice. The challenge, therefore, was to get managers to explore a different philosophy in the way the business operated and embrace a fundamental change in priorities. Although the five new areas of Contribution, Franchise Growth, Customer Satisfaction, Risk, and People were defined and prioritized, people were left to interpret these for themselves.

The challenge for HR was therefore clear: first, how should 65,000 individuals in the UK and more overseas cascade these priorities into meaningful individual plans? Second, how could HR alter individuals' perceptions around performance plans to move away from a surface-level reworking of current objectives to an appreciation of the strategic change in thinking required to formulate new scorecard objectives? The balanced scorecard is a tool for identifying and driving value creation within organizations. Allowing it to become simply a new label for a performance contract would have confirmed the perception of the minority who criticized its 'flavour of the month' hallmarks (Ward, 2005).

To address some of these issues the organization created a Head of Performance Management, Adrian Ward, to oversee implementation of the BSC and to regenerate performance management. One of Ward's first activities was to commission executive education seminars. These were half-day sessions aimed at the top 250 executives and attended by the entire HR business partner community. By the end of 2003 most of the Group-wide senior executive population had attended the education seminars, even though participation was on a purely voluntary basis, resulting in a greater awareness and understanding of both the scorecard itself and the strategic reasons behind the executive team's commitment to it.

THE PERFORMANCE MANAGEMENT PROCESS AT LLOYDS TSB

The traditional performance management process at Lloyds TSB had been untouched since the merger in 1995 and comprised a series of objectives and measures with a loose link to pay. These objectives tended to be extremely detailed 'tick lists', often describing the minutiae of a person's job. For example, some local directors and managers, who were being urged to be more entrepreneurial in running their business locally, had as many as 30 objectives and 50 'micro' measures of performance. Measurement was not towards goal accomplishment but task completion, and the process revolved around the bureaucratic process of form filling. A key step in the balanced scorecard journey was therefore to support people to drill the scorecard into much more focused individual objectives that concerned key accountabilities rather than task completion.

The first part of this process has been to state that only one objective (or a maximum of two) would be required under each of the five sections of the scorecard – a major cultural shift! Each of these objectives should be broad and generic, common to many people, enabling most individuals in the organization to sign up to a shared set of goals. For example:

I **finance**: maximize income and optimize cost to enhance profitability;

I **franchise**: maximize the number of new profitable customers and the products and services we sell to those we already have;

I **customer**: maximize customer satisfaction;

I **risk**: optimize operational, financial and reputational risk;

I **people**: maximize capability and motivation.

Next, people are asked to specify the measures for each objective, thereby differentiating how a particular job holder contributes to that overall objective. In the 'old world' this would have meant a measure such as 'Have no more than x people by y date.' However, in the new process the focus has shifted to a measure that is more along the lines of 'average cost per head of staff' – in line with the broader objective – and one that is not about headcount but about cost efficiency.

Each measure also has an associated target; for instance, in the example above, the target may be 'maintain within current budget'. Finally, the target has an associated set of actions, the activities that will be necessary to help meet the target. These may be detailed and could include specific tasks with milestones, and whereas in the new system this represents the end point, previously these would have been the goals set at the outset. Figure 12.1 shows the Lloyds TSB scorecard and provides some examples of measures and targets.

By realigning objectives away from tasks and closer to organizational goals, managers are now forced to consider what data they really need to measure individual contribution rather than simply what they already have at their disposal. Examples abound of what a striking difference this can make. In the Wholesale division, for example, senior executives were historically charged with 'raising profile in the business community' as a

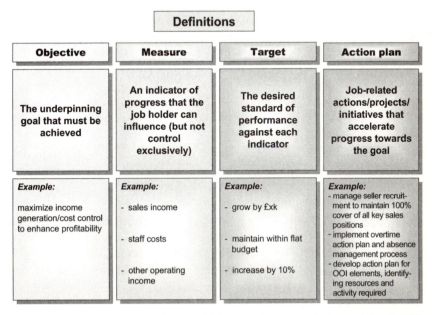

Definitions			
Objective	**Measure**	**Target**	**Action plan**
The underpinning goal that must be achieved	An indicator of progress that the job holder can influence (but not control exclusively)	The desired standard of performance against each indicator	Job-related actions/projects/initiatives that accelerate progress towards the goal
Example: maximize income generation/cost control to enhance profitability	*Example:* - sales income - staff costs - other operating income	*Example:* - grow by £xk - maintain within flat budget - increase by 10%	*Example:* - manage seller recruitment to maintain 100% cover of all key sales positions - implement overtime action plan and absence management process - develop action plan for OOI elements, identifying resources and activity required

Figure 12.1 Layout of the Lloyds TSB balanced scorecard. *Source:* Lloyds TSB, reproduced with permission

performance objective. When it came to measuring this, it was common to see such things as 'number of lunches' or even 'number of speeches'. Reword the objective to 'maximize new profitable customer relationships', however, and lunches and speeches quickly become irrelevant compared to metrics such as 'number of switchers' (customers switching their account to Lloyds) or '% of new customers becoming profitable by the end of first 12 months banking' (Ward, 2005).

Achievement of each overall objective around the five scorecard areas is rated according to a three-point rating scale: Exceeded Expectations, Met Expectations, or Partially Met Expectations. Whether particular objectives are weighted over others is left to the discretion of individual business units. The end of the performance management document also includes a development plan focusing on competencies and capabilities as well as skills and knowledge, where individuals are encouraged to set some goals for individual learning and development. The focus, however, is primarily around measurement and 'getting the measures right'.

The end point is an overall rating, again using the same three-point scale as above. The link to pay is indirect, relying on the judgement of line managers to distribute monies from an allocated pot. Line managers use a fairly standard process to guide decision making; judgements are based on balanced scorecard performance and on where people currently fall within the pay benchmark.

MANAGING PERFORMANCE VERSUS MEASURING PERFORMANCE

The performance management process at Lloyds TSB has undergone a significant transition, with a much greater alignment between the strategic priorities of the business and individuals' performance objectives. Additionally, the transition includes a deeper understanding of the value-creation factors around the business and people's own role, with an empowering of managers to focus on measures that are meaningful to them. All of this has greatly enhanced precision about what is expected of people and what they need to do to get there, beyond the previously over-engineered system where detail detracted from clarity.

However, while the performance management process has its benefits, it is essentially about measuring performance rather than encouraging managers to take ownership of managing people. Capability among managers to analyse the root causes of performance issues, to give constructive feedback and coach for high performance, while there, is variable within the organization. The next challenge for Lloyds TSB is likely to lie in transforming the conversations line managers have with people from the categories of Above Target, Met Target or Below Target to a more holistic discussion of performance, including the role of values, competencies and behaviours in driving performance; and additionally, to ensure that the people section of the balanced scorecard carries equivalent weight to other parts and that managers have incentives to focus on these outcomes as much as others.

THE SPEED OF CULTURAL CHANGE

As pressure from the City mounts to deliver greater shareholder return and capital growth for investors, senior leaders within any organization (and Lloyds TSB is no exception) need to hold their nerve in the implementation of any scorecard that is truly balanced. This is not as easy as it sounds, particularly when the culture of the organization has not kept pace with the speed of implementation of the scorecard. Cultural change takes time and is not the same as enthusiasm; if attempts are made to carry it out too rapidly, this may confound the situation further.

Inevitably at Lloyds TSB, although the majority of line managers have embraced the changes required, some managers were able (as the pressure mounted) to exploit the informal nature of the process to focus on short-term wins and 'revert back to type'. For these managers, it was easy to characterize the scorecard as 'another stick to beat us with' and to change their practice so that the day-to-day reality was somewhat removed from the rhetoric they publicly supported. It is hard in difficult trading times to maintain the sustainability argument and easier to revert to the status quo. This has resulted in the organization slipping back from some of the transformational changes it wanted to achieve at the outset of the balanced scorecard launch.

Lloyds TSB is typical of a number of organizations that have successfully implemented a balanced scorecard approach; it has brought greater alignment of individual and team performance to business priorities, but it has fallen short of some of the 'lofty ideals' talked of at its inception. It has provided clarity and enabled the business to track performance in a more meaningful way. The pitfall for any organization is whether the scorecard, as created by Kaplan and Norton to 'decode' strategy and interconnect the critical performance factors, has been truly realized, or whether it has merely provided a useful way of reordering measures and objectives.

13
Managing performance and development-based approaches

This chapter deals with the managing phase of performance management. This phase is the one where many of the 'big wins' of the process can occur, notably in the process of turning round underperformance as well as coaching for greater success. It may appear to be counter-intuitive to regard this as a separate phase, as performance management is fundamentally a structured way of thinking about a key and ongoing managerial responsibility. In organizations where 'good' management happens as a matter of course, it may be difficult or impossible to distinguish everyday conversations, coaching and feedback from the more procedural performance discussions that happen as a part of the performance management process. For this is how effective performance management should be. In organizations where this has not yet happened, it is important to build line management understanding that performance needs to be managed throughout the year; sound performance management does not start and finish with the annual review.

At its simplest, the managing phase is intended to encourage or enforce one or more interim reviews during the course of the year so that the final performance review presents no surprises. In many organizations these interim reviews are an ideal opportunity to focus in more detail on development planning and on giving (and perhaps receiving) feedback.

It is within the managing phase, therefore, that we examine those elements of performance management which are associated primarily with development and capability. We have already discussed the 'process' and 'metrics' circles from our organizing framework (presented in Figure 8.1). We now look at the capability circle. The topics we cover include the links between performance management and development planning in line with personal aspirations and job/organizational requirements. In addition, we discuss the impact managers have on the climate created within their team and some of the leadership qualities and skills required to deliver effectively the managing phase of the performance management process.

HOW PERFORMANCE MANAGEMENT LINKS TO DEVELOPMENT PLANNING

We have already suggested in our house model presented in Chapter 8 that performance management operates as the key element within an integrated HR management structure once individuals have been recruited and roles defined. Once the building blocks are in place, performance management should drive the higher-order processes of reward, training and development, promotion and career progression.

Competency-based development approaches

After producing a competency framework (as illustrated in Chapter 1), the next step for most organizations as they seek to include competencies in performance management is usually the profiling of roles in terms of their competency requirements. (An illustration of this approach is given in Chapter 8.) Profiling should help provide clarity for managers and employees to understand how the competency framework – all too often perceived as an abstract document written in HR jargon – translates into everyday roles and organizational requirements.

'Gaps' between job requirements and an individual employee's personal competency profile are likely to be discussed firstly in the planning performance meeting and followed up in the interim and end-of-year performance review discussions. Throughout the performance cycle the identification of any gaps may also be used to help to create a competency-based development plan along the lines of the example in Figure 13.1, or to inform decisions around job rotation, promotion or high-potential identification.

Role Profile	Key Account Management
Jo Smith Development Priorities	**Type of Development**
1. Relationship building	Competency
2. Leading performance	Competency
3. Interpreting financial reports	Skill/knowledge
Jo Smith Development Actions	**Date to achieve**
1. Relationship building:	
- Identify key individuals for priority accounts	End first quarter
- Develop long-term contact plan with key individuals	End second quarter
- Log contact activity	Review end of year
- Review with Ken every month for top 10 accounts	
2. Leading performance	
- Clarify priorities for each team member and review monthly.	Commenced by end first quarter
- Read 'How to give constructive feedback' guidelines from PM Handbook	Prior to review meetings in June
3. Attend FT workshop on how to interpret financial reports and accounts	Workshop booked for March in advance of budgeting process

Figure 13.1 Example of a competency-based development plan

Figure 13.1 builds on the example we explored for key account management in Chapter 10. If we look first at the training and development requirements we can see that *'relationship building'* and *'leading performance'* emerge as key competency development areas for this employee, coupled with the knowledge and skill area of *'interpreting financial reports'*.

For relationship building we see that the development suggestions are divided into four bullet points. These require the individual to put in place a process around key account planning in order to manage relationships with clients and ensure more repeat business. For leading performance and interpreting financial reports there are additional development activities.

Competency development suggestions
Focusing on client service

Level 1   Understands client and responds to stated needs

♦ Put yourself in your clients' shoes - when dealing with and discussing their issues, practise looking at the situation from their point of view. Ask yourself what they want and what business issues are driving their needs.

♦ At the beginning of each financial year organise a planning meeting that brings together representatives from your clients. Write up the findings and communicate to your team.

♦ How does your area interact with clients? What were the impacts of recent actions on your clients? Ask yourself how you could improve the quality and efficiency of these interactions.

♦ On completion of a client project, seek formal feedback on the quality of service provided by HR.

Level 2   Suggests fitting solutions

♦ Build a service level agreement through consultation with your clients: use this to ensure that you focus on continual improvement.

♦ On receiving a request from a client, consider if there is a way to add further value by going beyond their expectations; involve others if they have relevant expertise which will help.

♦ Look outside your area of the business for approaches to specific problems that have been used to good effect, and will help you to uncover and understand your clients' requirements.

♦ When responding to a client request, try to provide a range of options. Outline the pros and cons of each to enable the client to make an informed decision.

Level 3   Addresses underlying needs

♦ Gather together all of the available data on your clients; summarize this into a concise and meaningful presentation that will provide new clarity for your team.

♦ Bring together a group to look at your clients' HR needs, trying to link these to their underlying business issues: facilitate a brainstorming session to find practical solutions.

♦ When planning with your client, map out the peaks and troughs of their activities; use this information to provide additional support when it is most needed.

♦ List the issues which currently shape the HR needs of your clients, and the changes that you anticipate to these. Use these to consider what new solutions might be required in the future.

Level 4   Acts as a trusted adviser

♦ Ask to review clients' long-term business plans and understand their strategic goals.

   ♦Use this to tailor your offerings, ensuring that these align with their future requirements.

   ♦Review projects currently in progress and determine whether they will deliver future value to the client: if not, consider calling a halt to them.

♦ Seek to build strong relationships with key players in your clients: offer your services to them as an independent 'sounding board' for issues in which you hold expertise.

♦ Familiarize yourself with your clients' planning cycle, and ask to become involved in the next round with a view to shaping, and being better prepared for, future requirements.

Figure 13.2   Extract from a competency-based development guide

As competencies are introduced into organizations, the challenge for many managers is to understand how to diagnose competency gaps along the lines discussed earlier and then to advise on the sort of activities that will support the development of the required competencies. For this reason, many organizations have produced competency-based 'development guides'. These detail suggestions for developing each competency and contain a range of on-the-job and off-the-job training and development ideas as well as resources such as reference books, articles and

Competency development suggestions
Focusing on client service

Books Hyperlink to Amazon.com

Moments of Truth
J Carlzon (1987)
ISBN 0887302009

Winning the Service Game
B Schneider, D E Bowen (1995)
ISBN 0875845703

Customer Connections
New Strategies for Growth
R Wayland, Paul M Cole (1997)
ISBN 0875847994

Customers as Partners
C R Bell (1994)
ISBN 1881052540

Strategic Market Management
D. Aaker (1998)
ISBN 0471177431

The Experience Economy
B Pine II (1999)
ISBN 0875848192

Delivering Profitable Value
M J Lanning (1998)
ISBN 073820045X

Marketing Management
P Kotler (1996)
ISBN 0130156841

Business @ The Speed
of Thought
B Gates (1999)
ISBN 0141800429

The Discipline of
Market Leaders
M Treacy, F Wiersema (1996)
ISBN 0006387160

Customer Capitalism
S Vandermerwe (1999)
ISBN 1857882415

Audio/Video/CD ROM

A Passion for Customers
Video Arts

In the Customer's Shoes
Melrose Films

Managing Customers for
Profits
Harvard Business School
CD ROM

Courses/Seminars

Building Customer Focus
Forum International

Marketing for
Management
A Fast-track Guide for
Non Marketing Executives
Management Centre
Europe

Figure 13.2 *Continued*

videos/DVDs which illustrate the area in need of development and also support different learning styles. They make the point that attending training programmes is only one option and not always the best for modifying behaviour at work. An extract from a competency-based development guide can be seen in Figure 13.2.

This development guide shows how different competencies might be enhanced and provides an invaluable guide for managers and individuals in their search for appropriate ideas for the development of competencies that are not being displayed at the required level for job success.

Accepting the competency gap and producing their own development plan is one of the critical starting points in terms of revising individual behaviour. Figure 13.3 suggests that helping individuals to see the relevance of particular competencies to their role will generally help them to overcome barriers around development.

The model in Figure 13.3 illustrates how the mindset of the individual employee might react to the type of development need suggested for him or her. For example, someone needing to learn a new computer programming language might recognize this as a skill and knowledge gap and undertake a course of study. However, many of the roadblocks to development encountered by individuals cannot be addressed at the level of skills and knowledge. The model in Figure 13.3 suggests a hierarchy of attributes, of which skill and knowledge are closest to the surface. If we think of the layers below (role, self-image, traits and motive), we can see that motive and trait are the deepest attributes. They reflect aspects which are closest to an individual's core and are likely to be challenging (but not impossible) to change. Such changes are very

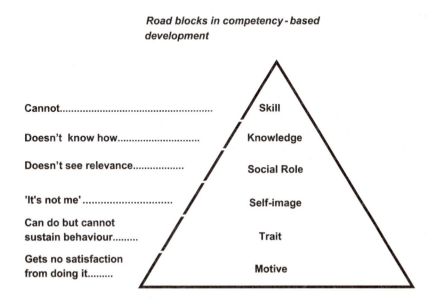

Figure 13.3 Overcoming 'roadblocks' in competency development planning
Source: Adapted from Marshall (1996)

unlikely to be achieved by skill and knowledge acquisition alone, because behaviours are the issue here.

Role profiling can help individuals to realize that something they have not considered important before is in fact key to their role. For example, many team leaders are promoted to take on a people management role not because of their people skills but because they have been the best salesperson or computer programmer. They do not, without development support, make the necessary behavioural shift required to move from an individual contributor to achieving through others. There may be a lack of understanding as to the change in self-image that is required, or more commonly there is an instinctive reaction, 'it is just not me'.

An important step towards closing these gaps is to provide reinforcement of what is crucial for performance within the role. This is an area in which a development-focused performance management discussion can play a key positive role.

From the *Fortune* research into the most admired companies we know that in these organizations people development is perceived to be a core accountability for line managers and that they spend a considerable proportion of their time on this activity (see Key Success Factor 4 in Chapter 7). This research also tells us that in the most admired companies leaders are kept informed about the capability of their management team and are confident that individuals are matched with appropriate roles.

Career development and high-potential management

Tools employed for career development and for the recognition and management of high potential can be used to support managers in optimizing the return they get from individuals holding key roles in their reporting line. We have already described, in one of our organizational stories, how high-potential recognition and management might be linked to performance management. Similarly, the leadership 'pipeline' at BAT, described in Chapter 11, operates a structured career development approach following the leadership pipeline steps. Some organizations have already defined various career pathways to map out how an individual might progress from one point within an organization to another, on the basis of appropriate skills, knowledge and competency. Within many organizations there are often formalized assessment processes along the way, such as structured assessment and development centres. However, it is predominantly performance management combined with managerial judgement that contributes to the decision making process around career development and high-potential recognition.

We illustrated how a computer-based system can capture the information to support career development (Chapter 8). In many organizations individuals are assessed for progression to the next level of work in advance of applying for a given vacancy. Once such a vacancy exists, they are deemed eligible for a move upwards. This is an approach that has in the past been most associated with the Civil Service where there was a practice (now much less used) of putting people through promotion boards and passing them into a 'pool' from which they moved to the next suitable higher-grade job. It also occurs within the private sector, as typified in our example below from a high-street retailer.

MINI CASE STUDY: CAREER DEVELOPMENT AND TALENT MANAGEMENT

Retail Co is a large retail company that has a career development and talent-spotting process with three key stages: resource planning, career discussion and talent planning. The starting point for the approach is a belief that everyone within the company is talented. A talent-spotting initiative is aimed at identifying those people who are ready to move to the next level and specifying within what timescale. The process involves initial self-assessment by an individual around his or her own performance in role and the self-completion of a form on which to indicate (among other things) readiness to move. The line manager then discusses the self-assessment forms with the individual, via a process which links to, but is separate from, performance management. The intention is for both manager and employee to agree whether the individual is ready to:

- progress to next work level (very small number);
- move to a new job within work level;
- stay in current role;
- needs further performance management

Any individual nominated for a move has to be put forward by that person's manager at a Talent Planning meeting. Here the manager presents the individual's case (four minutes per person/candidate). If this is agreed by the Talent Planning meeting the individual is then deemed 'ready' once a suitable vacancy becomes available.

UNDERSTANDING THE MANAGER'S IMPACT ON ORGANIZATIONAL CLIMATE

Key Success Factor 3 from the *Fortune* research found that the most admired companies were three times closer to achieving their ideal working culture than the other companies. The desired attributes include teamworking and treating all employees fairly – both of which are likely to be influenced by the performance management process of agreeing clear priorities within a team and being perceived as equitable in the objective-setting, review and reward elements. The overall culture of an organization may be determined to a large extent by the actions and communication of board members; however, for individual employees their immediate manager plays a key moderating role.

The impact of individual managers in determining the performance and productivity of the working environment for their immediate team is well captured by the 'climate' measure and we now turn to this.

Organizational climate

Organizational climate can be thought of as 'how it feels to work in a particular environment and for a particular boss'. More precisely, it is a measure of employees' perception of those aspects of their environment that directly affect how well they can do their jobs. It relates to the 'atmosphere' within a particular team and shows how members of a team experience the working environment created for them by their manager. It was first studied at Harvard by Litwin and Stringer (1968) and has most recently been linked to emotional intelligence by Goleman (2001). In motivational terms, when leaders get this right, they have a positive impact on 'discretionary effort' (that is, the extra contribution individuals give because they are engaged in their work and committed to success); when they get it wrong, it can result in the withdrawal of all effort – productivity plummets. Climate makes a difference to performance because it indicates how energizing the work environment is for employees. This motivational impact of a leader on those he or she leads can be quantified, providing a tangible measure of leadership effectiveness. Such measures have consistently promoted business performance criteria such as profit, sales and productivity (Hay McBer, 2000a, 2000b; Merritt *et al*, 1995).

Climate, the research tells us, comprises six key 'dimensions' that directly affect how well people can do their jobs (see Table 13.1).

Table 13.1 The climate dimensions

Climate dimension	Definition
Flexibility	Bureaucracy is minimized and innovation encouraged.
Responsibility	There is sufficient autonomy and reasonable risk taking is encouraged.
Standards	Excellence is the standard and continual improvement is encouraged.
Rewards	Good performance is recognized and rewards/recognition are performance based.
Clarity	The work unit's mission is clear and how roles relate to it are understood.
Team commitment	There is pride, dedication and cooperation among work unit members.

Source: Described in Watkin and Hubbard (2003) as well as in numerous Hay Group materials

The impact of climate on performance

A review of nearly 35 years of consulting research by Hay Group (up to October 2002) has clarified the link between organizational climate and performance. In short, this tells us that high-performance organizations have climates with specific measurable characteristics. The research has also consistently shown how organizational climate can directly account for up to 30 per cent of the variance in key business performance measures (see Watkin and Hubbard (2003) for a summary). Some organizations now use climate as a proxy measure when performance is difficult to quantify because they trust the results and their link to successful delivery. When used in this way, climate assessments provide an invaluable organizational 'profit and loss' statement on how well a company manages its people, as well as the individual contribution leaders make to that statement. As illustrated in Table 13.2 showing a case study from a global professional services company, small changes in climate can have a substantial impact on share price drivers such as profit and revenue growth.

This research example also confirmed what was thought intuitively by the CEO – that the poorer performers were growing revenue but they were not able to do this profitably.

Table 13.2 The earnings impact of creating a positive climate (2001 case study from global professional services company)

Managing directors (*n*=21) 2001 business results for the accounts (£m)	Profit margin	Revenue growth
Creating high performance or energizing climates	£710m	£0
Creating neutral or demotivating climates	£266m	£125m

THE IMPACT OF LEADERSHIP STYLES

Just as climate can account for up to 30 per cent of the variance in performance, up to 70 per cent of the variance in climate can be attributed to the leadership styles displayed by the leader or manager. The greater the ability of leaders to demonstrate a range of styles appropriate to the situation they face, the bigger the impact they will have on those they lead. The range of leadership styles is shown in Table 13.3.

There are no 'right' answers to the use of styles – directive can work very well in a crisis and pacesetting can be exhilarating among similar-ability professionals, but these two styles can prove demotivating when used where visionary or coaching would, for example, be preferable. However, research into the styles used by effective leaders indicates that the most effective leaders use a combination of the visionary, participative, affiliative and coaching styles.

Table 13.3 Leadership styles

Style	Definition
Directive	Getting immediate compliance
Visionary	Providing long-term direction and vision
Affiliative	Creating harmony
Participative	Building commitment and generating new ideas
Pacesetting	Accomplishing tasks to high standards of excellence
Coaching	Supporting long-term professional development

Linking performance management to the dimensions of organizational climate

If we consider the phases of performance management, planning, managing and reviewing, it is possible to suggest linkages between these and the six climate dimensions. These are listed in Table 13.4, starting with the aspects of climate where performance management is likely to have the most impact.

Interestingly, we can see (Kelner, Rivers and O'Connell, 1994; Williams, 1995; Goleman, 2000) that certain of the leadership styles are most likely to impact on certain climate dimensions. That is to say, adoption of an appropriate management behaviour can directly improve a poor organizational climate.

Table 13.4 Linking performance management to the dimensions of organizational climate

Clarity	This is the climate dimension where performance management approaches might be expected to have most impact, since the planning stage of performance management pays great attention to the clarification of goals as well as motivating the workforce behind these in terms of appropriately cascaded business and behavioural objectives at an individual level.
Standards	The objective-setting process of performance management will also impact this dimension as it is all about setting and agreeing standards of contribution and encouraging employees to define and go on to meet or exceed challenging goals.
Rewards	This third main climate dimension is important both to the managing and review phases of performance management. It is concerned with linking individual contribution and discretionary effort more directly to reward and recognition, in cash and non-cash terms.

To a lesser degree we might also expect effective performance management approaches to have a positive impact upon the remaining three climate dimensions:

Responsibility	Here we see individuals being encouraged to take responsibility for what they do. This is reflected both in the performance planning and managing phases of performance management since it is all about ownership of accountabilities.
Flexibility	Performance management can positively influence this dimension by encouraging individuals through the target-setting process and competency frameworks to focus on new ways of doing things and to innovate.
Team commitment	Performance management can reinforce and reward the importance of a cooperative working culture and engender pride in the organization.

Table 13.5 Leadership styles linked to climate and performance management

PM interaction	Leadership style	Climate dimension
Planning performance		
Defining business priorities	Visionary	Clarity and standards
Agreeing priorities with team	Participative	Responsibility
Managing performance		
Development planning	Visionary & Coaching	Rewards/Clarity
Ongoing reviews	Coaching	Standards/Clarity/ Rewards
Reviewing performance		
Reviewing performance	Visionary & Coaching	Clarity/Reward

In Table 13.5 we suggest linkages between the performance management phase and activity and the most appropriate leadership style. In addition, we make links to the climate dimension where there is likely to be a positive impact on climate.

Holding continuing and appropriate dialogue with direct reports lies at the heart of development-focused performance management practice and indeed we can see this reflected in the three styles illustrated in Table 13.2: visionary, participative, coaching. So, for example, the visionary style is a long-term style which is typified by articulation of goals and objectives, being firm but fair and giving regular feedback. It is likely to be appropriate for use in the performance discussions where business priorities are agreed and targets set for the year ahead. By making expectations clear and connecting them to overarching business objectives, managers can significantly improve clarity and standards for their employees. The participative style is another long-term style which involves listening and consensus building. In the context of performance management, it is likely to be an appropriate style when agreeing how to divide up work with team members in order to achieve overall goals. Through the delegation of tasks and holding individuals responsible for the outcomes, responsibility is likely to be improved. The coaching style is concerned with the long-term growth of performance through the development of individuals in line with company and personal needs, and we shall say more about this in relation to the development phase of performance management at the end of this chapter. What the three leadership styles discussed here have in common is the drive to communicate and build performance through others. This requires skills in giving feedback and coaching, which we go on to describe briefly now. Before moving on, however, it is important to stress that the affiliative style – the style used to foster harmony and good working relations – must not be overlooked in the face of more 'achievement'– and delivery-focused styles. It needs to be woven in with the use of the participative, visionary and coaching styles. It is an important style to use in building the respect and trust within organizations that make performance improvement possible. Managers need to use this style to get to know their employees, to understand where work fits into their life and to help them judge the moment to use the other styles in their repertoire. It is also a key style to use in building team commitment.

THE MANAGEMENT CAPABILITY REQUIRED TO BALANCE DEVELOPMENT AND MEASUREMENT APPROACHES

We have already stressed that managerial capability is a main contributor to the success or otherwise of a performance management process (see continuum diagram in Figure 1.1, for example). Although the planning stage requires an understanding of company strategy and a clear thought process in order to link this to individual team members, it is almost certainly the 'development and management phase' that relies most heavily on the level of managerial capability. This is the point at which line managers engage with and motivate their team, shielding team members from wider pressures and ensuring that they will feel valued and motivated to deliver what they understand to be their main priorities. This requires line managers to adopt a number of different 'personas' in terms of managing performance. These include:

I strategy decoder;

I operational leader;

I target identifier;

I coach;

I confidante;

I motivator;

I advocate;

I reviewer;

I disciplinarian.

As is clear from the thinking we have described on leadership styles, it is not expected that any one manager will necessarily feel comfortable across all these styles of interaction. However, it is important to recognize that there are a certain number of key skills that managers are likely to require in order to deploy the managing and development phase of performance management effectively. In particular, we focus here on the critically important skills of giving feedback and coaching.

Managerial skills and behaviours needed for development-based approaches

Giving and receiving feedback

Feedback is one of the central ways in which we give colleagues information on how well they are doing their work and how aspects of their behaviour impact on their work effectiveness. There are two main types of feedback that are appropriate in performance management: **positive feedback (praise)**, which tells the person what he or she did well; and **constructive feedback (advice)**, which tells the person what needs to be changed and how to do it.

For individuals to improve their performance in the workplace, they need to gain awareness both of what it is that they are doing well and also of where there are areas for development or issues around performance. Table 13.6 contains a checklist of advice for managers on giving feedback to an employee.

Table 13.6   Checklist for giving feedback

✓	**Focus on the changeable**. Avoid using vague or general comments that will be of little use to someone in terms of increasing their self-awareness or developing skills. Statements such as 'you're brilliant' may be pleasant to hear but are of no value in terms of personal learning. Best practice – try to pinpoint what the person did that made it brilliant, as unambiguous and explicit feedback gives greater opportunity for learning and is likely to be more readily accepted.
✓	**Emphasize observed behaviour**. Offering feedback on behaviour that you have seen, and the impact that it had, is likely to be most useful in terms of getting buy-in from the person to whom you are offering feedback. Best practice – be specific.
✓	**Take a balanced approach**. Simply overloading people with constructive criticism may be accurate but may not leave them feeling positive. Best practice – use a mix of positive and constructive feedback; this is more likely to be well received and leave people energized about development, eg linking their behaviour to your perception of what worked well and what worked less well.

Table 13.6 (*Continued*)

✓	**Elicit information**. If you simply present a series of statements to people there is a tendency for these to be seen as fact, and this may be difficult to accept. Best practice – ask questions and help others to see alternative ways of doing things for themselves; this leads to greater ownership for change.
✓	**Define ground rules**. Establishing the boundaries of feedback conversations will enable people to feel more comfortable with the messages you are providing, for example with confidentiality. Best practice – be explicit with the context and boundaries of your feedback.
✓	**Be selective and flexible**. Try not to overload people with messages, regardless of how valuable you feel they are. Best practice – ask yourself what will be the most useful for this individual and be prepared to adapt and be flexible as the conversation progresses.
✓	**Accept ownership**. Give feedback as if it is your own personal view rather than a globally agreed fact; eg 'it seems to me that', rather than 'you are'. All we are entitled to do is offer our own experiences of individuals, and along with that comes responsibility for the messages given. Best practice – own the feedback and speak from personal experience.
✓	**Know the key messages**. Along with being flexible, it is important to ensure that the key messages are heard, otherwise the feedback that would provide the greatest impact may be lost among some less crucial messages. Best practice – set yourself priorities for feeding back key messages.
✓	**Get to the point**. Sometimes it can feel uncomfortable to deliver constructive feedback and it is easy to wander off at tangents. This only makes it more difficult for the receiver to understand what you are saying. Best practice – say what you mean.
✓	**Suggest solutions**. If you do offer constructive feedback to others then it is helpful to be able to suggest what would have had a more beneficial impact; eg 'Arriving late for a meeting disrupted the schedule of a number of others, including myself. If you had contacted us in advance . . .'. Best practice – offer alternatives.

Receiving feedback, whether positive or constructive, may challenge an individual's sense of reality and self-awareness. One tool that may be useful to help provide awareness is the 'Johari window' developed by Joseph Luft and Harry Ingham (for a fuller account, see Luft, 1969). The Johari window can be used to ascertain how self-aware you are and how others perceive you. It divides the knowledge of behaviours into four areas, based on what is 'known to you' and 'known to others', thus providing a useful framework for feedback discussions and for showing why feedback and disclosure are necessary for performance improvement.

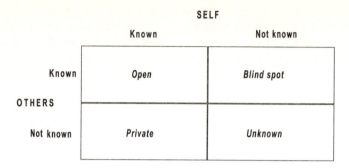

Figure 13.4 The Johari window. *Source:* Luft and Ingham (1955)

Figure 13.4 shows the four quadrants of the Johari window containing different combinations of knowledge about ourselves:

▌ Information that is known to ourselves and known to others is called the 'open' window because it is in the public domain and feedback about this is not likely to be a surprise to us.

▌ Information that is known to us but not known to others is called 'private' information because we choose not to share this with others. If we receive feedback in this arena, although this feedback is unlikely to be a surprise, it is important to pay attention to this, as keeping these elements hidden can be a source of stress.

▌ Information about ourselves that we do not know and that others do not know is called the 'unknown' window.

▌ One of the most important areas to focus on in feedback is the 'blind spot'. This refers to information that others know about us but that we do not know about ourselves. Feedback in this window is likely to provoke the strongest emotional reaction, as we can be surprised and can sometimes want to reject what we hear initially. The more that relevant feedback takes place, the more the open area displaces the blind spot. It is also the area that managers may find hardest to tackle, as it will often involve underperformance, where the job holder has not realized this is the reality of the situation.

An example from a study into leadership for the 21st century in the life insurance industry (Williams, 1995) illustrates how a manager might handle a blind spot when dealing with an underperforming team member. We are not suggesting this rather blunt approach as the way forward, although it doubtless brings to attention the issue:

> We've had a whole series of meetings where I've tried to help him... it is a constant series of feedback sessions. My last meeting with him was

very tough. I said, 'You've just got to keep track of the people. I'm willing to take whatever time I can to help you, I will sit down with you when I can'. I asked him, 'What kind of job do you think you are doing? How do you perceive you are doing?' And he said, 'I think I'm doing fine'. I said, 'There's just nobody but you that agrees with you'.

Feedback alone is unlikely to be sufficient in supporting people to change behaviour. For an individual who has difficulty accepting feedback, or for any employee wanting to pursue the career and personal development options available through the performance management process, managers are likely to need to invest time in coaching activities.

Coaching for performance

Coaching used to be synonymous with sports training – but in the past decade the concept of coaching has become far more widespread. According to Hargrove (2002: 1), 'coaching is hot! Companies like EDS, Chrysler, Herman Miller use coaching to create a culture of high performance. Xerox, IBM, Microsoft amongst others are training managers to become coaches.' An internet search engine in 2006 provides 9,800,000 results for 'coaching', illustrating how life coaches, executive coaches and the original sport coaches have proliferated. 'Line manager as coach' has become a phrase adopted by many organizations recognizing the potential benefits of moving people managers from a 'doing' or functional role to one which is about managing the personal performance of others.

Of the numerous models and frameworks for coaching now in existence, a common feature is the recognition of some sort of 'gap' in terms of desired performance. The coaching model illustrated in Figure 13.5 is drawn from Kolb and Boyatzis's research into self-directed change and described by Boyatzis in 2002. It suggests that once the gap between the

Figure 13.5 Managing – the coaching model. *Source:* Boyatzis (2002)

individual's current state ('me now') and desired state ('me future') has been identified, it is possible to formulate an action plan for change. This can be monitored and reviewed by the manager/coach working with the individual.

In our example from the life insurance industry above (Williams, 1995), we see a direct message being put across to an individual who has resisted hearing these messages before. However, we do not know from the excerpt if there was any follow-on coaching discussion around the apparent gap between the reality of the current situation and where the individual wants to be in the future. The coaching model suggests that this is then used as the basis for subsequent development actions which are jointly planned, monitored and reviewed with a coach.

For the line manager keen to use coaching to develop employees there are options about whether to employ the services of an accredited coach or to train and develop himself/herself and other line managers to fulfil this role.

In the UK in 2005 the Chartered Institute of Personnel and Development (CIPD), in recognition of this fact, produced a set of coaching and mentoring standards (Poole and Warren for CIPD, 2005). At the practitioner level these include performance indicators on:

1. the coaching and mentoring context;

2. planning a coaching or mentoring plan intervention;

3. working with external suppliers to deliver coaching/mentoring;

4. managing coaching/mentoring interventions;

5. delivering coaching/mentoring personally;

6. building and maintaining coaching/mentoring relationships;

7. collaboration with others to build coaching/mentoring;

8. evaluation of coaching/mentoring interventions.

In terms of personally delivering coaching/mentoring, the standards acknowledge a whole host of models and techniques of which the coach is likely to require an overview. Models and approaches include:

▌ cognitive behavioural;

▌ psychodynamic;

▌ gestalt;

▌ existential;

▌ neuro-linguistic programming (NLP).

Techniques include:

▌ questioning frameworks, such as the GROW (goals, reality, options and will) model;

▌ reframing situations;

▌ visualizations and mental imagery;

▌ relaxation;

▌ creating and maintaining positive states (pattern breaking, powerful anchors, etc);

▌ use of e-coaching technologies;

▌ 360-degree feedback tools.

Understandably, this is a very long list and for the line manager who wants simply to appreciate the ethos of what a coaching relationship should entail it might be helpful to focus on it as a style of management in its own right. This is supported by Whitmore (2002: 6), who advocates 'coaching as a management style rather than merely a tool for a manager or consultant to use occasionally'.

The main elements of coaching as a leadership style have been described by Kelner, Rivers and O'Connell (1994). They describe a leadership style that takes as its main focus the long-term development of others. It achieves this by:

▌ helping employees identify their unique strengths and weaknesses in the light of their aspirations;

▌ encouraging employees to establish long-range development goals;

▌ reaching agreement regarding manager and employee roles in the development process;

▌ providing ongoing instruction as necessary, with underlying rationales and principles as well as feedback to facilitate employees' development;

▌ accepting some possible shortfalls in performance during the learning process and accepting this as necessary to achieve long-term development.

While coaching may be used primarily as a tool to foster long-term development, it may also be a useful technique for managers faced with the perennial problem of dealing with underperformance.

Coaching is one of the tools which a manager might deploy in order to focus on performance improvement. However, as a starting point it is likely to be necessary to diagnose the type of underperformance in evidence (see Chapter 16 for a review of the most common causes).

If an individual is genuinely in the wrong role and could perform more effectively elsewhere, coaching may not be appropriate and an alternative role might be sought either within the department or beyond. In the case of external factors such as illness or family/relationship issues, it may be possible for the line manager to organize a reduction in duties for an agreed period and he or she may need to call on HR policies for support with these.

In the case of insufficient development, often a cause of inappropriate attitudes and leadership styles, these might be dealt with via a stronger development plan, particularly where development has been neglected in the past. Coaching may also be used to help 'fast track' performance improvement.

It is important to note that not everyone will find coaching a natural process or a motivational way of operating. Many authors, including Whitmore (2002) and Lee (2003), describe how coaching, done well, can bring clear business benefits. According to Anderson (2001), coaching has been shown to produce a 529 per cent return on investment as well as significant intangible benefits such as employee motivation. However, done badly, coaching is likely to frustrate and create cynicism. At worst, managers who believe they are coaching may actually be using a 'veiled' directive or pacesetting leadership style which individuals find disempowering.

Within most organizations looking to enhance their performance management practice there will be attempts to build the coaching capability of managers, often linked to ensuring a greater return from people resources more generally. This is important, as the organization's ability to develop the managerial skills and behaviours needed for the managing phase of the performance management cycle will be a key driver in ensuring the success with which it balances the measurement and development aspects. Achieving this balance is likely to be critical to the successful implementation of performance management.

In the following chapters we feature two organizational stories: the first is from Belron, an organization that has emphasized the managing and development phase of performance management through its focus on the climate created and leadership styles adopted by line managers. Our second organizational story, from the Irish Health Service, builds on this theme but moves away from a focus on the individual to team-based performance development and tapping into people's self-maturation through bottom-up involvement and buy-in.

14

Organizational story: a focus on development at Belron

In this chapter we showcase Belron, an organization that has adopted a primarily development-based approach to managing performance, particularly in the way that senior managers are measured and developed to improve business and personal performance.

Belron repairs and fits vehicle glass, with over 1.1 billion sales in 2004. It operates in 28 countries under a variety of brand names, for example in Europe under Carglass® or Autoglass®, and in the United States under Elite Autoglass™ and Glaspro™. It handles nearly 5 million customers a year and has 10,000 employees at over 1,000 centres, with 3,500 mobile repair vehicles. Impressive growth in profits over the past five years has meant an 18 per cent compound annual growth rate, achieved through a simple strategy of organic growth, new territories and driving efficiencies across the business.

Belron's journey started in 2000, when there was a realization by the CEO Gary Lubner that it would not be strategy, access to capital or opportunities to enter new territories that would stand in the way of Belron achieving further sustained growth. The constraint would come from the leadership capability of managers within the organization to realize the potential on offer. The organization then started on transforming its approach to leadership development. The journey has had a massive impact on the attitudes and behaviours of managers at all levels:

FROM	TO
'Don't go too fast with this.'	'This is part of my job.'
'We have a job to do.'	'How can I get my middle managers involved with this?'
'I can't spare my people for this.'	'I want to use executive development to leverage business performance.'
'If you tell me to focus on it, I will.'	'This is an important focus for my business.'

So what did they do to achieve this?

Sponsorship and personal commitment by Lubner has played a large part in driving Belron to put leadership development at the heart of its strategy to deliver business performance. His unshakable belief that this is the only way to transform the business has created the momentum that has enabled the rest of the organization to stay focused. Executive development therefore forms one of the five core corporate priorities and there is a commitment to measure leadership in the same way as business units measure productivity and customer satisfaction. Indeed it is the prime responsibility of one of Lubner's team.

The Belron measure of leadership capability and their impact as leaders on business performance is 'climate'. Climate as a measure has been developed by the Hay Group and has been shown, over 35-plus years of research, to link to bottom-line business performance. For more information on climate and leadership style, including definitions of supporting dimensions, refer to Chapter 13.

CLIMATE AND LEADERSHIP STYLES MEASUREMENT AT BELRON

The focus at Belron has been to manage the performance of leaders at an individual level and to measure their progress on development through the climate they create for their teams; and also to collate the picture of climate across Belron to gauge how well the organization as a whole is positioned to progress towards its objective of profitable growth.

To do this, managers have undertaken a three-day development programme introducing them to the concepts around climate and leadership styles and the link to performance. Having established a baseline measure and produced a development plan, managers undergo annual diagnostic assessments on climate and leadership styles. Individual coaching and feedback sessions for each manager within the executive population are carried out by two full-time internal coaches acting as a dedicated resource, signalling the Belron commitment to developing leadership capability.

The Belron approach to performance management through the use of climate and styles has given the CEO the confidence to say that 70 per cent of managers have improved their leadership capability. This approach is probably best exemplified by examining a couple of case studies.

CASE STUDY

As the general manager of one of Belron's most important business units, Alex (not his real name) was shocked when he received his first set of leadership style and climate data. This showed a heavy reliance on the two dissonant leadership styles – directive and pacesetting. The effect, unsurprisingly, was to create a demotivating climate for his team; the feedback showed big gaps between what the team needed to perform to the best of their abilities and what they actually got from Alex.

Over the course of two years Alex set a plan, working with his line manager (the CEO) and an internal Belron coach, to change his behaviour in a way that would drive a positive climate.

In the first year Alex set out to provide more feedback on performance through regular one-to-one meetings with his team, and use these as an opportunity to demonstrate visionary and coaching leadership styles. He sought to build team commitment by establishing cross-functional teams where possible, constantly focusing on the links to the vision and annual operating plan (both of which were developed with his team), and particularly encouraging his executive team to look for synergies. He also worked with his team to understand some of the constraints to progress.

But Alex found what many executives find – that behavioural change is difficult to achieve. A year after his initial feedback, Alex retook the leadership style and climate survey and found that, while he had started to improve the climate through a more balanced set of leadership styles, he still had considerable progress to make.

Undeterred, Alex refined his plan, focusing on the visionary style. But his new plan was also typical of those executives that make genuine progress – it addressed his own attitude and behaviour as much as a list of tasks. He decided to 'step back' rather than believing

'I know what to do'; he planned his interventions with his team, reflecting on which leadership style would be most effective; he sought opportunities to experiment with different styles; and he constantly looked for feedback on his behaviour and its impact.

Two years after his initial feedback, Alex retook his leadership style and climate survey for a second time, and this time it showed a significant swing in his leadership style to the four styles that link to high performance – visionary, coaching, participative and affiliative – with the directive and pacesetting styles diminishing to a 'background' level. What was the climate created by these styles? High performance – with no significant gaps between what the team needed in order to perform and what they received from Alex.

But what about business performance over the two years? Belron's focus on leadership development is due to its passionate belief that this is what drives performance. The business unit had been focused on achieving significant expansion over the two years – both through organic growth and through a complex acquisition. These required a wide range of leadership skills from Alex to drive change and growth while taking his team with him. The result? Operating profit increased from 3.1 million to 4.8 million over the two-year period, for example (see Figure 14.1). And the CEO is very clear – 'without this focus on Alex's leadership this level of growth would simply have been unachievable'.

The graphs in Figures 14.2 and 14.3 show the results of the climate feedback for Alex from his direct reports. The dotted line (Ideal) represents what people would ideally like, while the straight line

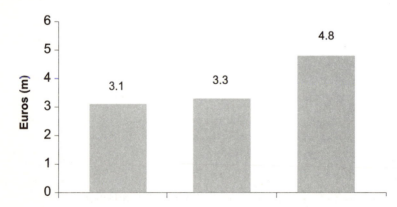

Figure 14.1 Profit growth of Alex's business unit. *Source:* Belron, reproduced with permission

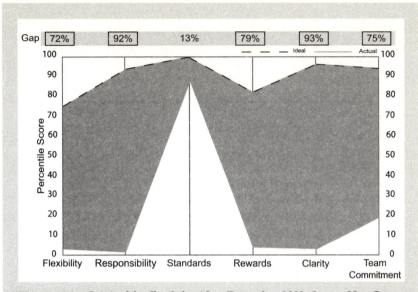

Figure 14.2 Original feedback for Alex, December 2002. *Source:* Hay Group

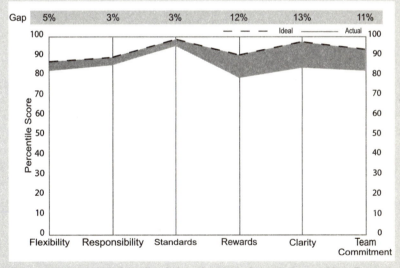

Figure 14.3 Updated feedback for Alex, March 2005. *Source:* Hay Group

(Actual) is what people feel they currently experience. The graphs show the gaps in perception between Actual and Ideal for the six Climate dimensions. Figure 14.2 shows a large grey area indicating very substantial gaps, while Figure 14.3 shows only small gaps between the climate people would like and what they actually experience.

CASE STUDY

This is a tale of two similar operations with two very different leaders. Two of Belron's business units, both with similar operations, recently undertook a major change initiative. The two leaders were very different: one operated with a set of leadership styles that led to long-term sustained performance (the visionary, coaching, participative and affiliative styles), creating a high-performance climate for his team; the other operated from a set of short-term leadership styles (directive and pacesetting), creating a demotivating climate. The result from the change initiative? The leader with the greater range of long-term styles delivered a seamless transition – costs were controlled and customer service remained outstanding. But the business led by the leader with the short-term styles struggled; performance was poor, costs escalated, and customer service dropped.

It is examples like this that have reinforced the CEO's belief in their approach to leadership and provided additional momentum.

THE BELRON PERFORMANCE MANAGEMENT PROCESS

The use of climate and styles at Belron is restricted to its executive population, comprising general managers and their direct reports, as these are the people who will make the biggest difference in terms of the impact of their leadership capability. The data is integrated into the performance management process for these managers, although it forms only one part of the total process.

Targets and KPIs relating to the operating plan for each business unit form the first part of the review. However, a large part of the review is focused on required behaviours defined through nine leadership competencies. Belron uses these competencies to recruit managers, to develop and coach people, to review performance and to action plan for the future. During the review meeting, 360-degree feedback on the competencies focuses managers' attention on two to three competency areas that provide role model behaviour and the two to three areas that require improvement. The climate and leadership styles feedback is used primarily to inform the discussion around the two competencies of Leadership and Developing Talent, and other competencies such as Strategic Outlook rely more heavily on the 360-degree competency feedback.

While climate and styles has focused on developing managers to manage 'downwards' in terms of building effective teams, it has not necessarily emphasized the skills around managing upwards, across the organization or externally with key stakeholders. These are also important areas of performance for leaders within Belron, and work in the future will focus on addressing these more closely through the other seven competencies.

The Belron approach to performance management is to move away from a form-based bureaucratic procedure towards allowing line managers autonomy around how they conduct the process. Thus while they are clear that the review needs to be annual, one-to-one, involve 360-degree feedback, and be documented, there is no further prescription about tight timescales or the method of feedback collection. There is a tolerance of the inconsistency and variations among regions this inevitably produces.

Belron is one of the few organizations we have come across that deliberately makes no link between performance and reward. The individual bonus at a senior level is linked to company performance, and in particular to business unit performance. The same bonus is received by either everyone or no one within a business unit executive team, depending on annual performance. The absence of a link to individual performance appears to stem from a collegiate mentality and traditionally autonomous business units. There is a belief that to alter this would be divisive, although this is in the context of a business that is performing extremely well. If Belron failed to hit its profit targets in future years, it is not difficult to imagine a situation where questions were asked about the individual contributions of certain individuals compared with others.

The use of the climate and styles data has also enabled Belron to manage poor performance. The data has enabled some managers to see a poor fit between their primary strengths and those skills and abilities required and valued by the organization. The organization is also prepared to tackle those managers whose behaviour does not conform to the behavioural standards it requires, even if financial performance is sound. It is interesting to note that of the 11 people that Belron lost last year from an executive population of 140, 8 had demotivating climates.

DEVELOPMENT AS A KPI (KEY PERFORMANCE INDICATOR)

In line with their belief in leadership development as a key driver of performance, Belron has recently developed a 'leadership KPI' that measures the extent to which a business executive team is leveraging performance through leadership. This involves composite climate graphs being generated for general managers on the climate created by people in their team as well as the percentages of people who have particular leadership styles. Composite data runs the risk of encouraging action at a team or global initiative level and Belron is careful to stress the need to work at an individual level with managers to produce real behavioural change. It is the latter that research has shown is linked to business performance, not change initiatives concerning the whole team.

The intention is to ensure that leadership is taken as seriously as other, more established Belron business measures. When the CEO views the new leadership KPI, the links between business performance and the measures are evident. Leadership has become a 'strategic lever' within Belron, just like the other traditional measures.

The move towards measuring leadership has transformed development from a 'soft' skill, which involves faith in the link to bottom-line performance, to a business-critical KPI. As a consequence it is, however, viewed as a 'score' and has led to a sense of competition at Belron. The challenge will therefore be to maintain the message that the intervention is essentially about development and not evaluation.

The focus on development to manage and improve performance is one that requires a long-term view; developing a leader may not happen through one climate and styles re-run of data. It is all too easy to lose sight of this as the pressure to quantify the impact of behavioural change increases, and holding firm to the view that personal development will lead to business performance improvement requires holding one's nerve regarding the belief as well as the timescales to realize it.

15
Organizational story: team-based performance management at the Irish Health Service

In our second organizational story around the 'managing' phase, we move away from a purely individual focus to showcase a team-based approach to performance management within the Irish Health Service. The scheme sponsored by the Irish Health Service Employers Agency (HSEA) was initially piloted in 2004 and in 2005 was being implemented by approximately 360 teams nationally, with ambitious targets for further roll-out. The scheme emanated from a recognition that the delivery of the changes required for the Irish Health Service required a new strategy for human resources, outlined in the 'Action Plan for People Management'. Of the seven themes identified in this document and later developed, performance management was seen as a key enabler to achieving the necessary reforms. Consultation with key stakeholders within the Health Service, including the unions, led to an agreement that the approach taken should be team based or unit based.

The reasons for the approach being team based appear to stem in part from cultural appropriateness and 'fit-for-purpose' issues within the Irish Health Service. The Health Service has no tradition either of individual performance appraisal or of formal discussions around performance.

Feedback has not been given directly and, in the main, people are uncomfortable with open discussions about performance issues.

There is an exception to this in the practice of certain health professionals who undertake clinical supervision. However, they see this as part of a process of continuing professional development rather than an HR or management-sponsored activity.

Additionally, the old system of 11 Health Boards led to fragmentation and a lack of clear standardization with regard to effective management development, such that managers continued to focus on making the service run rather than on developing or managing staff. Team-based performance management therefore was seen as a move towards performance management that had the attraction of avoiding the thorny issue of individual appraisals.

WHAT IS TEAM-BASED PERFORMANCE MANAGEMENT?

In the Irish context, performance management has been defined as: 'a strategic and integrated approach to delivering sustained success to organizations by improving the performance of the people who work in them and by developing the capabilities of teams and individual contributors' (Health Service Employers Agency, August 2003).

In the Irish health sector the process was aimed at ensuring that teams and the individuals within them were clear about their roles and objectives and could relate these to the wider organizational goals as represented in the service and operational plans.

Team-based performance management has not been taken up in many organizations in the public or the private sectors, despite the emergence of teamwork as a critical success factor governing the achievement of organizational success. Work in this area has primarily focused on team-based pay. Indeed, in the health sector, a major 'team-pay' project was conducted by Hay Group and the Institute for Employment Studies in the UK National Health Service from 2002 to 2004. The team-pay pilots have helped to extend the picture of team rewards in three ways, as chronicled by Armstrong and Murlis (2004):

▌ While results produced by the team can be significant, the biggest gain is at the performance planning phase.

▌ Team rewards do not have to mean payment to individuals but can be in the form of a common fund for the team to spend collectively.

▌ It is possible to work with teams of 100 or more members as long as they have a coherent identity, and to agree a mixture of targets – some for the broader group and some for sub-teams.

While some work has been done at the team-pay level, we have come across very few examples where the focus has been on team-based performance management with no links to reward.

KEY PRINCIPLES OF THE IRISH HEALTH SERVICE SCHEME

A key tenet of the new approach was articulated at the outset by the Health Service Employers Agency: 'The performance management process is designed to achieve a quality service, through the achievement of organizational goals, rather than to implement a performance appraisal system. The process is not linked to an employee's pay, probation or promotional opportunities' (HSEA, 2003).

The system was to be focused on team/unit/department performance. A team was defined as 'a group of people who share a common objective and who work together to achieve them'. Teams within the health sector are various, ranging from a team providing services for children at risk in the community, to a team providing acute in-patient care, to a team providing IT support and services. Teams are often multidisciplinary, with staff from different professional groupings such as nurses, doctors, social care workers and healthcare assistants all in the one team. The leader of the team may not always be the line manager of all the team members. For the purposes of performance management, however, the teams in this case were to be defined at the lowest levels where operational plans could be developed.

The introduction of the performance management scheme was not intended as an 'add-on' to the relationship between the line manager and his or her team. A clear strand of the process is the emphasis on putting more structure and focus on what is already an integral line management role. The process is a means of helping people clarify what their jobs are about and what their objectives are. However, this should not be done in isolation but be informed by the service planning process. Service planning is intended to set goals that translate as plans for areas, distinct team/units and departments. Team leaders and team members should then collectively consider their objectives for the year ahead in the light of the content of the Service Plan. A key design principle was that all staff should receive training to implement the process, and this has ranged from half a day to five days.

Participation is another key tenet of the Irish Health Service Scheme. While the line manager or team leader should initiate and lead the process, there is a heavy emphasis on eliciting the views and inputs of all team members and crafting objectives that are jointly agreed by all members of the team. Involvement, buy-in and communication are key parts of the process. There is also a focus on generating objectives that can be expressed numerically, and performance indicators that can be expressed as a rate, index or percentage are encouraged.

THE TEAM-BASED PERFORMANCE MANAGEMENT PROCESS

The performance review period is set to be the calendar year. This allows the Service Plans (normally completed in December/January) to be used in the setting of team objectives. The process follows an annual cycle as set out below.

January meeting

The team leader and team members review last year's performance and set objectives for the forthcoming year. At the core of the process is the team setting its own performance targets. This involves the team identifying the few critical areas in which it needs to do well in order to meet the needs of the Service Plan. These have been alternatively referred to as 'critical success factors' or 'key performance indicators' (although a subsequent evaluation of the scheme has recommended one common terminology). Once these critical success factors have been identified, two or three specific targets are agreed in each critical area and the means of measuring the achievement of these defined. An example of the key performance indicators agreed by a team with supporting targets is shown in Figure 15.1.

It is very unlikely that all team members can be present at this meeting – particularly for those clinical teams that operate a 24-hour, seven-days-a-week service – and therefore one-to-one 'catch up' sessions or smaller sub-group meetings also play an important part in making the outcomes to this meeting feel as if they are genuinely joint outcomes, and owned by all members of the team. Preparation for this meeting by the team leader has also emerged as another critical success factor; taking the time to read

---

Hospital of the Assumption

The team responsible for **health promotion** identified the following KPAs:

Key Performance Area 1: Move forward with Health Promotion Hospitals initiative

Key Performance Area 2: Identify appropriate needs analysis of residents and staff in the format of questionnaire focus groups

---

KPA 1
Objectives for first quarter:

1.1   Establish group – targeting multidisciplinary team/skill mix

1.2   Set ground rules – 1. Frequency of meeting
                                  2. Role identification/responsibility
                                  3. Terms of reference

1.3   Evaluation of performance

KPA 2
Objectives for first quarter:

2.1   Complete and audit questionnaire/focus groups

2.2   Set objectives on data obtained from questionnaire/focus groups

2.3   Liaise with Health Promotion Hospitals network and other Elderly care sites

---

Figure 15.1 Hospital of the Assumption. *Source:* Hospital of the Assumption, Irish Health Service, Western Region

relevant parts of the Service Plan and to consult with senior management prior to the meeting enables the team leader to facilitate the meeting more effectively. The trust that the leaders demonstrated in allowing team members to suggest objectives for the team was also a key success factor in a subsequent evaluation of the process (Hay Group and Institute of Public Administration, 2004). The output of this meeting is a Performance Management Form summarizing key objectives, accessible to all team members.

Interim review meetings (April, July and October)

The style of the interim review meetings is the same as that in January, with the meetings again focusing on a review of progress in relation to targets set. Open discussion leads to the team either agreeing necessary action to correct any shortfalls, adjusting some targets, or even completely resetting objectives based on a shift in operational priorities. The progress made on each target is tracked and recorded on the Performance Management Form after each interim review meeting. Although only three interim reviews are suggested, in reality teams meet much more regularly to check on progress, embedding the process as part of daily management practice, and meetings have a development rather than monitoring or 'policing' orientation.

Ongoing

Any one-to-one discussions around individual learning needs or personal development will take place at the line manager's discretion, or at the request of team members. Similarly, any underperformance issues are dealt with under the disciplinary process.

THE KEY BENEFITS ACHIEVED

The use of team-based performance management within the Irish Health Service has led to a number of key benefits thus far:

▌ The ability of the scheme to tap into people's self-motivation (we saw the importance of this when we discussed motivational perspectives on performance management in Chapter 2, in particular process theories that focus on 'how' performance is initiated, directed and sustained). By focusing on the involvement of all and the bottom-up identification of goals, people feel they truly 'own' their goals and that they have a genuine say in service delivery and improvements.

▌ A focus on quality improvements and change for the benefit of the service, patients and clients, rather than on individual gain or self-advancement.

▌ Staff have a greater input into organizational goals than they would have under a more traditional one-to-one appraisal system where the focus is on aligning their own activities with predetermined organizational or team goals. This is an important conclusion for those who want to increase participation in organizational goal and objective setting.

▌ It formalizes as a matter of course, through structure and a recording mechanism, some of the activities to improve the service initiated by staff. It is therefore easier to 'sell' to staff in a culture where performance appraisal is resisted, and is a way of managing and measuring performance that is incremental in its introduction.

▌ The process has provided focus for planning and reviewing performance and teams have achieved effective clarity around priorities and necessary actions.

▌ The empowerment of front-line managers in terms of accountability and authority has been a major outcome of the process. Team-based performance management has drawn out front-line supervisors, who have traditionally deferred to superiors in decision making and objective setting, to take responsibility and assume more of a managerial role. This has in turn required a cultural shift, for example on the part of site managers/directors of nursing who have had to actively 'let go' of the previous way of working.

▌ In some cases there have been considerable financial savings; for example, an administrative team working with a clinical team saved 25,000 euros in Q1 of an ongoing project to recycle medical and surgical appliances (Doyle, 2005).

▌ The process has fostered a better understanding of teamwork and what it involves, including a greater appreciation of the problems faced by staff members from different disciplines in the team.

WHAT HAS BEEN MISSING?

While team-based performance management has had benefits in the Irish example – most notably around performance planning – future developments have already been identified by those responsible for the scheme to join up hitherto isolated initiatives (such as learning needs analysis, personal development planning and management development) with the new process.

What has been missing is what is often termed a 'grandparent role', a check and balance within the system where objectives are checked for a degree of challenge and stretch, and local objectives are balanced in accordance with wider service priorities. Under the current arrangements, performance plans drawn up by teams do not have to leave the team (although in reality plans have usually gone to the site manager/director of nursing). The emphasis has been on the team setting objectives it considers will improve service delivery in line with the Service Plan, and on the internal monitoring and policing of these. Any external monitoring has been performed thus far by corporate learning and development, reinforcing the scheme as an HR initiative, and future recommendations are to push this to local health office managers (county managers) or directors. These senior health managers can then take a lead role in approving the key performance areas and objectives of teams before the annual team-based performance management process cycle begins, and thereafter in monitoring performance on a quarterly basis.

The issues raised here around senior sponsorship and reporting mechanisms will be a key critical success factor in the sustainability of the process. It is only through the closer connection between service planning and its cascade into the team-based performance management process that the new scheme will act as a strategic tool for service improvement rather than as a staff consultation exercise. This will be necessary if the scheme is to move beyond the implementation of local 'good' ideas to achieving a whole-system change in line with the intended health service reforms.

Team-based performance management will not be a substitute for individual discussions relating to recognition of individual achievement, learning needs, career aspirations and personal development. Individuals should also receive feedback on their contribution to the team and their level of performance in terms of team-working competencies.

In this case study team-based performance management has been a means to manage and monitor performance in an environment where this would otherwise have been difficult to achieve. It represents an incremental approach to the introduction of a performance management scheme based on the unit of a team rather than on individual appraisals, an approach that many other organizations wish to move towards. The lessons learnt will apply to any organization seriously considering the adoption of a team-based approach. The introduction of a link to pay or promotion will add another dimension not considered within this case study. It is interesting for us to note, however, that even here team performance measures tend to focus on output measures – such as quantity of work, improvements to measurable service levels, cost savings – rather than input or process measures – such as levels of team-working, skills and knowledge developed, degree of participation, etc. Striking the balance between measurement and development represents just as significant a challenge in team-based approaches as it does in individual performance planning and review.

16

Reviewing and rewarding performance

Contributed by Helen Murlis, Director, Hay Group

This chapter is concerned with the fourth and final circle of our organizing framework in that it considers how performance management is linked to review and reward. We start with a brief overview of the background in order to understand how these processes have evolved. We then proceed to look at what is needed in psychological terms to create an effective performance review and describe the principal kinds of review and dialogue currently available. The chapter then continues to assess the implications of different kinds of performance rating, looks at why performance rewards have underperformed, reviews which performance pay mechanisms are used for different purposes and discusses the criteria for successful implementation. The chapter concludes with a review of how the concept of total reward is changing perceptions of reward and its place in the creation of a motivated and engaged workforce.

THE LINKS BETWEEN PERFORMANCE REVIEW AND PERFORMANCE REWARD – BACKGROUND

In examining the link between reviewing performance and rewarding it, it is useful to understand the historical background that has inevitably influenced how organizations pay for performance. Performance-related pay is not new and goes back to the time when employment replaced slavery. Early forms of performance reward were, as far as we can tell, directly related to units of production, with some penalties for poor quality as time wore on. Things stayed that way into the 20th century when major employers in the United States and elsewhere, seeking to operate on a more rational basis, started to develop more complex incentive schemes for non-manual employees. With this came the need to do more than check production records before payout. For management levels the needs of succession and workforce planning as well as the implementation of bonus schemes required some record and justification for decisions on pay progression, bonus allocation and, very importantly, promotion. Performance appraisal as a practice began to spread. The performance review and appraisal processes and documentation that started to be introduced in the middle of the 20th century owe much to the annual confidential review processes then in use in institutions such as the UK Civil Service and the armed forces – used as underpinning for career management decisions.

The arrival of 'management by objectives' in the 1960s, promulgated by John Humble of consultancy firm Urwick Orr and his colleagues and further fostered by the then British Institute of Management (now the Chartered Management Institute), had a key role in the development of more widespread performance appraisal. It was the process by which objectives were given, recorded and tracked, and reviewed at the end of the appraisal year. These appraisal records provided the data for bonus and pay progression decisions – insofar as these were rational rather than purely discretionary. Appraisals were completed by line managers and may or may not have been shown in full to the individuals they covered. They tended to be rather a 'parent–child' process (using the terminology of transactional analysis), reflecting the emphasis on status and hierarchy of the time. They generally focused on objectives (definitely in the measurement school as discussed throughout this book), although some un-researched behavioural qualities were added in some cases for managers and professionals. The UK Civil Service, for example, had 'penetration' (intellectual) as a desired quality in the 1970s for its middle/senior ranks. This was the beginning of development-focused appraisals and was generally accompanied by an assessment of training needs.

Performance-related pay increases the pace

This picture persisted into the 1980s when the progressive introduction of performance-related pay for managers, professionals and some non-manual support staff in the private sector, following the ending of government incomes policies, acted as a catalyst for changes and improvements to appraisal processes and documentation. Alongside this, the employee relations climate of the late 1970s onwards encouraged more transparency in pay and performance decision processes as a result of equal pay, equal opportunities and related legislation (and some well-publicized tribunal cases). Concurrent pay decentralization and the break-up of industry-wide collective bargaining put much more emphasis on line management accountability for developing, appraising and judging the performance of people.

Focus on financial motivation

Most of the thinking driving performance-related pay was economic – generally the 'effort bargain' theory, ie I will pay you x if you deliver y. For executive incentives this was overlain by principal agent theory, which focused on the measures that should be used to focus and drive the performance of executives as the agents of the owners/shareholders (Sappington, 1991). Both of these theories are based on a concept of 'economic man' making rational choices to maximize his (or her) financial gain from reward opportunities. This thinking underpinned implementation of executive share options in the UK, first made tax-effective in the 1984 Finance Act, the (subsequently withdrawn) performance bonus scheme for Grades 5–7 of the Civil Service or the proliferation of merit-pay schemes for managers and white-collar staff that spread across the UK economy. Money and personal wealth accrual was assumed to be the dominant driver. Respectable academic research on employee priorities, pointing to a more complex pattern of motivation at work, was often ignored. This one-dimensional view of motivation spilled over into the appraisal systems that were increasingly being used as the evidence base for performance rewards.

The narrow focus of early appraisal training

Training in appraisal processes too often focused on how to fill in the forms and, if you were lucky, how to tackle a couple of tricky performance issues by role playing with colleagues. Effective training in coaching and feedback for the managing part of performance management only really came into its own in the 1990s, along with the approaches to understanding leadership styles and the creation of a high-performance organizational climate described in Chapters 13 and 14.

THE PSYCHOLOGY OF A GOOD REVIEW

In previous chapters we have stressed the importance of a sound dialogue between manager and individual in the planning and managing stages of performance management. This imperative carries through into performance review and reward.

Recognition for contribution

The outcome of a successful performance review should be that individuals feel that their contribution for the review period has been fully considered and recognized and that they have a sound basis for performance planning for the future. Managers should feel that the review has been thorough, that the individual understands and accepts how his or her contribution has been valued and that the dialogue that has continued through the previous review period has been built on positively for the future. Good performance will have had full recognition and performance issues will have been appropriately addressed.

For far too many organizations, the focus for design of the review process has been on the design of the forms that go with this and the support or guidance material for reviewer and employee. Important as these are, they in no way compensate for the creation of an environment in which individuals welcome and use feedback of all kinds given by managers and leaders skilled in delivering good and difficult messages while maintaining motivation and engagement. We have already looked at the practical issues around giving (and receiving) feedback in Chapter 13.

Creating the right climate for review

If the management and development phase of performance management has gone well, the review and reward phase should be a much easier and indeed shorter process. In essence, it should be a summary of the dialogue during the year, with no surprises on either side. The right climate for this dialogue is set by leaders who use appropriate leadership styles (as described in Chapters 13 and 14) to create a climate of openness and trust between themselves and the people they manage.

Preparation on both sides is essential. Reviewing managers need to review and summarize what has been delivered and developed over the review period – which may be quarterly, six-monthly or (generally) annually. They will also, increasingly, take views on a confidential basis from a sample of people with whom the individual has worked, using either a formal 360-degree process or informal soundings. Individuals need to review their achievements against the targets they have agreed to and the development areas on which they have been working. They need to take a view of what has gone well and what has gone less well or could have been done differently. They also need to feel they understand what has influenced performance, including the unforeseen events that almost inevitably affect most people's plans for future achievement. Thoughts will also be needed on what to aim for in the coming PM cycle as the process starts again.

The review dialogue

Performances reviews should be conducted in an environment suitable for confidential discussion, away from the interruptions of work, and might be expected to last one to two hours. Reviewers skilled in feedback and coaching generally tend to encourage individuals to take time to describe how the review period has gone for them. They can then probe why elements of work have gone a particular way, summarize understanding and build a common view of how both development and delivery have gone. Reaching this common view is essential whether performance ratings are used or have been replaced by a written summary of the contribution over the period. If performance ratings are used, individuals nowadays are often encouraged to give a realistic view of how they have performed against the rating scale. This helps build ownership and acceptance of the rating eventually agreed and any performance rewards that follow. It is not uncommon for individuals to give themselves a tougher, ie lower, rating than their manager might have done.

Documentation in support of performance reviews

Whatever form of documentation is used, the written record of the review should be completed after the review interview has taken place, then given to the individual to consider and comment on prior to approval and sign-off. Unpublished research conducted by the author, evaluating performance management and pay systems over the past 15 years for a number of clients in the public service, suggests that this point is critical to the maintenance of trust and positive dialogue.

The arrival of electronic HR systems has led to major changes in the way the documentation used to support performance management and review systems is designed. Most providers of HR software have generic approaches to 'appraisal forms' and can produce bespoke applications as required. Generic approaches should always be scrutinized carefully to make sure they reflect both the values and organizational language in use by the specific employer. For bespoke approaches, it is always helpful to involve the stakeholders, ie a sample of managers and individual employees, in the design to make sure that local needs are met.

The key elements that performance review documentation should contain are:

▌ employee data – typically name, role, location, duration of time in role;

▌ performance plan, measures or outcomes agreed, and a review of achievements;

▌ development plan and review of achievements – generally linked to a competency framework;

▌ agreement/sign-off by individual and line manager.

Some web-based approaches also provide for stakeholder input – soliciting feedback from a small number (four to six is not uncommon) of individuals nominated by the employee with agreement from his or her manager. Some provide for 360-degree feedback, where trust in this approach has progressed to the point where individual and line manager share the information and use it for joint performance planning.

Some processes (generally in the public sector) provide for a 'grandparent' or 'countersigning officer' comment. The purpose here should be both to enable senior managers to ensure the consistency of performance reviews and also to consider the contribution and development of those below their direct reports in achieving the targets set for their whole area of responsibility.

Long, complex guidance notes on performance reviews have a tendency not to be read. Therefore the simpler, clearer and more directly focused on managers' and individuals' needs these are, the better. Increasingly, such guidance is online and has to be written and laid out screen by screen for the intranet. Again this is an area where testing the guidance out with stakeholders before 'going live' can pay off in terms of usability, cultural sensitivity and frequency of eventual use.

THE NATURE AND IMPLICATIONS OF PERFORMANCE RATING

Until the mid-1990s, some form of performance rating was the norm. The use of ratings represents the visible face of the measurement approach to performance management already described at length in this book. The use of ratings went largely unquestioned until formal and academic evaluations of performance-related pay systems called ratings into question. From evaluations conducted by Marsden and Richardson (1994), among others, the key issues with ratings appear to be:

▌ the number and nature of ratings used;

▌ the use of forced distributions;

▌ managerial consistency in allocating ratings;

▌ discomfort with tackling underperformance.

Each of these is now considered in turn.

Number and nature of ratings

First, it is important to consider a couple of cultural issues. A major problem with ratings is that they can all too easily look and feel like a school report, and as such may be associated with varying degrees of pleasure and motivation. Use of lettering and numbering systems, 1–5 or A–E, for example, often directly replicates the systems used on a school report and compounds the problem. If 3 or C attracted parental concern or disapproval, then it is hardly surprising that even where these are supposed to be the 'fully acceptable' ratings allocated to the majority of employees, they are tainted by earlier experience and tend to be rejected. Words are likely to be better than numbers or letters as long as they are culturally acceptable, and the terminology attached to performance rating is important. Calling ratings 'achievement levels' is an altogether different proposition to calling them 'box markings', for example – still a prevalent term in the parts of the UK Civil Service that still use performance rating. One implies an adult–adult approach, the other parent–child.

In deciding the number of ratings to use (if any), as well as the words that go with them, it is important to be clear how many levels of performance or contribution can actually be discerned by managers and individuals for the purposes of performance review. We deal with the main approaches and their use below:

▌ **No rating but an agreed summary of contribution** – this approach has been used increasingly by some leading employers where there has been a genuine desire to get away from what is regarded as the artificiality of performance rating. Such organizations feel that to reduce a year's contribution down to a single letter or number is to oversimplify the 'texture' of individual achievement and development. Success with this approach depends on very high-quality performance management and equally high levels of trust in managerial consistency between individuals performing at similar levels. Under such approaches, performance-related pay will be allocated by managers deciding how best to spend their pay increase budgets across the individuals for whom they are responsible. There may, however, be a separate (usually flexible) system of guidance on performance 'tranches' to enable the fair allocation of performance-related pay. This is the approach used in the UK Senior Civil Service – one of our case studies (see Chapter 18).

▌ **Three ratings** – which are typically:

- Exceeded expectations
- Fully met expectations
- Has not met expectations

The main advantage of this approach is that it is easy to understand and in most circumstances reflects recognizable levels of contribution. Truly outstanding performers are recognized and the vast majority of dependable performers fit into the middle tranche, with the few underperformers placed in the 'Has not met expectations' category. It can, however, mean that there is a lack of fine performance definition, which can make pay decisions difficult where some of those in the middle tranche who think they should be towards the top may resent the idea of probably all being paid the same.

▌ **Four ratings** – which typically comprise:

- Highly effective
- Effective
- Developing
- Basic – which might also be 'learner/developing' for those new in post

This is an approach adopted by organizations working hard on the motivation of employees, and who therefore wish to ensure that all ratings are positive. As and when unacceptable performance occurs, individuals are taken out of the rating system and tackled under the processes in place for handling underperformance. It is easier to have differentiated and systematic links to pay than the three-level option.

▌ **Five ratings** – which typically comprise:

- Exceptional
- High performance
- Good all-round performance
- Fair performance
- Poor/unacceptable performance

Using five levels has the advantage of providing for two superior performance levels, a fully acceptable level and two shades of less than effective. It is based on the view that managers can effectively discriminate between five levels and that this level of differentiation facilitates the links to pay, notably the use of merit-increase matrices which underpin many approaches to base-pay increases in middle management, professional and support staff.

❚ **Six ratings** – generally involving:

- Exceptional
- Excellent
- Well balanced
- Reasonable
- Barely effective
- Poor/unacceptable

This approach can be helpful in organizations where fine differences in levels of performance can easily be distinguished and where it is helpful to have this amount of variation in recognition of achievement.

Very few organizations use more than six levels. Those that do tend to be in technical fields, focused more on the measurement approach and given culturally to fine levels of precision. Once again, the choice of words is important; the wording attached to different levels of performance can, of course, vary considerably. The most important consideration here is that the maximum numbers of fully acceptable and high performers feel recognized and motivated by the wording used.

Any organization wishing to make a sound decision about how many performance levels to opt for needs to take account of:

❚ historical data about performance distributions for the population to be covered;

❚ the degree of flexibility it wishes to give line managers around rewarding different 'types' of performance;

❚ key messages it wishes to give about identifying (and tackling) poor or mediocre performance;

❚ the capability of existing line management to make fine distinctions/ judgements about the performance of their people.

The use of forced distributions

One of the besetting problems of performance ratings is the tendency over time for ratings to creep up – the process of 'ratings drift'. This happens for understandable reasons as managers try to reward progress year on year with a higher rating. Ratings themselves have become a form of reward. This drift seems to occur despite the fact that for most organizations the performance bar is raised every year by competitor or stakeholder pressures, which should mean that to achieve the same rating in a following year is to make progress at the rate of the organization.

A common way of tackling rating drift and injecting a bit more realism into performance distributions is to provide guidance on the range of distributions expected. At its most stringent this may resemble the 'Vitality Curve' approach adopted by General Electric (GE) under the leadership of Jack Welch in the 1990s. Under this approach, managers at GE were directed to rank all their direct reports in terms of the top 20 per cent, the core 70 per cent and the bottom 10 per cent. The bottom 10 per cent were then expected to be removed from the organization, so raising the bar for the year ahead and enabling a certain amount of 'ventilation' of the culture of the organization by moving people around and through new recruits. Welch exposed his rationale in an interview with the *Financial Times* ('He's got the power', *FT Magazine*, 29 October 2005: 16–19) as follows:

> I have seen it transform companies from mediocre to outstanding. And it is as morally sound as a management system can be. The thing is, protecting people who don't perform hurts the people themselves. For years, they are carried along with other people looking the other way. At appraisals they are told they are doing just fine. Then a downturn occurs and these under-performers are almost always the first to go, and always the most surprised because no one has ever told them the truth. The awful thing is that this often happens when underperformers are in their late forties or fifties. Then suddenly, at an age when starting over can be tough, they are out of a job.

Welch is very clear about what needs to be in place for this approach to work. He was quoted by Lawler (2003) as saying:

> Our vitality curve works because we have spent over a decade building a performance culture that has candid feedback at every level. Candour and openness are the foundations of such a culture. I would not want to inject a vitality curve 'cold turkey' into an organization without a performance culture already in place.

Readers tempted to go down this route have been warned!

There are two continuing challenges for the use of forced distributions, which are typically based on a statistically normal curve. First, where absolute ratings of performance are being used, is it in the organization's interest for performance to be normally distributed – in key areas, it might need to be skewed towards the high-performance level to achieve competitive advantage? Second, and this applies to relative/ranked performance ratings – how easy is it to give fair and consistent ratings across a whole, large international organization – or a large public service one, when the rankings will inevitably mean different things in different places? A lowly ranked individual in a very high-performing area might actually be performing better than a middle-ranked individual in a more humdrum environment. This outcome can affect both development opportunities and relative rewards.

Managerial consistency in allocating ratings

A less aggressive approach that can be used to support line management decision making on the fair and consistent allocation of performance ratings is illustrated in Figure 16.1.

This is essentially a tool that supports the development of a performance culture and considers overall performance in terms of objectives, competencies and also development objectives and potential. The mix can, of course, vary according to organizational need and culture. Its purpose is to encourage the line manager to go through each objective in turn and consider whether for each one the individual has met, exceeded, or not fully met the agreed target. Once this process has been completed, the manager can consider objectively how to relate this information to the ratings scale. Exceeding one objective, for example, while missing out on one and hitting all others might equate to 'meeting objectives' on balance. The rating tool can also be tailored to encourage the reviewer to consider any 'legitimate shaders' that should be taken into account in reviewing performance against each objective. It may, for example, become apparent in the course of the year that one of the objectives has become even more stretching because of difficult business or operating conditions outside the individual's control. Also, the use of the matrix serves to help managers record their thought process prior to any calibration or other internal consistency checking.

In summary, flexible guidelines seem to work better than fixed/forced distributions of ratings. Performance is rarely distributed normally in organizations, and fixed/forced distributions that reflect this may go against the grain of what is required and delivered. More flexibility allows line managers to reflect this.

Overall ratings: A B C D
Performance against objectives   (exceeded/met/not met)
Competency rating (1–4)

Objectives and competencies	1	2	3	4	5	6	7	8	
Overall performance — Performance against objectives									
Competencies									
Development objectives/potential									Tentative rating:
Factors to take into account — Stretch									
Skills shortages									
Support needed									Provisional rating is:
Exclude distorters — Age, friendship, etc									

Figure 16.1   Rating tool

Discomfort with tackling underperformance

Critical to the acceptability of any form of performance rating or review is the way in which underperformance is handled. This needs to fit the specific causes of underperformance involved. Armstrong and Murlis (2005) identified the most common causes as:

▌ capability:

 – promoted beyond personal ability to develop and change (most common for senior roles);
 – insufficient development input either recently or earlier in career;
 – the individual is currently in the wrong role for his or her actual level of skills/capabilities that can be developed;

▌ inappropriate attitudes or behaviours (eg resistance to change, inappropriate leadership style, 'coasting' – doing just enough when there is clearly capability to make a much greater contribution);

▌ interference of personal issues:

 – family (parents/children), unforeseen care responsibilities;
 – marriage/relationships in difficulty;

▌ illness – medical conditions other than long-term disability that impact on presence at work, concentration and energy levels;

▌ poor management/clarity of direction:

 – being allowed to 'do the wrong things right';
 – being set unrealistic objectives;

▌ lack of support from manager/colleagues/others who should contribute to achievement levels;

▌ substance abuse – alcohol/drugs;

▌ insufficient self-confidence/self-esteem – sometimes related to discrimination, harassment or bullying.

Clearly, each of these requires handling in different ways by line management with the support of HR, either to deal with the causes or put the individual through disciplinary procedures which allow the issue to be tackled fairly, consistently and speedily. Most other employees resent having to 'work around' an underperformer for long and expect action to be taken.

TRUST AND THE LINKS TO PAY

Performance-related pay has attracted a mixed reaction since it began to become more widespread in the private sector in the 1980s and in the public sector in the 1990s. The criticisms have centred around:

▌ lack of clarity about performance standards;

▌ insufficient foundations in terms of performance management;

▌ poor management capability to assess performance outcomes;

▌ insufficient training for leaders, managers and individuals on the 'why' and 'how' of performance rewards;

▌ inconsistent/unfair performance assessments;

▌ insufficient funds to pay for meaningful performance rewards;

▌ too much/not enough differentiation in rewards;

▌ failure to reward teamwork/overemphasis on individual contribution;

▌ poor communication – failure to sell the benefits of an improved performance focus and rewards for those who do well.

These criticisms are as much about the quality of performance management as they are about the pay mechanisms themselves. But fundamentally they are about levels of trust – between leaders, managers and individuals – to do the right thing and provide financial recognition consistently and fairly. They have led to the failure of many performance-related pay systems, especially in the UK public sector where there was strong resistance and adverse publicity at the outset as well as restricted funds for the rewards themselves. Not that the UK public sector is moving away from some form of performance rewards: the newer approaches take account of the learning for the most part and local government and the National Health Service have shifted the ground slightly to focus on paying for contribution. 'Contribution' implies discretionary effort freely given in place of the 'carrot and stick' implications of performance-related pay. It also specifically included inputs as well as outputs – although in practice many traditional performance-related pay schemes and performance management practices that lay behind them catered for inputs too. We deal with this in more detail below.

In reality, in the private sector at least, performance-related pay appears to have become an accepted part of the reward picture and certainly the basis for most annual pay reviews and progression. The concerns listed above are being or have been tackled and significant work on leadership and organizational culture means that in many major employers levels of trust have risen – as has the quality of performance management. Over the past decade, it is clear that a new perception of pay equity has evolved where most employees feel it is unfair to pay someone the same in relation to themselves, even if they have the same role, experience and service, if they are not performing at the same level.

They feel that the clarity of performance standards and requirements has improved and that fair differentiation is possible.

There is a continuing debate as to whether performance reviews and pay should be handled at the same time. It is argued that waiting to hear a performance rating and pay outcome detracts from the usefulness and quality of performance reviews and dialogue. Better perhaps to keep the performance review separate?

The reality is that there is, and should be, a recognizable link between performance reviews of individuals and any performance rewards they get. If they trust the process and it is handled on an adult–adult basis, this should not be an issue. So if ratings are used and the individual contributes views on this and an agreement is reached, then the pay outcome should be easy to communicate too. There is something to be said, however, for communicating the size and nature of pay or bonus awards separately from the review, if only to reinforce the messages given at the review and focus on raising motivation and engagement for the future. This is yet another part of the continuing performance dialogue. There is also the operational reality that reviews need to be complete in order to finalize pay or bonus distributions.

WHAT ARE ORGANIZATIONS PAYING FOR – AND WITH WHAT?

Rewards for performance vary, from the just noticeable difference from a fixed increment or annual cost-of-living award on base salary up to aggressive annual and longer-term cash bonuses and share incentive schemes. We list the principal forms of performance reward architecture and their uses below:

▍ **Base salary progression** in the form of performance-related fixed increments or performance-related pay increases for individuals within pay scales – used for employees of all levels to reflect overall performance in the year. May be used on their own or with cash incentives or bonuses/other performance rewards.

▍ **Annual performance incentives** – typically related to the achievement of specific personal objectives. Used for managers and staff (notably senior managers and sales staff) who have direct personal control over the outcomes of the areas to which their personal targets apply.

▍ **Annual bonuses** – paid to reflect achievement levels but not incentives because they do not relate to specific targets – discretionary bonuses fall in this category.

▍ **Long-term incentives** – payments in cash or shares designed to reflect sustained performance where payment/award is deferred until the performance targets are delivered. These typically cover periods from three to five years and are used for top and senior management teams in direct control of business outcomes.

▌ **Team awards** – payments in cash or kind which reflect team contribution. Can only be used where team membership is consistent over the period in question, where the team has control over outcomes and there are no issues arising from outlying contributors or other factors.

▌ **Profit shares/gainsharing** – essentially a collective award or share in success with no strong link between individual performance and overall organizational performance. This approach is valuable as a means of communicating how the organization is doing and how success is achieved. It supports the development of a performance culture.

▌ **Recognition awards** – individual awards in cash or kind that reflect exceptional personal contributions. To work well, these depend on having clear criteria for awards and being implemented within a culture that celebrates success.

▌ **Competency and skills-based approaches** – in the 1990s, there was much discussion and development activity around competence and skills-based pay. This came from a desire to pay for people's ability to grow and to demonstrate the behaviours required to reflect a high-performance culture. Skills-based pay (paying additional amounts for validated skills acquisition in a specific area) proved valuable where organizations wanted to foster multi-skilling and a learning culture – generally on the shop floor. It proved problematic when organizations found they were paying for skills that were not being used or needed. Such schemes appear to have a limited life unless there is steady progression into different roles requiring new skills and a significant influx of new recruits to be trained in competency-based approaches. These approaches, which reward the development and use of behaviours (and are therefore directly related to the development-focused approach to performance management), have proved problematic and are not, in their purest form, at all widely used (CIPD Reward Management Surveys, 2004, 2005). For a good illustration of a skills-based pay approach in action, refer to Chapter 17, which describes such a scheme at British Airports Authority. Many organizations have not gone down the road of creating balanced scorecards related to cash payments for competency development. This has proved too complex, especially in addition to the measurement of achievement of business objectives. A 'middle way' has emerged, often referred to as **'contribution-related pay'**, where both development input and target achievement are reviewed together and the base salary increase or annual bonus reflects them both. In addition, the term 'contribution-related pay' appears not to be tainted with the 'search, find and punish' overtones sometimes linked with performance-related pay and is therefore more acceptable to employees and the trade unions that represent them. For this reason, this terminology has figured prominently in recent reward strategy proposals in the UK in both local government and the National Health Service.

In designing performance rewards it is important that the vehicle used fits with market practice for the kinds of people involved, the business sector involved, what the organization can afford and the messages the organization wants to give. It is important to avoid paying twice for the same thing and to be specific about what payments and awards are for and how they can be achieved. Figure 16.2 illustrates a basis for making decisions on reward architecture based on the elements at risk and those that are dependent on individual and organizational performance.

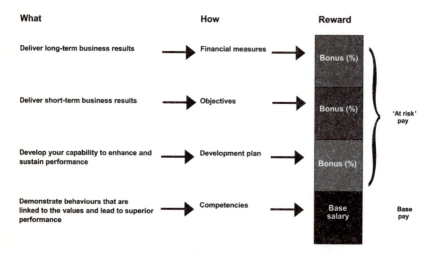

Figure 16.2   Elements of reward architecture

THE TOTAL REWARD DIMENSION

The more that organizations conduct employee opinion research into what motivates and engages employees and what their priorities are, the stronger the rationale becomes for considering total rewards. By 'total rewards' we mean everything that employees perceive as their 'deal' with their employer, the reasons why they choose to work for them and the reasons they stay and contribute. People are more or less engaged with their work in relation to the perceived quality of their deal. Figure 16.3 illustrates a model of total reward developed by the Hay Group in the late 1990s, reflecting its employee opinion research on the components of Engaged Performance®.

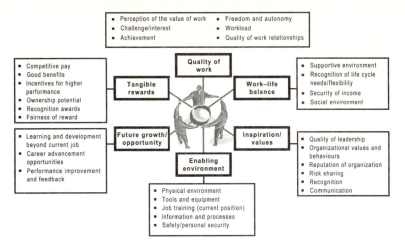

Figure 16.3 The Hay Group Model of Engaged Performance®. *Source:* Hay Group (2000) *Engage Employees and Boost Performance,* Hay Group working paper, see www.haygroup.co.uk

Engaged Performance is defined as a result that is achieved by stimulating employees' enthusiasm for their work and directing it towards organizational success (Hay Group, 2000). It is not just about investing financially in employees through pay and benefit increases. It is about striking a new contract in which the organization invests emotionally in its workforce.

Within this model, it can be seen that there are several elements related to performance management and reward that matter. Hay Group research (2000) suggests that in many organizations the 'inspiration and values' cluster is of greatest importance – and within this the way in which organizations provide for recognition of achievements. Often second as a priority is the 'future growth and opportunity' cluster, within which opportunities for performance improvement and quality of feedback feature strongly. Tangible rewards tend to come third or later in the employee priority listing. They are nevertheless important, and getting the financial reward architecture and its communication right is a significant contributor to engagement – though not dominant. These findings, together with those of other researchers in this field such as Purcell, Guest, Armstrong and Baron, and Brown, combine to suggest that effective performance management and development are of themselves perceived as rewards and components of the creation of employee engagement.

For this last part of the performance management cycle, as before, we feature two stories from practice of organizations that illustrate a particular approach to reviewing and rewarding performance. Chapter 17 describes a skills-based pay approach at British Airports Authority (BAA) and Chapter 18 highlights the process used within the UK Senior Civil Service to separate the performance review and summary from pay allocation.

17

Organizational story: rewarding development at BAA

The previous chapter has discussed how performance management is linked to review and reward. It has considered the principal forms of performance reward architecture, including competency and skills-based approaches, which are the topic of this organizational story. In her chapter Helen Murlis has described how skills-based pay (paying additional amounts for validated skills acquisition in specific areas) has proven valuable in organizations wanting to foster multi-skilling and a learning culture – particularly on the shop floor. The example we showcase provides an excellent illustration of this, as it focuses on a 'shop floor' population and describes a process which has been developed in conjunction with the workforce and Amicus and the Transport and General Workers Union (TGWU). It is particularly noteworthy since it has succeeded in avoiding the sometimes punitive or divisive overtones which often make performance management, particularly linked to reward, unacceptable within this environment.

Our example is drawn from the experience of BAA plc's engineering and maintenance division. With revenues of around £2 billion, BAA has grown since privatization in the mid-1980s to become the world's leading airport company. It owns and operates seven UK airports – Heathrow, Gatwick, Stansted, Southampton, Glasgow, Edinburgh and Aberdeen, serving over 141 million passengers each year, and employs either directly or via the airports over 125,000 people in the UK. In addition, BAA has developed interests and operational responsibilities in numerous other airports around the world, including Italy, Australia and the USA where it serves over 40 million passengers a year.

Continued innovation and improved customer focus have been identified as key strategic priorities. This has led to a number of internal reorganization and change initiatives, including those in the area of airport maintenance. Between 2002 and 2005, as a result of such a change programme, the whole approach to team structures, managing performance and reward was redesigned for the engineering population working across the three southeast airports in the UK (Heathrow, Gatwick and Stansted).

THE TECHNICIAN PERFORMANCE DEVELOPMENT REVIEW

The initial focus of the Maintenance Change Programme was to resolve issues relating to the leadership population, maintenance process and supporting infrastructures and systems. Once complete, the focus moved to developing a new performance management process for the technician population. The existing process had last been defined and agreed with the unions in the 1990s, and although this had resulted in a performance review 'form' being in existence, its actual use and impact were limited.

Chris Ricketts, the Head of People and Organization for engineering in the UK, worked with the unions to design and roll out a new performance management process, which better met the needs of both the technician workforce and the more customer-focused strategy at BAA. The new process has the following features:

- A review and feedback on both WHAT you do as a technician (the role accountabilities and outcomes) and HOW you do it (the technical and behavioural competencies required to deliver high performance).

- A personal development plan based on the training and development needs in their current role.

- A discussion around future skills development and their career (subject to good performance in their current role) and recommendation by their manager that they work towards one of the enhanced Skill-Based Pay modules.

- The maintenance team managers would lead the discussion with each technician, although in the longer term this may move to the team leader owing to the size of the technician teams.

- Performance management 'cycle' includes the three meetings typically associated with the planning, managing and reviewing phases of performance management.

▌ The year-end review involves a discussion of both the extent to which outcomes are met and reviews the personal development plan. In the first years of operation the review does not include a summative rating, although a four-level rating scale is planned to be rolled out subsequently.

▌ Documentation includes a section which invites the technician to give feedback on the review and rate the maintenance team manager's performance in conducting the review.

ENHANCED SKILLS-BASED PAY FOR TECHNICIANS

The rationale behind the enhanced skills pay approach is to support the development of a flexible and responsive workforce where technicians' skills are deployed on the basis of their competency, rather than their position within the department's hierarchy. To support the development of this culture and create career paths for core technicians, two new roles were created – technician engineer and team leader. Each position comes with specific additional accountabilities and technical and behavioural competencies, for which the technician will receive additional payment in recognition of their value to BAA. However, in terms of position, both roles are considered as being at the same organizational level as the core technician. This is summarized in Figure 17.1.

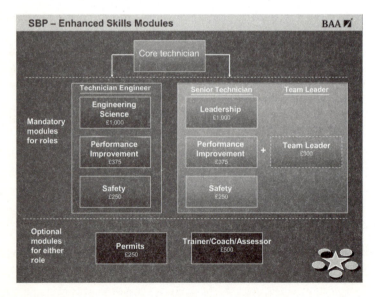

Figure 17.1 The enhanced skills modules and link to roles

Should an individual technician opt to go for skills-based pay, their performance would be reviewed against the accountabilities and competencies contained in the 'Enhanced Skills-Based Pay Modules'. The skills modules comprise:

▌ Performance Improvement;

▌ Leadership;

▌ Engineering Science;

▌ Safety;

▌ Permits;

▌ Trainer/Coach/Assessor.

Figure 17.1 summarizes how the development modules link to the enhanced roles.

Once the technician has completed an enhanced skills-based pay module they will be expected to be able to deliver and display the additional technical and behavioural competencies at an assessment and, if successful, will be paid the additional amount on their base salary (highlighted in Figure 17.1) and take on the additional accountabilities associated with it. For example, the additional accountabilities and competencies for the Performance Improvement Module include (this is not the full list):

▌ Accountabilities include:

 – Set up small groups of technicians to identify and prioritize opportunities for 'productivity performance improvement'.
 – Analyse equipment and team performance information; identify and communicate performance improvement opportunities and progress.

▌ Technical competencies include:

 – Facilitation of performance improvement groups, including appropriate people and facilities.
 – Organize and present data to team using appropriate techniques such as fishbone and balanced scorecard.

▌ Behavioural competencies include:

 – Being courageous (eg constantly seek to stretch productivity and quality targets and outperform the norm).
 – Being curious (eg look broadly at problems and consider a wide range of factors before homing in on the best solution.

By opting for skills-based pay a technician may, subject to the needs of the business, choose to develop along the Technician Engineer or the Team

Leader route, each of which requires the completion of a different set of modules. The Technician Engineer route involves the successful completion of the technical science, performance improvement and safety modules. The individual will be expected to take on the additional accountabilities associated with these and display the associated competencies on an ongoing basis, in addition to their accountabilities and competencies as a core technician.

The Team Leader route includes:

▌ successful completion of three modules: leadership, performance improvement and safety;

▌ appointment to a team leader role once a role is available. This requires the individual to take on a number of additional accountabilities, including:

  – conducting 'start of shift meetings';
  – reviewing team performance;
  – providing a constructive challenge to technicians who do not have a full workload.

The BAA example is an interesting one which illustrates how the 'typical' performance management cycle of 'plan, manage and review' may be implemented with a strong emphasis on development. In the past, the organization had struggled to promote the value of performance management processes, particularly for front-line and non-managerial positions. Here is a novel approach which seems to have won approval from both the workforce and managers but which has also been accepted by the unions, as it clearly provides their members with opportunities for development and the chance to earn more as a result of this development. Interestingly, at the time of writing, members of the maintenance workforce have the option of choosing to take the skills-based pay route or not. This reflects the fact that some of the longer-serving members of the team may not be focusing on ongoing career development, but still are keen to have the chance to discuss the priorities of their role and how well they are doing, a facility the revised performance management process offers. Interestingly, without the use of ratings there is no clear link between 'high performance' and being offered the chance of development (and job enhancement). BAA intends to move to the use of ratings once the maintenance team managers have further developed their performance management skill sets and the business is confident that they can use the ratings process consistently and fairly both within and across the airports. In doing so they should avoid some of the pitfalls of a 'development alone' approach, which, as we have discussed earlier, can result in development for development's sake.

18
Organizational story: paying for contribution within the UK Senior Civil Service

In this chapter we look at what is happening to the performance management and reward arrangements applied to UK Senior Civil Servants. This case study is an interesting example of an approach to rewarding senior managers that started a decade ago with tightly fixed pay based on grade and has progressively moved towards a variable pay regime based on contribution.

The UK Senior Civil Service (SCS) was created in 1996 and comprises all staff from permanent secretaries (ie heads of government departments) to deputy directors (what used to be called Grade Five level). It includes chief executives and top-level Civil Servants and specialists – operational managers and policy advisers of government departments and agencies – and is currently about 3,800 people. Although SCS members work for a particular government department, they are seen as a 'corporate' resource and their pay and conditions are covered by a single set of service-wide arrangements. The UK Cabinet Office develops policy and provides advice and guidance for departments on the design and operation of the SCS performance management and pay framework. It also submits the government's evidence to the Senior Salaries Review Body (SSRB) who make recommendations on SCS pay.

THE PERFORMANCE MANAGEMENT PROCESS FOR THE SCS

At the beginning of the year the individual and his or her line manager discuss the job to be done and reach a performance agreement for the year ahead. The guidance for this annual performance agreement has been fairly open, typically up to six key personal business objectives or targets are to be defined which clearly reflect departmental priorities and define the individual's in-year deliverables and the way in which performance against targets will be measured. Recently, more structure has been required in specifying objectives which are to be identified in three broad areas:

▌ what to deliver – to reflect priorities for SCS members focused on service delivery, a number of key objectives derived from each department's Public Service Agreements (PSAs), defining performance and service delivery;

▌ building capability – to focus on continual growth and development, objectives that relate specifically to senior staff building the capacity of their team or building more organization-wide capability;

▌ personal development – linked to increasing 'professionalization'; each SCS member is expected to work towards achieving a set of core skills, professional expertise in what they do, as well as acquire broader experience either within or outside the Civil Service. This is guided by the Professional Skills for Government (PSG) initiative launched by the Head of the Home Civil Service to enable the further raising of professionals standards across the top of the Civil Service.

In addition to the above, the performance agreement includes a requirement for an objective related to the Civil Service's priorities in respect of diversity. Departmental management may also moderate personal objectives or targets to take account of relative 'stretch' and to ensure alignment with overall business plans and departmental performance agreements.

During the course of the year, reviews to evaluate progress are encouraged, in line with the normal process of business monitoring. At the end of the year, performance reviews take place in April when the individual and his or her line manager review performance over the whole year and lay the foundations for the next year. Both are asked to prepare for the review session, line managers by gathering feedback from multiple sources. The emphasis is on honest face-to-face discussion of performance rather than form filling and the SCS has made significant progress over many other parts of the public sector by moving away from a lengthy and bureaucratic form to a simple, free-text, two-page performance review record.

In the light of the review discussion, the manager records on, or attaches to, this record the overall job purpose and agreed personal objectives. Managers also summarize their assessments of achievements against all objectives or targets, the individual's overall contribution throughout the year and his or her growth in skills and leadership competence. Performance ratings (formerly called box markings) are no longer used.

Where line managers judge that there is a performance shortfall, they may draw up 'performance improvement plans' setting out specific areas of progress in performance urgently required, how this will be monitored and the support that will be provided by themselves and others who need to be involved.

Recommendations on pay and bonus are dealt with separately. Some managers may make recommendations on pay and bonus, while in other cases pay committees 'interpret' their performance assessment summary. The approach depends on departmental practice. Some departments have additionally retained the traditional role of a 'countersigning officer' both to check on review standards and to oversee the performance management process. This enables a more informed overview to be taken of the way in which the SCS members are developing delivery and so contribute more effectively to the reward and talent management processes.

The SCS performance management approach this is a relative assessment process in which SCS members' contributions are compared with each other. Rather than use a pure ranking arrangement, SCS members are placed in one of three tranches and there is a predetermined distribution of tranches.

The recommendations about 'tranches' inform reward for the SCS, to which we now turn our attention.

SEPARATING THE REWARD ELEMENT FROM PERFORMANCE MANAGEMENT

The SCS scheme works on the premise that it is important to inform and moderate pay decisions across SCS members working at a similar level. This is especially important within large departments such as the Ministry of Defence or Her Majesty's Revenue and Customs (HMRC) where hundreds of SCS members are involved. Base pay and bonus decisions are therefore handled by pay committees, at a departmental level. These committees take as their input the narrative summaries of performance from line managers (and any reward recommendations) and place SCS members into one of three 'pay tranches'. Pay committees comprise a mix of line manager representatives and external members, for example senior managers from other departments or non-executive directors. Often, there may be a hierarchy of committees within a department; for example, within the Cabinet Office the senior committee membership includes the Head of the Cabinet Office (Permanent Secretary) and the senior management team, while other pay committees operate below this level.

Base pay

Salary recognizes an individual's continuing value to the organization and sustained contribution as a member of the SCS. Increases in salary reflect individuals' tranche and position in their pay band. The allocation of individuals to one of the three tranches is based on three base criteria that define the 'contribution' an individual has made that year:

▎ how well the job has been performed in relation to the challenge within the job (contribution in relation to 'job loading' – rather than the 'job size or weight' in job evaluation terms);

▎ growth in competence;

▎ sustained performance (to give confidence of future performance); for example, if an individual has consistently delivered above expectations for the last three to four years, then the likelihood this will continue is higher than for a high performer who has just moved into a position and is therefore unproven in the new role.

Guidance, with some flexibility, is provided to departments on the proportions of people expected within each tranche:

▎ The top tranche should comprise the 25 per cent of the SCS who have contributed most to departmental success in the year.

▎ The middle tranche should be the 65–70 per cent who have contributed well and delivered effectively.

▎ The bottom tranche are the 5–10 per cent who have contributed least compared to peers.

In practice, feedback to the Cabinet Office has indicated that some departments feel it is difficult to identify people in the bottom tranche, raising issues around managers' capability to identify and confront poor performance and cultural issues around a lingering discomfort with ranking and rating people according to performance.

The annual bonus

Non-consolidated cash payments or bonuses reward SCS members' delivery of personal business objectives or other short-term personal contributions. At the beginning of the year, individuals agree with their line manager the achievement of which priority business objectives or targets will ensure eligibility for consideration for a bonus. Everyone who meets their targets fully, while demonstrating the agreed competencies and behaviours, can expect to be considered for a bonus regardless of tranche allocation, although bottom-tranche performers would receive a bonus only in exceptional circumstances.

In the past, the Cabinet Office has given the advice that only the top two tranches should be eligible for a bonus, but more recently it has been left to departments to decide, within the general guidance to differentiate more strongly in favour of stronger performers. This gives flexibility for departments to give a bonus to those who, for example, may have exceeded their goals for the year but who has been placed in the bottom tranche (resulting in little by way of pay rise) since their job was not particularly challenging, their competence has not grown and their past performance has been more patchy than sustained.

The pay committee process – current issues

Pay committees are rightly concerned about being consistent and following good process well. In this context they need to consider more broadly the relative 'value' of an individual and his or her contribution within a performance year. For example, the guidelines for pay on promotion are that rises should be 'at least 10 per cent': the tendency has been to give a straight 10 per cent increase, not less and not more, rather than stand back and decide what the right position in the pay band should be.

Pay committees work hard to provide the rigour necessary to make judgements about pay increases and bonus allocation as objective as possible. They may spend many hours over decisions, but the amount of differentiation in monetary terms remains relatively small. The system does not primarily incentivize (since there are not, generally speaking, large amounts of money on offer which might provide a genuine financial incentive), but it does draw attention to the importance of performance in specific areas and reinforces management communication about what constitutes successful achievement. In this sense it is a clear form of management recognition – people who are judged to be the highest performers are paid more – in a culture where variable pay is a relatively new phenomenon.

The SCS performance management and reward process takes place within the context of a 'dual market' where external recruits into the Civil Service may get paid more for the same contribution owing to the need to offer higher salaries to bring them in – usually from the private sector. The impact of this on pay decisions and pay committee operation, as well as its impact on SCS members with more traditional career paths, is an area to which the Cabinet Office is giving continuing attention.

Additionally, while pay committees operate at a departmental level to ensure moderation and consistency, this process is not replicated across departments (although there is analysis by the Cabinet Office after the review and reward process).

Dealing with underperformance

The tranche system has led to some departments becoming much better at recognizing their poor performers and managing them towards the achievement of higher levels of performance. However, the overall statistics for SCS members being 'managed out' of the service has remained fairly static at approximately 10 per cent a year, with most of these handled through the early retirement route. The feedback from departments around difficulties allocating people to the bottom tranche is also indicative of the challenges of managing underperformance. Line managers within the SCS shy away from giving feedback and dealing with poor performance face-to-face, and investment by the Cabinet Office to improve the performance management process has been directed, among other things, to helping these managers handle difficult conversations. The tendency to avoid these discussions may be exacerbated for some departments by the separation between the performance management process and reward decisions, where some line managers hide behind the pay committee, placing the responsibility on the latter for differentiating performance rather than taking it upon themselves to tell people where they really stand in performance terms. On the other hand, other line managers may feel disempowered at not being able to follow through directly on their performance reviews with pay and bonus decisions. Whichever viewpoint is taken, Senior Civil Service reward practice has come a long way from its origins as a system where everyone at a particular grade received the same pay, for the same service in post, and everyone knew how much it was, to a system that rewards according to level of contribution, where there are broader rewards on offer and where line managers are progressively being entrusted to make these decisions on behalf of the service. It is important, too, to remember that a senior management cadre of 3,800 is a large one in worldwide terms. Changing practice for a group of this size, particularly given the historical starting point, to a more performance-focused and differentiating environment while retaining strong underlying values of integrity, fairness and consistency is a considerable challenge – if a necessary one to support continuous improvement in public service delivery.

19

Future directions and conclusions

The evidence given in this book shows clearly that performance management, while not a new phenomenon, is experiencing a resurgence in terms of its perceived organizational importance and its levels of acceptance and use by managers. We now go on to look at what recent developments mean and what the future might hold.

Our literature-based research, together with survey and case-study data, provides an overview of the performance management terrain from a range of different data sources. We have then explored how best to implement measurement- and development-based approaches in a balanced way and illustrated this with seven organizational stories. In this final chapter we suggest what the future might look like for both the measurement and development dimensions of performance before pulling together the main threads of our debate and offering conclusions on optimum approaches for the future.

PERFORMANCE MEASUREMENT: FUTURE DIRECTIONS

We begin our crystal ball gazing by looking first at measurement-based approaches to performance management before considering those which are development based.

The world in which many organizations now operate is much changed; while the need to achieve a balance of measures remains a priority, organizations have become more complex, with multiple reporting lines, 'matrixed' relationships and overlapping accountabilities. The task of leaders is complex as they strive to achieve a balance of measures to help them focus on successful delivery of all their responsibilities. There is a need to set accountabilities that recognize interdependencies across different areas of the business rather than maximizing performance within one area, as well as set accountabilities for others within a 'virtual' team where there may be 'dotted' lines of responsibility.

Initial balanced scorecard implementations involved working down from strategy in a cascade of dependent measures across the four scorecard areas. It is an approach which is logical and essentially deductive, usually resulting in a multitude of measures. Experience of implementing balanced scorecard projects over the past decade suggests that although they work in principle they may be problematical to implement (see Chapter 2 for some of the theory around this and Chapter 12 for an example of one organization that has striven to overcome some of the problems).

One of the main problems is the usual proliferation of measures which follow their design. As the 'traditional' approach to a scorecard involved the focus on four 'perspectives': finance, customer, process, and learning and growth, management teams could spend much time debating which was the most appropriate perspective for a certain strategic priority and also working through the hierarchy of the causal links. More recent work on scorecards has suggested a more streamlined approach. In place of the four perspectives, Lawrie, Cobbold and Marshall (2004) have suggested using only two 'perspectives': activities and outcomes, reflecting a maximum set of 24 short- to medium-term priorities. By adopting the more general terms of 'activities' and 'outcomes', organizations are able to identify more clearly what actions are likely to lead to the desired (and measurable) outcomes, thus doing away with the need to identify lead and lag measures. Once the 24 objectives have been selected, the management team of an organization might opt to allocate them into the original four scorecard perspectives, but this is not a requirement.

Within Hay Group a similar approach has been described (DeVoge, 2005) as 'strategic scorecards'. Again the emphasis here is on streamlining what could become an overly complicated process in order to encourage leaders to focus on the 'must-win' battles necessary to deliver the corporate strategic goals of the organization rather than all of the measures on a scorecard. These 'must-win' battles are likely to be smaller in number, perhaps three to five, representing the priorities a top team or set of senior leaders 'must win' together in order to achieve the strategy successfully. These are distinctly different from what each senior leader must do apart, to maximize performance in his or her own area, sometimes to the detriment of other areas of the business. Thus the first step needs to be decoding the strategy into these key 'must-win' areas that require shared strategic accountability (since they cannot be met by working individually). This might be achieved in a way which is more inductive (knowing what must be done) and not therefore requiring the intricacies of a full balanced-scorecard strategic map. Having identified the must-win battles, the second step is articulating the strategic accountabilities for which each leader is responsible. Since these can only be achieved collaboratively, nearly every team member has responsibility for achieving some element of the must-win battles, as well as key accountabilities that relate to his or her own area of the business.

The strategic scorecard directs the organization to lead strategically rather than operationally. It is shown in Figure 19.1 and focuses much more clearly on the strategic goals of the organization and aligning performance and compensation to the delivery of these.

Balanced scorecard	Strategic scorecard
■ focus on a balanced perspective of performance	■ delivering results that make a substantial difference to performance
■ focus on medium- and longer-term performance	■ focus on 'must-win' battles
■ set performance objectives on operational objectives	■ getting synergies and cross-organizational efficiencies
■ focus on the metrics that have to be achieved	■ getting breakthrough innovations
	■ interdependencies
	■ different for every organization

Figure 19.1 Balanced versus strategic scorecards. *Source:* Hay Group (2005)

Time will tell how successful the strategic scorecard proves to be. For those readers interested in comparing the extent to which processes within their own organization match or fall short of this kind of thinking, we present a short audit tool below.

AUDITING YOUR MEASUREMENT PROCESSES – THE STRATEGIC SCORECARD CHECKLIST

1. How do you define your performance goals? To what extent do they reflect the key performance drivers in your business? To what extent, by contrast, do you set performance targets in

relation to either overall financial outcomes, or short-term operational performance?

2. Is there a sufficiently strong and robust process of debate and challenge in relation to your strategic goals? Is accountability for strategic goals clearly defined and 'owned' by each member of the leadership team? Do you genuinely hold people to account for delivery of the goals to which they have agreed?

3. Are your strategic performance goals stretching and well communicated? Is there alignment between overall corporate performance goals and those for each part of your organization? Do your people have 'line of sight' between their own goals and those of the organization as a whole?

4. Do your reward policies and practices, particularly variable reward arrangements, drive and reinforce the achievement of strategic goals? Is there alignment between reward arrangements at every level in the organization, so that directors, executives and employees generally are incentivized to achieve common goals?

Source: Hay Group (2005)

PERFORMANCE DEVELOPMENT: FUTURE DIRECTIONS

In the *Fortune* study we saw that talent management, dovetailed with development, seems to be one of the differentiating themes between the most admired organizations and the rest. However, the challenges relating to talent management are increasing; for example, bigger increments between roles, fewer 'builder' roles, shorter time in role before 'big wins' are expected, and 'matrix' roles that are harder to define. Successful talent management means investing heavily in developing people for the long term and focusing equally on the success requirements of specific roles, not just considering the development needs of the individuals within them.

We have given examples already that suggest how this might be achieved. In Figure 13.1 we considered an example of a competency role profile. Such competency profiles rely on the assumption that it is possible to predict the requirements for success in different types of role across the organization. Thus, via performance management it becomes realistic not only to profile employees in terms of development for their current position but also to identify the more senior roles they might possibly grow into and those for which they would require more development or which are unlikely to be suitable. This requires more than a profile for any

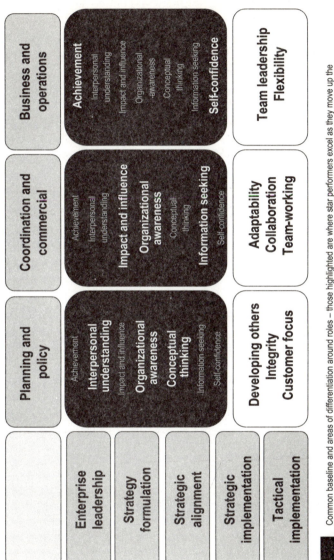

Figure 19.2 Example of a roadmap. *Source:* Hay Group (2005)

one job; instead a 'roadmap' across all organizational roles needs to be considered. A roadmap such as that described below can enable organizations to understand the challenges of different roles within the organization and to map workable career paths to develop its talent.

Figure 19.2 shows an example of a roadmap containing the three main families of executive roles (planning and policy/co-ordination and commercial/business and operations), each requiring its own unique set of leadership skills and behaviours. Despite similarities between roles there are a variety of significant differences, depending on the 'shape' of the job, its proximity to organizational results and the levels of operational and strategic focus.

By combining a robust evaluation of talent with an understanding of levels and types of roles, organizations can aggregate the position of all employees in order to gain a 'big picture' of their talent pool. This can be used to determine the gaps and successors against specific roles, as illustrated in Figure 19.3, where we indicate for an individual employee (Jo Smith) the ease with which he or she will be able to move into different, more senior roles.

For most organizations the challenge of defining a coherent roadmap would be the start of this process. Some organizations have already embarked along this road. However, in the course of this research, few have come to our notice as really placing as much emphasis on the achievement of the development aspects as on the measurement elements. It is our belief that a blind faith in measures alone will always limit the long-term success of an organization's people management processes and

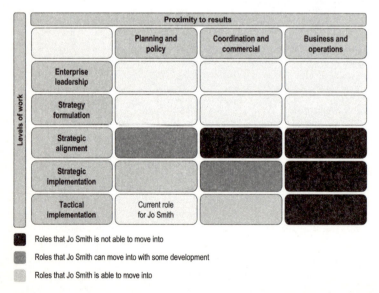

Figure 19.3 Mapping individuals to the roadmap. *Source:* Hay Group (2005)

hence its long-term business performance. Instead we look to combine measurement more fully and constructively with development practice.

CONCLUSIONS

In Part I, we summarized the evolution of performance management and looked at the underpinning academic disciplines relevant to understanding why performance management has evolved as it has. We also introduced the 'performance measurement/performance development framework', and started to pose the question as to whether these very different philosophies are discernible 'on the ground' by providing a framework for understanding the driver and primary character of performance management systems. After deciding that they could both be discerned, we began to examine whether they were in fact irreconcilable countervailing forces. Our initial thinking was that given the different value base and philosophies upon which the two styles of performance management reside, they must by nature inhabit different domains.

Our survey of line manager perceptions, reported in Part II, confirms a trend towards 'harder' approaches, with links to pay and measurable outputs being in vogue. We found a clear emphasis on defining measures and monitoring them, a tendency to link this to a rating of individual performance, and a recognized link between performance management systems and reward.

Despite the heavy emphasis that we found on measures, this does not appear to be at odds with motivation or development. Indeed, the emphasis on measures seems to be used to provide a clear link to organizational imperatives. Here we begin to detect resonances with the *Fortune Magazine*/Hay Group surveys (2004, 2005) reported in Part II. Findings from this research indicated that the most admired companies focus their performance management energies on:

▌ strategy clarification and implementation;

▌ holding people accountable;

▌ achieving congruence between desired and actual working culture;

▌ developing and managing talent;

▌ balancing measurement and development with a 'rounded' set of measures, rather than purely financial performance; and

▌ integrating strategy, performance and compensation.

In our survey, line managers' perceptions seem to suggest that measures provide an opportunity to focus on 'what is important around here', driving accountability throughout the organization and focusing employees on delivering their part of the organization's overall strategy. Within the arena of HR research we can see similarities with the notion of a unifying 'big idea' (which drives purpose, activity and motivation) as being a key variable in the achievement of business success through people management (Hutchinson *et al*, 2002).

From the mini case studies summarized in Chapter 5, we were able to deduce the following:

▌ There is continuing change and flux within organizations in terms of their performance management practice.

▌ Organizations are working extremely hard to make a link between organizational strategy and individual accountabilities.

▌ There is an increasing trend towards measurement as well as measuring or 'hardening' the intangibles (eg competencies).

▌ Organizations are striving where possible to 'standardize' their approaches across different countries or business units.

▌ Real efforts are being made to hold people accountable and to address poor performance.

▌ Linked to attempts to deal with poor performance, energy is being invested in revised ratings, improved, more flexible approaches to forced distribution of ratings and differentially rewarding employees based on their contribution.

The mini case studies combined with the later, more detailed organizational stories confirmed our observation that, despite its often mixed press, performance management does not appear to be receiving criticism from all sides. Our results from both survey and case studies largely concur with Armstrong and Baron (1998: 203) who report a picture that: 'Many people in organizations believe performance management is worthwhile and appear generally to be comfortable with the processes involved.' In their updated research for the CIPD in 2005, they found that 42 per cent of their 451 respondents believed that their performance management processes are very or mostly effective in improving overall performance and 49 per cent believed it was partly effective – only 4 per cent found it ineffective (Armstrong and Baron, 2005: 15).

What we observe is that organizations that perceive performance management to be well done are increasingly learning from the lessons of the past – they may have experienced poor 'management by objectives' approaches or unsuccessful balanced scorecard implementations, and as a result know all about the pitfalls of measurement dysfunction and have worked out strategies for avoiding it. On the other hand, perhaps they have also spent time on development-focused approaches where a disconnection exists between the performance management process and organizational objectives, and are therefore keen to link development investment to key organizational deliverables.

Performance management trends

Based on our research to date as well as that of the CIPD and others, we can conclude that managers are largely positive about the effectiveness of performance management systems and their motivational aspects. The swing over the last five to seven years towards harder, measurement-based approaches would appear to be in line with developments in HR more generally. These changes themselves perhaps reflect the trend in the UK towards a target culture; this has been reinforced by the 'New Labour' governments that have been unusual in both their power and their commitment to modernization and measurement (Pollitt, 2005). Against this backdrop we conclude that measures and being measured are currently perceived as both good practice and fashionable. Figure 19.4 suggests how we can begin to plot these trends.

What the process of researching and writing this book has reinforced for us is that performance management practice, as it is conceptualized and articulated by the majority of HR practitioners, is very much the product of a mixed heritage. We have an increasingly strong sense of the multidisciplinary nature of performance management. It was perhaps

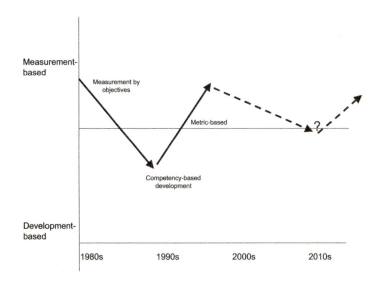

Figure 19.4 Mapping performance management trends

accurate to see the limited intervention that was annual appraisal reside within the personnel function. However, if performance management is a fully integrated and strategic player as a core organizational and management process, then it must be acknowledged that it owes its allegiance to many sources: operational scientists, economists, psychologists, learning and development specialists. If this is the case, perhaps each can contribute to the future of the discipline in dialogue with the others. As we suggested in Chapter 2, the disciplines and theoretical underpinnings of performance management have a more established heritage than the 'newcomer' that is HRM, but the tendency has been for these groups to operate within and write for their own communities, rather than to recognize the cross-disciplinary nature of managing employee performance. It is perhaps not surprising, therefore, that the reflective HR practitioner tasked with 'owning' the performance management process within his or her organization finds that it means one thing to the finance director and quite another to the head of employee development. One of the key future challenges is to bring these together to mutual benefit.

In this book we have described many of the external influences which have shaped practice by establishing fashions and trends; so, for example, we believe that the ascendancy of accountancy-based practices, coupled with government concerns (in the UK) to raise standards, has led to the increased popularity of measurement-based approaches. Figure 19.4 charts the main performance management trends over the past quarter of a century. We can see that in the late 1980s performance management practice was largely about setting objectives in line with organizational strategy. These were the days of 'boom and bust' and recession, so a hard-nosed focus on managing performance is not surprising. During the 1990s there appears to have been a move towards 'softer', more development-focused approaches. This is not necessarily due to more caring/sharing concerns, although the nineties are sometimes typified as being about that; it is also due to 'new technologies' raising the standards of development initiatives in the form of competencies, which were favoured at this time as organizations sought to understand what behaviours to invest in to best deliver business success. Organizations that developed their own competency frameworks were left with the dilemma of 'what to do with it'. An application of competencies to performance management, via development, was a logical next step in the majority of cases.

We then see the pendulum swing again in the late 1990s and early part of this century. We observe the world's most admired companies using performance management as a vehicle for driving strategic changes or hammering home key messages about what is important and what needs to be delivered. This represents a significant shift from the 1990s – performance management is no longer predominantly focused around managers and employees having high-quality conversations; it goes beyond this as a baseline and is rather about ensuring these conversations are aligned to what needs to be done to deliver the organizational strategy. The view seems to be that there is little point in having a good conversation about something that doesn't matter; what works best is 'focused' dialogue. This approach manifests itself, at its best, through the consistent cascade of key deliverables (the 'stick of rock' analogy) and, at its most negative, through an over-reliance on measurement and a rigid forced distribution of performance ratings, the proxy tool that rewards or punishes for delivery of what matters. The latter approach carries, of course, some management style implications that are far from motivational in the longer term.

The availability of the balanced scorecard and other strategic tools perhaps also played a part in the swing away from 'purely' development-based approaches (although learning and development/talent management are contained within the most effective scorecards). Also, the political impetus behind measurement since the late 1990s has been a major factor within the UK, as at the same time the increasing 'professionalization' of the human resources function has been accompanied by a drive to measure its contribution. Pollitt (2005) found that performance indicators were more intimately connected in the UK to the other main management systems, including HRM, than they were in the other European comparison countries.

In Figure 19.4 we suggest that the future would appear to be around a more balanced view than has been seen in the past. We conclude that although the development/measurement framework is useful at a conceptual level, both for diagnosing current practice and understanding theoretical underpinnings, it is an artificial barrier if we assume the two cannot be combined in practice. Indeed, findings from the *Fortune Magazine* Research 2004 confirm that the most admired companies are already balancing the different elements of performance management by measuring more than traditional 'hard' measures and by maintaining a link to talent management processes in such as way as to make development strongly aligned to organizational imperatives.

Although the most admired companies appear to be achieving this ideal, our research suggests that for the majority of other organizations, there is still a tendency predominantly to measure. It is our observation that although many organizations believe they have a 'rounded' process that incorporates both measurement and development aspects, in fact this balance is skewed and the reality 'on the ground' is at odds with the strategic intent of the process. The ability to achieve this 'balance' – in practice rather than rhetoric – will determine the long-term success of most performance management systems. After the extended process of researching and writing this book, we believe that the two manifestations of measurement and development are in fact reconcilable and that the secret of reconciling them lies in not falling into the trap of extremes.

Appendix

Performance measurement/ development audit: a quick self-test

Presented below is a list of statements relating to the performance management process.

Consider how <u>true</u> each of these statements is for your organization using the following scale:

High	Medium	Low
3	2	1
(True to a high extent)	(True to a medium extent)	(True to a low extent)

Please place score in unshaded box	A	B
As a result of my last review discussion I felt motivated to improve my performance		
Business needs and priorities are well communicated through the PM process		
I have regular discussions with my manager about my personal development		
In my last review, I was given the chance to say everything I wanted		
Managers/supervisors in my organization have a good understanding of their employees' jobs		
Managers in this organization motivate staff to develop and achieve their goals		

Statement		
Managers/supervisors in my organization tell employees when they are doing a good job		
Managers/supervisors in my organization tell employees when they are doing a poor job		
Monitoring standards of performance is a regular management activity in this organization		
My manager coaches me to improve my performance		
People in my organization agree together on their performance targets with their immediate manager/supervisor		
People in my organization are clear as to how their role links to the company's plans		
People in my organization are clear as to how they could improve their performance		
People in my organization are held fully accountable for the end results they produce or fail to produce		
People in my organization have a clear idea of what is expected of them in their role		
People in my organization have a good understanding of how the appraisal review links to reward		
People in my organization know how their performance is measured		
People in my organization receive constructive feedback on their performance		
People in my organization receive feedback on how they are performing against targets		
People in this organization are in no doubt that performance is what matters		
Poor performance is not tolerated in this organization		
The performance management system in my organization focuses on career development		
The measures used to monitor performance are the most appropriate for the role		
The measures used to monitor performance in my organization are clearly linked to business objectives		
The organization provides sufficient time and resource for its performance management process		
The performance management process allows us to give managers feedback on their performance		
The performance management system is linked to producing sustainable long-term performance		

There is a clear link between corporate goals and team/ individual goals

This organization focuses on achieving measurable targets

This organization focuses on raising personal capability

This organization has a development programme to improve skills

This organization insists on high quality work from its employees

TOTAL (Please add up the scores in each column)

A	B

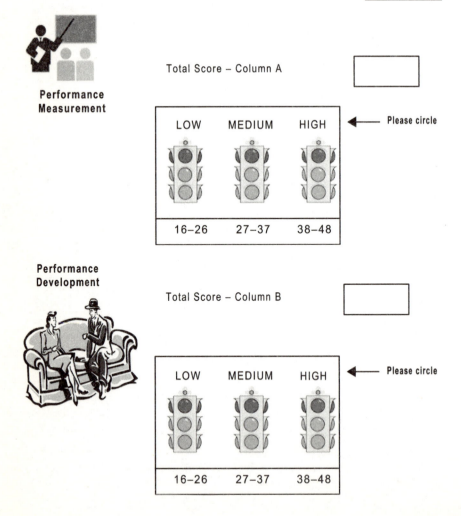

Performance Measurement

Total Score – Column A

Performance Development

Total Score – Column B

LOW	MEDIUM	HIGH
16–26	27–37	38–48

Please circle

LOW	MEDIUM	HIGH
16–26	27–37	38–48

Please circle

References

Adams, J S (1965) Inequity in social exchange, in *Advances in Experimental Social Psychology*, vol 2, ed Leonard Berkowitz, pp 267–99, Academic Press, New York

Anderson, M C (2001) Executive Briefing: Case study on the return on investment of executive coaching, MetrixGlobal, Iowa, USA

Armstrong, M (2002) *Employee Reward*, CIPD, London

Armstrong, M and Baron, A (1998) *Performance Management: The new realities*, IPD, London

Armstrong, M and Baron, A (2005) *Managing Performance: Performance management in action*, CIPD, London

Armstrong, M and Murlis, H (2004) *Reward Management: A handbook of remuneration strategy and practice*, Part 6, pp 275–406, Kogan Page, London

Armstrong, P (1987) The rise of accounting controls in British capitalist enterprises, *Accounting, Organisations and Society*, **12** (5), pp 415–36

Baladamus, W (1961) *Efficiency and Effort: An analysis of industrial administration*, Tavistock, London

Barlow, G (1989) Deficiencies and the perpetuation of power: latent functions in performance appraisal, *Journal of Management Studies*, September, pp 449–517

Beardwell, I, Holden, L and Clayton, T (2004) 4th edn, *Human Resource Management – a Contemporary Approach*, FT Prentice Hall, London

Beer, S, Mills, D Q and Walton, R E (1985) *Human Resources Management: A general manager's perspective*, Free Press, New York

Boyatzis, R E (2002) Unleashing the power of self-directed learning, in *Changing the Way We Manage Change: The consultants speak*, ed R Sims, pp 13–32, Quorum Books, New York

Chan Kim, W and Mauborgne, R (2003) Fair process, managing in the knowledge economy, *Harvard Business Review*, January, **1**, pp 127–36

Charam, R, Drotter, S and Noel, J (2001) *Toward the Leadership Pipeline: How to build the leadership-powered company*, Jossey-Bass, San Francisco

Childs, M (ed) (2005) *CIPD Reward Management* (Looseleaf), 1st edn, Section 2 Reward Theories (contributed by Murlis, H), CIPD, London

CIPD (2004) *2004 Annual Survey Report, Reward Management*, CIPD, London

CIPD (2005) *2005 Annual Survey Report, Reward Management*, CIPD, London

Corvellec, H (1997) *Stories of Achievements*, Transaction Publishers, New Brunswick

Corvellec, H (2001) For a narrative criticism of organisational performance, paper presented at the second New Directions in Organisational Performance conference, March

Deci, E L (1985) *Intrinsic Motivation and Self-determination in Human Behaviour*, Kluwer Academic Publishers (now Plenum), New York

Deming, W E (1986) *Out of the Crisis*, Cambridge Press, Cambridge, MA

DeVoge, S (2005) The Strategic Scorecard, Hay Group Internal Paper, London

Dinesh, D and Palmer, E (1998) Management by objectives and the Balanced Scorecard: will Rome fall again? *Management Decision*, **36** (6), pp 363–9

Doyle, R (2005) Team based performance management: how to move the process forward in 2006, Working paper, Health Service Executive Western Region, October

Eccles, E G (1991) The performance measurement manifesto, *Harvard Business Review*, January–February, pp 131–37

Fletcher, C (2002) Appraisal: An individual psychological perspective, in *Psychological Management of Individual Performance*, ed S Sonnentag, p 116, John Wiley and Sons, Chichester

Fletcher, C and Williams, R (1992) *Organisational Experience, Performance Management in the UK: An analysis of the issues*, Institute of Personnel, London

Fombrun, C, Tichy, N and Devanna M (eds) (1984) *Strategic Human Resource Management*, John Wiley and Sons, New York

Fortune in association with Hay Group (2004) The world's most admired companies, *Fortune* (Europe edition), **149** (4, 8), pp 30–46

Fortune in association with Hay Group (2005) The world's most admired companies, *Fortune* (Europe edition), **151** (4, 7), pp 40–53

Friedman, R, Sherman, D and Welch, S (2004) Differentiating the best from the rest: the world's most admired companies. Presentation at Hay Group International Client Meeting, Vienna 21–23 April

Goleman, D (2000) Leadership that gets results, *Harvard Business Review*, **78** (2), March–April, pp 78–90

Goleman, D (2001) *Primal Leadership*, Bantam Books, New York

Gomez-Mejia, L R, Tosi, H and Hinkin, T (1987) Management control, performance and executive compensation, *Academy of Management Journal*, **30** (1), pp 51–70

Goold, M and Campbell, A (2002) *Designing Effective Organizations: How to create structured networks*, Jossey-Bass, San Francisco

Guest, D (1987) Human resource management and industrial relations, *Journal of Management Studies*, **24** (5), pp 503–21

Hargreaves, G (2000) The review of vocational qualifications, 1985 to 1986: an analysis of its roles in the development of competence-based vocational qualifications in England and Wales, *British Journal of Educational Studies*, **48** (3), pp 285–308

Hargrove, R (2002) *Masterful Coaching*, Pfeiffer Wiley, San Francisco

Hay Group (2005) white paper, *Talent Management: What the best organisations actually do*, London

Hay Group (Ireland) and Institute of Public Administration (2004) Evaluation of the health service performance management system, Final Report, April, Dublin

Hay McBer (2000a) white paper, *Bonus Payments and the Organisational Climate Dimensions*, pp 14–15, Boston, MA

Hay McBer (2000b) white paper, *Operating Income and the Organisational Climate Dimensions*, Boston, MA

Health Service Employers Agency (2003) Performance management – the process and how it will work. Arrangements for the introduction of performance management as a pilot basis in the health service (Guidelines document), Dublin

Hendry, C and Pettigrew, A (1986) The practice of strategic human resource management, *Personnel Review*, **15** (5), pp 3–8

Hendry, C and Pettigrew, A (1990) Human resource management: an agenda for the 1990s, *International Journal of Human Resource Management*, **1** (1), pp 17–44

Huselid, M, Jackson, S and Schuler, R (1997) Technical and strategic human resource management effectiveness as determinants of firm performance, *Academy of Management Journal*, **40** (1), 171–88

Hutchinson, S, Kinne, N, Rayton, B and Swart, J (2002) *Sustaining Success in Difficult Times*, research summary, CIPD, London

IDS (1997) *Study 667: BT as an example of company practice in performance management*, April, London

Jackall, R J (1988) *Moral Mazes: The world of corporate managers*, OUP, New York and Oxford

Kaplan, R S and Norton, D P (1992) Putting the Balanced Scorecard to Work, *Harvard Business Review*, January–February, pp 71–79

Kaplan, R S and Norton, D P (1996) Using the Balanced Scorecard as a strategic management system, *Harvard Business Review*, **74** (1), January–February, pp 75–85

Kaplan, R S and Norton, D P (2000) *The Strategy-focused Organization: How balanced scorecard organisations thrive in the new business environment*, Harvard Business School Press, Boston, MA

Keenoy, T (1990) Human Resource Management: rhetoric, reality and contradiction, *International Journal of Human Resource Management*, **1** (3) Review Article pp 363–84

Keenoy, T. (1996) Human Resource Management: rhetoric, reality and contradiction, *International Journal of Human Resource Management*, Review Article

Keenoy, T (1999) HRM as Hologram: a polemic, *Journal of Management Studies*, **36** (1), pp 1–23

Kelner, S P Jr, Rivers, C A and O'Connell, K H (1994) *Managerial Style as a Predictor of Organisational Climate*, Hay Group, Boston, MA

Lawler, E E III (2003) *Treat People Right! How organisations and individuals can propel each other into a virtuous spiral of success*, Jossey-Bass, San Francisco

Lawrie, G, Cobbold, I and Marshall, J (2004) Corporate performance management system in a devolved UK governmental organisation: a case study, *International Journal of Productivity and Performance*, **53** (4), pp 353–70

Lee, G (2003) *Leadership Coaching: From personal insight to organisational performance*, Chartered Institute of Personnel and Development, London

Legge, K (1978) *Power, Innovation, and Problem-solving in Personnel Management*, McGraw-Hill, London

Legge, K (1989) Human Resource Management: a critical analysis, in *New Perspectives on Human Resource Management*, ed J Storey, Routledge, London, pp 19–40

Legge, K (1995) *Human Resource Management: Rhetorics and realities*, Macmillan Business, Basingstoke

Litwin, G H and Stringer, R A Jr (1968) *Motivation and Organizational Climate*, Harvard University Press, Cambridge, MA

Locke, E A (1968) Towards a theory of task motivation and incentives, *Organisational Behaviour and Human Performance*, **3**, pp 157–89

Luft, J (1969) *Of Human Interaction*, National Press, Palo Alto, CA

Luft, J and Ingham, H (1955) *The Johari Window: A graphic model for interpersonal relations*, University of California, Western Training Lab

Luthans, F and Kreitner, R (1985) *Organisational Behaviour Modification and Beyond*, Scott, Foresman & Co., Glenview, IL

Marsden, D and Richardson, R (1994) Performing for pay, *British Journal of Industrial Relations*, **32** (2), June, pp 243–62

Marshall, P (1996) Why are some people more successful than others? in *People and Competencies*, ed N Boulter, M Dalziel and J Hill, Kogan Page, London, pp 49–60

Maslow, A H (1943) A theory of human motivation, *Psychological Review*, **50**, pp 370–96

Mayo, A (2001) *The Human Value of the Enterprise*, Nicholas Brealey, London

McClelland, D (1973) Testing for competence rather than for intelligence, *American Psychologist*, **28**, January, pp 1–14

McGregor, D (1960) Theory X: The traditional view of direction and control and Theory Y: the integration of individual and organizational goals in *The Human Side of Enterprise*, Mcgraw Hill, London

McGregor, D (1971) Theory X and Theory Y, in *Organization Theory: Selected readings*, ed D S Pugh, Penguin Books, Middlesex

Merritt, L G, Leshner, M, Baker, D A, and Larrere, J B (1995) *Leadership for the 21st century: Life insurance leadership study*, LOMA and Hay Group, Boston, MA

Meyer, J P and Allen, N J (1992) *Commitment in the Workplace*, Sage Publications, London

Meyer, M W and Zucker, L G (1989) *Permanently Failing Organisations*, Sage, Newbury Park, CA

MSC/DES (1986) *Review of Vocational Qualifications in England and Wales*, Her Majesty's Stationery Office, London

Neely, A (1998) *Measuring Business Performance*, The Economist/Profile Books, London

Neely, A D and Griffith, R (2006) *Does the Balanced Scorecard Work: Empirical investigation*, British Academy of Management Performance Measurement Special Interest Group, Cranfield, January

Nethersell, G (2005) *Organisation Design*, Hay Group internal paper, London

Neumann, J, Morgenstern, O and Kuhn, H W (2004) *Theory of Games and Economic Behaviour (Commemorative Edition)*, Princeton Classic Editions, Princeton University Press, Princeton, NJ

Patterson, M, West, M, Lawthorn, R and Nickell, S (1997) *The Impact of People Management Practices on Business Performance*, IPD, London

Pfeffer, J (1998) *The Human Equation*, Harvard Business School Press, Boston, MA

Pollitt, C (2005) Performance management in practice: a comparative study of executive agencies, forthcoming in *Journal of Public Administration Research and Theory*

Poole, E and Warren, D (2005) *The new coaching and mentoring standards*, CIPD, London

Purcell, J, Kinnie, N, Hutchinson, S, Rayton, B and Swart, J (2002) *Understanding the People and Performance Link: Unlocking the black box*, Research report, CIPD, London

Richardson, R and Thompson, M (1999) *The Impact of People Management Practices on Business Performance: A literature review*, IPD, London

Sappington, D F M (1991) Incentives in principal–agent relationships, *Journal of Economic Perspectives*, **5** (2), pp 45–66

Sonnentag, S (2002) *Psychological Management of Individual Performance*, John Wiley and Sons, Chichester

Stiles, P, Gratton, L, Truss, C, Hope-Hailey, J and McGovern, P (1997) Performance management and the psychological contract, *Human Resource Management Journal*, **7** (1), pp 57–66

Storey, J (1992) *Developments in the Management of Human Resources*, Basil Blackwell, Oxford

Storey, J (2001) *Human Resource Management: A critical agenda*, Thomson Learning, London

Thorpe, R and Holloway, J (due for publication 2007) *Perspectives on Performance*, Palgrave, Basingstoke

Torrington, D, Hall, L and Taylor, S (2001) *Human Resource Management*, FT Prentice Hall, Harlow

Townley, B (1993) Foucault – power/knowledge, and its relevance for human resource management, *Academy of Management Review*, July, pp 518–45

Townley, B (1994) *Reframing Human Resource Management: Power, ethics and the subject at work*, p 72, Sage Publications, London

Truss, C, Gratton, L, Hope-Hailey, V, McGovern, P and Stiles, P (1997) Soft and hard models of HRM: a reappraisal, *Journal of Management Studies*, **4** (1), pp 43–74

Ulrich, D (1998) A new mandate for human resources, *Harvard Business Review*, **76** (1), pp 124–34

Ulrich, D and Brockbank, W (2005) *HR Value Proposition*, Harvard Business School Press, Boston, MA

Vroom, V J (1964) *Work and Motivation*, John Wiley and Sons, New York

Ward, Adrian (2005) Implementing the balanced scorecard at Lloyds TSB, *Strategic HR Review*, **4** (3), pp 16–19

Watkin, C and Hubbard, B (2003) Leadership motivation and the drivers of share price: the business case for measuring organisational climate, *Leadership & Organization Development Journal*, **24** (7), pp 380–86

Weiss, T and Hartle, F (1997) *Re-Engineering Performance Management*, St Lucie Press, Boca Raton, FL

Welch, J and Byrne, J (2003) *Jack: Straight from the gut*, Warner Books, New York

Whitmore, J (2002) *Coaching for Performance: Growing people, performance and purpose*, London, Nicholas Brealey

Williams, D (1995) Leadership for the 21st Century – Life Insurance Leadership Study, Boston

Winstanley, D and Stuart-Smith, K (1996) Policing performance: the ethics of performance management, *Personnel Review*, **25** (6), pp 66–84

Further reading and other sources of information

There is a large body of literature about performance management. This section is intended as a guide to the main sources and a limited selection of the key recent literature. It is certainly not exhaustive. The fact that a particular source or organization is listed here does not imply the authors' recommendation.

BOOKS AND REPORTS

Ainsworth, M, Smith, N and Millership, A (2002) *Managing Performance, Managing People*, Longman Publishing Group, Harlow

Armstrong, M (2002) *The Performance Management Audit: An eight-step audit to help analyse, develop and improve performance management processes so that the organisation achieves its business goals*, Cambridge Strategy Publications, Cambridge

Armstrong, M (2006) *Performance Management: Key strategies and practical guidelines*, 3rd edn, Kogan Page, London

Armstrong, M and Baron, A (2005) *Managing Performance: Performance management in action*, Chartered Institute of Personnel and Development, London

Bacal, R (2003) *The Manager's Guide to Performance Reviews*, McGraw-Hill Education, Maidenhead

Baguley, P (2002) *Performance Management in a Week*, 2nd edn, Hodder & Stoughton, London

Baguley, P (2003) *Performance Management*, Hodder Headline, London

Bentley, T J (2001) *Effective Personal Appraisal: A management guide*, Chandos Publishing, Oxford

Carter, E and McMahon, F (2005) *Improving Employee Performance through Workplace Coaching: A practical guide to performance management*, Kogan Page, London

Coens, T and Jenkins, M (2003) *Abolishing Performance Appraisals: Why they backfire and what to do instead*, Berrett-Koehler Publishers Inc, San Francisco

Cokins, G (2004) *Performance Management: Finding the missing pieces to close the intelligence gap*, John Wiley, Hoboken, NJ

Concise Management Guides (2003) *Stay Up to Speed: Performance management for decision makers*, Format, Norwich

E-reward Research Report (2005) *What is Happening in Performance Management Today: Part 1 – survey findings*, April (32)

E-reward Research Report (2005) *What is Happening in Performance Management Today: Part 2 – the e-reward toolkit*, October (37)

Fletcher, C (2004) *Appraisal and Feedback: Making performance review work*, 3rd edn, Chartered Institute of Personnel and Development, London

Grote, D (2002) *The Performance Appraisal Question and Answer Book: A survival guide for managers*, Amacom, New York

Grote, D (2005) *Forced Ranking: Making performance management work*, Harvard Business School Press, Boston

Hale, R and Whitlam, P (2000) *Powering Up Performance Management: An integrated approach to getting the best from your people*, Gower, Aldershot

Hartle, F, Everall, K and Baker, C (2001) *Getting the Best out of Performance Management in Your School*, Kogan Page, London

Hunt, N (2004) *Conducting Staff Appraisals: How to set up a review system that will ensure fair and effective appraisal and improve individual performance and organisational results*, How To Books, Oxford

Incomes Data Services (2005) *IDS Study: Performance management*, IDS, London

Industrial Society, Bingham, C (2001) *Managing Performance*, Managing best practice 86, The Industrial Society, London

Jones, J (2001) *Performance Management for School Improvement: A practical guide for secondary schools*, David Fulton Publishers, London

Kearns, P (2000) *Measuring and Managing Employee Performance: A practical manual to maximise organisational performance through people*, Financial Times/Prentice Hall, London

Kressler, H W (2003) *Motivate and Reward: Performance appraisal and incentive systems for business success*, Palgrave Macmillan, Basingstoke

Naisby, A (2002) *Appraisal and Performance Management*, Spiro Press, London

National Extension College Trust (2002) *Managing Performance*, Prime Training, Cambridge, UK

Personnel Today and Peoplesoft (2004) *Performance Management Survey*, Personnel Today Management Resources, Reed Business Information, Sutton

Sandler, C and Keefe, J (2003) *Performance Appraisal Phrase Book*, Adams Media Corp, Avon

Webb, J (2003) *Putting Management Back into Performance: A handbook for managers and supervisors*, Allen and Unwin, Crows Nest, NSW

Whitmore, Sir J (2002) *Coaching for Performance: Growing people, performance and purpose*, Nicholas Brealey Publishing, London

Williams, R S (2002) *Managing Employee Performance: Design and implementation in organizations*, new edn, Thomson Learning, London

JOURNAL ARTICLES

Axelrod, B, Handfield-Jones, H and Michaels, E (2002) A new game plan for C players, *Harvard Business Review*, **80** (1), pp 80–9

Baron, A and Armstrong, M (2004) Get into line, *People Management*, **10** (20), pp 44–6

Bates, S (2003) Forced ranking, *HR Magazine*, June, pp 65–8

Cunneen, P (2006) How to … improve performance management, *People Management*, **12** (1), pp 42–43

Elliott, S and Coley-Smith, H (2005) Building a new performance management model at BP, *Strategic Communication Management*, **9** (5), pp 24–9

Financial Times (2004) Understanding performance management, Supplement, 6 October, *Financial Times*

Gammie, A (2001) What does performance management mean?, *Topics*, no 85, pp 2–7

Goodge, P (2005) How to link 360° feedback and appraisal, *People Management*, **11** (2), pp 46–7

Goodridge, M (2001) The limits of performance management, *Topics*, no 85, pp 23–28

Greenberg, R and Lucid, L (2004) Beyond performance management: four principles of performance leadership, *Workspan*, **47** (9), pp 42–45

Grote, D (2002) Forced ranking: behind the scenes, *Across the Board*, **39** (6), pp 40–45

Industrial Relations Services (2002) Welcome Break: motorway services chain introduces competency-based management, *IDS Report* (854), April, pp 20–22

Industrial Relations Services (2003) Performance management: policy and practice, *IRS Employment Review* (781), 1 August, pp 12–19

Jackman, J M and Strober, M H (2003) Fear of feedback, *Harvard Business Review*, **81** (4), pp 101–07

Kearns, P (2000) How do you measure up?, *Personnel Today*, 21 March, pp 21–22

Kochanski, J and Sorensen, A (2005) Managing performance management, *Workspan*, **48** (9) pp 20–27

Lawler, E E (2003) Reward practices and performance management system effectiveness, *Organizational Dynamics*, **32** (4), pp 396–404

Lawler, E E and McDermott, M (2003) Spotlight on performance management – current performance management practices: examining the varying impacts, *WorldatWork Journal*, **12** (2), pp 49–60

Loren, G (2004) Performance management that drives results, *Harvard Management Update*, 1 September

Mitterer, S (2004) How to support high performers, *People Management*, **10** (16), pp 46–47

Morris, E and Sparrow, T (2001) Transforming appraisals with emotional intelligence, *Competency and Emotional Intelligence Quarterly*, **9** (1), pp 28–32

Murray, H (2002) Solving performance problems: diagnosing the causes, *Training Journal*, July, pp 22–26

Nelson, B (2000) Are performance appraisals obsolete?, *Compensation and Benefits Review*, **32** (3), pp 39–42

Peiperl, M A (2001) Getting 360 degree feedback right, *Harvard Business Review*, **79** (1), pp 142–47

Risher, H (2005) Getting serious about performance management, *Compensation and Benefits Review*, **37** (6), pp 18–26

Rose, M (2000), Target practice, *People Management*, **6** (23), pp 44–45

Swinburne, P (2001) How to use feedback to improve performance, *People Management*, **7** (11), pp 46–47

VanderHeijden, B I J M and Nijhof, A H J (2004) The value of subjectivity problems and prospects for 360 degree appraisal systems, *International Journal of Human Resource Management*, **15** (3), pp 493–511

Warner, J (2001) A mature performance management system: Abbey Life Assurance, *Competency and Emotional Intelligence*, **8** (2), pp 29–33

Warner, J (2002) A twin track to refocused performance management at HM Customs and Excise, *Competency and Emotional Intelligence*, **9** (4), pp 11–17

Weatherly, L A (2004) Performance management: getting it right from the start, *HR Magazine*, **49** (3), Special Section, 1 March, pp 2–9

Williams, A (2002), Making the truth work for us: giving feedback compassionately in performance management, *Topics*, no 87, pp 14–16

Williams, V (2001) Making performance management relevant, *Compensation and Benefits Review*, **33** (4), pp 47–51

Willmore, J (2004) The future of performance, *Training and Development (USA)*, **58** (8), pp 26–31

Wingrove, C (2003) Developing an effective blend of process and technology in the new era of performance management, *Compensation and Benefits Review*, **35** (1), pp 25–31

JOURNALS AND ONLINE RESOURCES

e-reward
33 Denby Lane
Heaton Chapel
Stockport
Cheshire SK4 2RA
Tel: (0161) 432 2584
www.e-reward.co.uk

Human Resource Management Journal
LexisNexis/Butterworths/IRS
London WC2A 1EL
Tel: (020) 8662 2000
www.ingentaconnect.com/content/irs/hrmj

IDS Studies
Incomes Data Services
77 Bastwick Street
London EC1V 3TT
Tel: (020) 7 250 3434
www.incomesdata.co.uk

IRS Employment Review
Lexis Nexis IRS
2 Addiscombe Road
Croydon CR9 5AF
Tel: (020) 8686 9141
www.irsemploymentreview.com

People Management
Personnel Publications Ltd
Benjamin Street,
London EC1M 5EA
Tel: (020) 7296 4235
www.peoplemanagement.co.uk

Personnel Today
Reed Business Information
Quadrant House
The Quadrant,
Sutton SM2 5AS
Tel: (020) 8652 3500
www.personneltoday.com

Team Performance Management
Emerald Group Publishing Limited
60/62 Toller Lane
Bradford BD8 9BY
Tel: (01274) 777700

WorldatWork Journal and Workspan
WorldatWork
14040 N. Northsight Blvd.
Scottsdale, AZ 85260
USA
www.worldatwork.org

ORGANIZATIONS

Chartered Institute of Personnel and Development (CIPD)
CIPD House
Camp Road
London SW19 4UX
Tel: (020) 8971 9000
www.cipd.co.uk

Chartered Management Institute (CMI)
Management House
Cottingham Road
Corby NN17 1TT
Tel: (01536) 204 222
www.managers.org.uk

Incomes Data Services
77 Bastwick Street
London EC1V 3TT
Tel: (020) 7250 3434
www.incomesdata.co.uk

Institute for Employment Studies
Mantell Building
Falmer
Brighton BN1 9RF
Tel: (01273) 686751
www.employment-studies.co.uk

Performance Measurement Association (PMA)
The Centre for Business Performance
Cranfield School of Management
Bedford MK43 0AL
Tel: (01234 751122)
www.som.cranfield.ac.uk/som/research/centres/cbp/pma

Roffey Park Institute
Forest Road
Horsham RH12 4TD
Tel: (01293) 851644
www.roffeypark.com

Society for Human Resource Management
1800 Duke Street
Alexandria, VA 22314
USA
Tel: +1 703 548 3440
www.shrm.org

WorldatWork
14040 N. Northsight Blvd.
Scottsdale, AZ 85260
USA
www.worldatwork.org

The Work Foundation
Peter Runge House
3 Carlton House Terrace
London SW1Y 5DG
Tel: (0870) 1656700
www.theworkfoundation.com

Index

NB: page numbers in *italics* indicate tables and figures in the text